FIRST OF THE FLOOD

A Fishy Tale

Dedication

This book is dedicated to the fishing community of the 'Bottom End' in Scarborough, in the days of my youth. To the larger than life, wonderful characters and a unique way of life which has gone forever.

One ship drives east, another drives west,
With the self-same winds that blow.
'Tis the set of the sails, and not the gales,
That tell her the way to go.

Like the winds of the sea are the winds of fate,
As we voyage along through life.
'Tis the set of the soul that decides the goal,
And not the calm or strife.

Fred Normandale April 2003

FIRST OF THE FLOOD

A Fishy Tale

FRED NORMANDALE

Bottom End Publishing
Scarborough

First published October 2002

Reprinted November 2002

ISBN 0 9543686 0 6

Cover design by Barry Perks Design

Cover photographs (left to right): Bill 'Jitta' Sheader, Walter 'Pellett' Eves, Ernie 'Soapy' Williamson, 'Filey' Bill Cammish, John 'Johnny Nom' Normandale, Bill 'Blondie' Wood, 'Dickie' Elliott and Bob Kitto.

Prepared and printed by:
York Publishing Services Ltd
64 Hallfield Road
Layerthorpe
York YO31 7ZQ
Tel: 01904 431213; Website: www.yps-publishing.co.uk

CONTENTS

THANKS

This book would not have been written without the encouragement of my long suffering wife Dorothy, whose initial "you've been talking about it for long enough, get on with it," gave me the impetus required.

The Arvon Foundation at Lumb Bank, near Hebden Bridge where I was given time, space and helpful advice from other aspiring writers and successful authors to make a start on this book. Thanks especially to Nicholas Royle for his positive attitude, which helped me to transform dozens of short anecdotes into this volume during his tutorial period.

My sister, Jan Palmer for her patient, professional proof reading and helpful corrections. To my sister, Sue Wood, Sid Magson, the late Peter Barton, Gilly Gray Q C, Douglas Schar, Ian Forbes, John Steel, Caroline Chapman and Terry Pearson for their constructive comments of earlier drafts.

To all who have loaned or assisted with photographs:

Ken Wigg, George Scales, Max Payne, the families of the late Bill Sheader, Bill Cammish, Bob Kitto, Denk Mainprize, Walter Eves, Dickie Elliott and Ernie Williamson, The RNLI, Grimsby Telegraph, Bob & Ann Walker, Jason Dobson, landlords and landladies of the Leeds Arms, Leeds Hotel, Newcastle Packet, Dolphin Hotel and Anchorage Club.

To all the remaining 'Bottom Enders' for keeping the memories alive with constant re-telling of the 'old' stories which I have unashamedly reproduced, notably, my Mum and Dad Fred and Doris Normandale, Rusty Drydale, Major Clark, Walt Crawford, Bill Scales, Eddie Temple, Tom Rowley, Bob Walker, Barry McNally, Ray Trotter, Mickey Watts and Brian and Herby Nicholson.

Last but by no means least, Dave Mercer, Duncan Beal and the staff of York Publishing Services who were able to produce this book when dozens of agents and publishers had given a negative or no response.

AUTHOR'S NOTES

My reason for writing this book is to document the way of life in the 'old town' of Scarborough in my boyhood days, as seen through my eyes, and to record some of the folk who inhabited the 'Bottom End'. The people of this fishing community were insular, seldom travelling far from their own environment. They were not articulate; indeed some of the older folk could neither read nor write. Their meagre livelihood was hard-gained from the sea.

As a boy I grew up among some wonderful characters, big men with big hearts. They were extremely hard working and when ashore, hard drinking, though never mixing the two pursuits. I thought this was a normal background, that everyone lived in a world such as mine. I couldn't have been more wrong; it was unique.

My father was a fisherman, working on a coble. In the winter he fished for cod with lines and hooks, in summer for lobsters and crabs with pots. I loved the historic harbour, spending every possible minute on the piers or on board the many boats that plied their trade, either fishing, or taking trippers around the bay in small motor or rowing craft. From an early age I knew all the fishermen and was known to everyone. To some this must have seemed a rough environment for a small boy, but from my vantage point, I was surrounded by larger than life characters who could find humour even in extreme adversity.

Fishing has always been an arduous occupation and even with modern technology, the risk and battle with the elements is still ever present. Now there is another, much more ruthless enemy, the bureaucrats. The few remaining fishermen are fighting a paper war against legions of 'experts' using licenses, permits, quotas, logbooks, surveys and a host of other technical measures for ammunition. These men are fighting a losing battle, defending the right to pursue the only way of life they've ever known and cannot survive much longer.

This book relates to a less complicated time, when by sheer hard work, a community was able to pursue a lifestyle in which they found contentment. I consider myself fortunate to have been born, brought up and to have spent my life in the fishing community of Scarborough.

Fred Normandale (Freddie Nom)

CHAPTER I

WINTER FISHING

It was an early January morning. The bitter east wind blowing off the sea made me shiver. Surf breaking on the rocks close to where I was crouching filled the air with a fine penetrating spray. I was cold, damp and could feel no sensation in my fingers. Sniffing, I wiped my nose on my jacket sleeve; it was wet. The old woollen socks on my hands seemed of little use now they too were wet. I put my bucket and knife down on a flat rock, removing one of the improvised mittens with chattering teeth. The biting wind attacked the back of my hand with added zeal as I plunged it into my jacket pocket, seeking out the remaining piece of chocolate. Quickly stuffing it in my mouth, I fumbled to replace the sock. They must be doing some good I thought, giving another large sniff.

Picking up the knife again with difficulty, I looked into the bucket. It was only half-full though I'd been chipping at the rocks for what seemed hours. I began to despair, knowing I wasn't going to fill it today. The limpets I was gathering, known as 'flithers' to the fishermen, were scarce in this area. Someone had been there in the past few days taking the best pickings. Ring marks on the rocks where the flithers had been were clear to see. It took effort to chisel each limpet from its location. Occasionally misjudging the resistance I would propel one several feet, losing it in a rock pool. Infrequently I shattered a shell or missed my aim completely, hitting only rock. The haft of the little knife dug into the palm of my hand again and again as I chiselled one and then another limpet from the rocks. The rag tied around the handle had helped to absorb the impact but this was now holed with the constant pressure and my hand was hurting. Why was it the only bit of my hand I could feel was hurting?

I was fifteen and had become proficient at flithering. Time was short, the tide wasn't out for long and I would look daft if I were to get trapped as it flowed back in. It didn't occur to me that it was dangerous. I looked to the water's edge; Coffee Pot Rock was just visible in the haze. This pinnacle, which must have seen a million storms, was surrounded by water. The tide was flowing quickly so I decided to quit. It wasn't a difficult decision, though I'd have liked to have filled the bucket. A full bucket would be worth a pound but I was cold, wet and someone had beat me to the best ones. Still I had more than half a bucket now. I hoped to get twelve bob for these. Flithers were good bait for cod and haddock which the fishermen caught on the miles of lines 'shot' each day, weather permitting, during the winter months.

I looked up; it was at least thirty feet to the railings on the Marine Drive which followed the cliff face around the castle headland. Beyond the railings the towering cliffs were white from the droppings of kittiwakes which nested each spring. They would be back soon. I glanced down again, to where I'd left my bike leaning against the railings; it was still there. I knew it would be. There wasn't another soul to be seen on this freezing cold morning. Scrambling across the few hundred yards of rocks with my haul of flithers, I gingerly climbed the seaweed-strewn steps to the Marine Drive, the bladderwrack popping under every footstep. I'd have to ride my bike with one hand, holding the bucket in the other. There was too much weight in the bucket to hang it on the handlebars. I'd fallen off before doing that.

The handle of the bucket bit into my tender palm as I pedalled into the wind along the Marine Drive to the harbour. 'Think of something to take my mind off the pain.' The waves will be breaking against the wall along here at high tide if this wind keeps blowing. When the wind was northerly or north easterly I came here with my friends to have fun 'wave dodging'. The waves sometimes shot a hundred feet into the air when they hit the Marine Drive wall. Cars were occasionally washed across the road, out of control as they were driven around the headland. It was exciting attempting to flee these huge breakers and we usually finished the day thoroughly wet through. I stopped reluctantly to change hands. Once stopped it was hard to get going again.

I visualised the baiting shed that I was making for. There'd be a roaring coal fire; the pot-bellied stove would be glowing red, a blackened kettle singing atop. Four or five men and women would be working away at various tasks, preparing the long lines for the next day's fishing for the *Rosemary*, the boat my Dad worked on. I hoped the men wouldn't laugh at me or call me a softy for not filling my bucket. I knew the women wouldn't, they were always cheerful and kind. Keep pedalling, keep pedalling. I must remember to take the socks off my hands before going in the bait shed or they'd laugh at me for sure.

Reaching the harbour I turned to ride along the North Wharf. With the wind now at my back, I was able to glance at the keelboats tied side by side as I passed. Some were named after family members, *Mary Joy*, and *Margaret Jane* but others had more dramatic titles, *Floreat*, *Progressive*, and *Brilliant Star*. One day I'd be skipper of a keelboat, I promised myself. Arriving at Sandgate Corner slipway, the furthest point from the harbour entrance, I passed a group of men surveying the harbour scene. There was always a small gathering on this corner, regardless of adverse weather conditions. Dad said they were the harbour critics. They'd never achieved anything themselves but would always criticise anyone else attempting to succeed. He said most were reluctant to leave the corner, less they in turn be sneered at by those remaining. It was very confusing, whenever I stood listening to their conversation they seemed to have lots of knowledge on all manner of subjects. One day while hovering at the edge of the group I overheard talk of a boat tied up near the slipway, which they were referring to as the 'Olympic Flame'. "Why d'ya call it that?" I asked the nearest man.

"'Cos t' bloody thing never goes out," he said, before turning to his colleagues to address more serious matters.

I was pedalling into the wind again as I turned left, passing the gathering at Sandgate Corner. I rode onto the West Pier, not far to go now. I heard one of the critics say "daft young bugger," he can't have meant me, keep pedalling. On my left now were the big square doors at the rear of the fish market. These were opened following the fish auction each day, allowing the merchants access to load their vehicles with newly acquired purchases.

On my right was Harry's tea shack, an ancient, though well-maintained, wooden construction, where fishermen would congregate for a cup of tea and a yarn. The proprietor, a small, neat man with straight combed hair, clad in a khaki overall, had been a prisoner of war following capture in North Africa. Meticulous and regimental, his premises were just so, everything was clean and in its place. Harry had only one teaspoon and it was kept in a specific place on his worktop. He'd used it constantly for so many years it was worn at the end from stirring countless cups of tea.

On the right, having passed the tea shack, was the first of the numerous baiting sheds, each brightly lit by several unshaded light bulbs. Though called baiting sheds, they were actually two-storey brick buildings with concrete floors. They were built by the Harbour Authorities to accommodate the many line fishermen. The upper stories were used as dry storage for all manner of fishing gear. I glanced through the windows in turn as I rode past; the scene was almost identical in each. Two or three women sitting around a large tray, piled high with live mussels. A similar number of men standing, baiting lines at waist high, wooden benches. These baiting and skeining operations began for most people at five o'clock each morning. Some women, my Mum included, preferred to skein mussels at home. Dad would tip half a sackful into the kitchen sink before he left for the harbour each morning. Someone from the baiting shed would collect the resulting bait from the house as it was required. Approaching the end block of baiting sheds, I noticed a woman, head down, dressed in headscarf, raincoat and fur-topped boots scurrying towards me; it was Charlotte. Having completed her quota of mussels for the day she was returning home. The swelling under her coat gave the impression she was heavily pregnant. She wasn't really, it was a cushion. Charlotte's daughter, Emily, was pregnant and unmarried. Emily had left town, she'd been sent away to live with relatives till the baby was born. On her return with child the cushion would disappear and Charlotte not Emily would have had the baby. I

4

don't know why they were bothering, everyone knew.

I finally arrived at my destination, the last door in the row. Putting my bucket on the ground I dismounted, leaning my bike on the pile of hundredweight sacks of mussels, stacked high against the wall of the building. I wanted to get the wet socks off my hands before opening the door. Pulling them from my frozen hands with my teeth again, I clumsily stuffed them in my jacket pocket. Picking up the bucket with both numb hands, I shook it vigorously. The flithers had settled in the bucket, sticking together, as limpets were bound to. My twelve bob had settled to ten and had to be reinstated. When I was satisfied the two shillings were back in the bucket I lifted the sneck on the door. I entered the brightly lit room and a wall of heat from the stove hit me.

The five inhabitants, three ladies and two men, all looked in my direction as I entered the spartan, twelve feet square working space. As in the other sheds the ladies were skeining mussels, the men baiting lines. On all sides of the brick walled room, a high, wide shelf was stacked with unbaited lines awaiting attention. The three ladies Mrs Coward, Mrs Wright and Mrs Messenger were sitting on padded wooden stools around a central tray of barnacle-coated, black mussels. Each was wrapped in an oilcloth apron and wore a headscarf.

"Come on in lad," Mrs Wright said quickly, beaming on recognising me. She was a tall, friendly, bespectacled woman. I knew her name was Violet but I always respectfully called her Mrs Wright. "Y' look 'alf frozen t' death young Freddy." Her glasses were streaked with mussel juice. I wondered how she could see through them.

Mrs Wright lived across the street from our house in Friargate. She always had time to stop and talk when I met her. She treated me as a grown up, asking sensible questions such as which boats were at sea? Who had landed fish most recently and what was Dad catching? Her brother Eric was the coxswain of the Whitby Lifeboat. She was very proud of her brother and enjoyed telling me of his exploits and his latest rescues. In her home there were photographs of the lifeboat ploughing through massive seas at the entrance to Whitby Harbour. I stared at these in awe whenever I visited her house. One day I would be in the Scarborough

Lifeboat, I knew the coxswain Bill Sheader. He was admired and respected by everyone around the harbour.

"Get sat by t' fire 'oney, y' look nithered," said Mrs Coward in a soft voice. Beckie Coward was a plump, elderly lady with rosy cheeks and twinkling eyes. A wisp of silver hair protruding from under her headscarf shone, reflecting the bright naked bulb above her head.

"Poor bairn," joined in Mrs Messenger. I didn't know her too well. She was a widow and lived alone. Esther Messenger was quite an attractive lady with bottled blonde hair. She was always dressed well and even in her working attire seemed well turned out. The men often said suggestive things to her, most of which I didn't understand but it was clear she enjoyed the attention. Mrs Coward would tut when the men paid special attention to her. "They wouldn't 'ave carried on like that in my day," she would say.

The floor surrounding the ladies was running with water from the tray. Their short sharp knives flashed as they swiftly separated each mussel from its shell. The meat was deftly flicked into a dish with the knife blade; the empty shell dropped into a bin that each had at their side. It took three to four hours to skein a sack of mussels, depending on their size, though mostly the sacks were pooled, enabling the ladies to finish together. They often complained when the mussels were small. Their pay was seventeen shillings a sack.

The men, now with their backs to me, were again concentrating on their work. Micky Scales and Ernie Eves, also wearing aprons which overlapped their short rubber boots, were standing on small wooden pallets, which insulated their feet against the concrete floor. On the bench, stacked high in front of each man, the coils of brown line were passed from hand to hand. As each hook was encountered, attached to the main line on a short length of light cord, it was filled from the selection of various baits in dishes before them. Today there were mussels, whelks and flithers. Some days there would be scallops, squid and big black lugworms, depending on availability. The worms were so big that only a half of one could be threaded onto a hook. When the hook was full the remainder of the worm was broken off with thumb and forefinger to fill a subsequent hook.

A 'fast baiter' could bait a line with over two hundred hooks attached in slightly over an hour, depending on the type of bait used. It took longer to bait the hooks with mussels, as sometimes four or five were needed to fill one hook. The men were paid seven shillings for each line baited. On the few occasions I'd attempted to bait a line, it took more than three hours to complete, yet it looked so easy when I watched others at work.

Though neither mentioned it, both these men had been part of the crew of the Scarborough Lifeboat, *ECJR* when it capsized close to the harbour entrance in December 1954. Three of the crew were drowned. The lifeboat, with a crew of eight, was escorting several fishing vessels back to port in a severe south easterly storm. When these boats had sailed, long before daylight, there wasn't a breath of wind but a very heavy frost hung over the coast. The wind increased rapidly to gale force, catching everyone unaware, as the frost broke. The Scarborough lifeboat, as always, had been manned by a crew of volunteers, though a small annual retainer was paid to the coxswain and mechanic.

The lifeboat was housed in a large brick building at the eastern end of the beach, where she was kept at ready on a trailer. The boat was launched into the sea, pushed by a heavy-duty tractor.

Micky, the head shore-man placed a juicy, mussel-filled hook in sequence, in the row of tempting baits on the line stacked to his right. The empty hooks were on the coils of line to his left. Crossing the floor he looked in my bucket. "Is that all you've got? It was 'ardly worth goin', there isn't 'alf a bucket. I'll give you nine bob for 'em." He was smiling and probably teasing but I was immediately defensive.

I countered, "there's at least twelve bobs worth, t' bucket's well over 'alf full, nearly three-quarters." I was glad I'd shook them up on arrival. Blowing on my reddened, clenched hands, inviting more sympathy from the women, I went on, "it's bloomin' freezin' out there, an' somebody 'ad been there before me an' got all t' best uns."

"Aye alright," he said "you 'avn't done bad." Reaching up he took a tobacco tin from the corner of the shelf; it was his cash tin. Tom, the skipper of the boat gave him an amount of cash each week for casual expenses. Micky took a ten-shilling note from it, then poking his finger among the numerous coins, looked in vain for a two-shilling piece. Finally he selected a half-crown. Tutting he said, "I've no change, I'll give y' twelve an six if y' skein 'em."

I agreed. It wouldn't take long, skeining flithers was easy and I liked being in the baiting shed listening to the conversation. I was warming quickly, so I took off my jacket, hanging it on the back of an old chair, not too close to the glowing fire, then arranged my bucket and dish for ease and comfort. A knife could be used but it was quicker with a teaspoon. Picking one up from the tea tray near the stove I sat down to my task. It was a good feeling to be among grown ups doing something useful, to be accepted as part of the team. Holding an upturned flither in one hand, I put the point of the spoon, held with thumb and forefinger of the other hand between the meat and shell then twisted. The meat remained on the spoon and was easily flicked with thumb into the dish. The empty shell was discarded into a bucket.

Micky had been in the Royal Navy during the war, then skipper of a steam trawler, fishing in Scottish waters in later years. His two brothers were keelboat skippers. He told wonderful stories, so when he began to speak I listened avidly. "I was talkin' t' Georgy Kennedy this morning. Y' know, t' fella that lives on Castle Crescent, t' one wi' t' bad limp."

There was a brief discussion among the ladies as they identified the man in question. Micky continued, "he was tellin' me 'e's bought a twenty foot motor boat t' tek trippers 'round t' bay durin' t' summer." There followed a discussion on George's ability with his infirmity to manage a boat of this size, which was capable of carrying eight passengers. The consensus being that he'd manage but would find it difficult.

Micky turned briefly in my direction as he filled his bait tray once more from the selection of baits by the door. "D' y' know 'ow 'e got 'is bad leg young Nommy." (All our family were called Nom or Nommy. It was the shortened version of Normandale. Dad and I were both Freddy Noms, my uncles were Johnny Nom, Robbie Nom and Georgy Nom).

I looked up, pleased to be involved in the conversation. "No, I know t' man you're talkin' about, 'e's always 'ad a bad leg as long as I can remember."

Micky returned to his station. He had everyone's attention now as he went on. "He was in t' *Cape Pallister* a minesweeper, durin' t' war. They were near t' Norwegian coast an' were blown up. 'Is ship was bombed, there were a few killed. Everyone thought George was dead; 'is legs were smashed up and t' top of 'is 'ead 'ad been badly damaged. 'E was laid on t' deck with t' other bodies and was about t' be buried at sea. Someone saw 'is eyes move an' 'e was saved but even then nobody thought 'e'd live. It was years afore 'e could walk again."

The ladies joined the storyteller, debating what year and month the incident took place and who George was related to. Ernie joined in the conversation, saying that he was in Lowestoft at the time, also in a sweeper. Micky continued, saying that before the war George had been a tough man, sailing as 'third hand' in Arctic trawlers from Hull.

Micky was a fountain of knowledge, and for my benefit explained that all the deep sea trawlers from the major fishing ports in Britain were requisitioned by the government during war time. They were converted for use as minesweepers or anti submarine ships in both world wars, for use by the Royal Navy. Their deck arrangement and winches made them ideal vessels for this work. Fishermen, on joining the Navy, were detailed to the Patrol Service and became crew for these ships. The men were familiar with these vessels and there was little difference between handling fishing and sweeping gear. Micky said no capital ships or convoys ever sailed until the 'sweepers' had swept the port entrances and approaches.

I sat on the stool listening intently but was quietly feeling guilty. I could recall on more than one occasion, when accompanied by friends, being cheeky to George Kennedy, knowing he'd never be able to catch us. He seemed a little strange to us; never ever removing his cap and often used piratical expressions, calling us 'young swabs' among other much stronger language. I was a little subdued for the remainder of my skeining session, then left to cycle the short distance up the hill home for my Sunday dinner. I hoped Mum wouldn't miss the table knife, which I'd borrowed from the kitchen the previous day, for chipping the flithers from the rocks. There was no point in returning it now, the blade had been reduced by half and was now chisel edged.

Mum always cooked a traditional midday Sunday dinner for our family, though Dad was usually at sea. He'd have his meal later in the day when he arrived home. This was my favourite meal of the week. It consisted of a roast joint of meat surrounded by crisp brown roasted potatoes with separate vegetables, plus the most wonderful Yorkshire puddings that it was possible to taste. Dad would have a plate full of these with rich onion gravy first, before eating his meat and vegetables. The remainder of the joint would make a stew for Monday's dinner.

Several days each week throughout the winter we ate fish. We were a large family and fish was free. Dad brought a cod home from the catch most days. My sister Christine said she didn't like cod so Mum told her it was haddock; it was eaten without question. I was the eldest and only boy, next came Susan, Christine then Janet. In the spring and summer Dad brought home crabs, small (undersized) lobsters or sea trout, depending on the type of fishing being pursued. We would complain bitterly at this constant assortment of seafood. My sisters and I considered sliced corned beef and chips to be a treat.

When the meal was finished there was no time to lose. The boats would be returning with their catches. I set off at a run back down the hill to the harbour. Approaching the fish market, I could see there were already two small cobles tied to the quay. These were two-man boats, which fished with only a few lines. I knew their names immediately; each boat was easily identified by shape, size and colour. These two were the *Nellie* and the *Constance*.

I'd learned at school that cobles were directly descended from the Viking long ships. Unique to the coast of Yorkshire and Northumberland, they were clinker built, open boats, approximately twenty to thirty feet in length, carrying a crew of two or three men. Built by local craftsmen without reference to plans or drawings, they were designed to work from open beaches. Traditionally, they were propelled by oars or a single square sail but more recently were fitted with engines and mostly worked from harbours. At Flamborough, Filey and a few other small villages along the coast, cobles are still operated from beaches and are launched from trailers with the aid of a tractor.

I'd heard old coblemen say that in years past, when working from beaches, wives would carry their menfolk into their boats once afloat, so the men would be dry to start their day. I also heard women chose small husbands and men picked big wives.

As I approached the harbour I could see hundreds of large, raucous, black- backed and herring gulls, fighting in the water at the boats' sides for the offal, as the fishermen in their shining, blood-streaked, yellow oilskins and sou'westers gutted their lifeless catch. The noise from the gulls was deafening. Kittiwakes swooped for the titbits, as the larger birds struggled for the big pieces of refuse.

I hurried along the pier to look down into the first boat. It was the *Constance*. Her skipper, Bill Sheader, was drawing buckets of water from the harbour, forcefully throwing the water onto the fish, which were liberally strewn in the boat. His long powerful arms reached effortlessly over the small boat's side, hauling water by the gallon. When washed, the catch was ready to be unloaded. The large quantity of water now accumulated under the bottom boards would later be pumped from the vessel by hand.

The catches were landed from the boats in cane baskets, each holding approximately five stones of fish; the biggest fish were landed first. Some of these cod would weigh fifteen to twenty pounds even when gutted. Each basket was hauled from boat to pier top by a small crane. Revolving at the base, this new construction had an electric capstan attached. Four of these cranes had recently been installed at the quayside to aid fish landing operations. Prior to this, boats waited in turn to be unloaded by a noisy, little, petrol-driven mobile crane or fishermen with small catches would haul each basket from the boat by rope. This new equipment was a great improvement.

Bill Sheader was a local celebrity with a wonderful sense of humour. He was able to combine his work as a coble fisherman and lifeboat coxswain quite well. The lifeboat was needed mostly during periods of bad weather when the sea was rough. Cobles didn't sail in poor weather, though they could be caught out if it changed quickly. All the skippers monitored the shipping forecasts from the BBC before sailing. Bill had a weather-beaten face, bright, alert eyes and slightly thinning, straight hair. Standing over six feet tall, he was thin and slightly stooped. A large, hooked nose dominated his face. Like all coble fishermen he had huge hands. He spoke very quickly with a broad accent and slight nasal voice, which even his friends found difficult to understand when he was excited.

Some of his quick wit was lost unless the listener concentrated but Bill always laughed at his own jokes and his laughter was infectious. Bill or 'Jitta' as he was known, was a skilful seaman and very popular with everyone. There were many stories told about him, mostly of his sense of humour.

He and Bill Cammish had been partners in the *Constance* for years. They fished with long lines throughout the winter and in the summer months worked with crab and lobster pots. Both modes of fishing required floating buoys at the ends of the gear, marking its location in the sea. These were not always easy to find. Glare on the water from the sun, poor visibility or a rough sea surface were all conditions which hampered the location of these markers. Whatever the conditions, it was always Bill C who saw the marker buoys first. "Can't y' see it?" he'd say, "it's clear enough."

This irritated Bill S, whose eyes were beginning to fail after a lifetime at sea. One afternoon, when they'd hauled their pots and finished work for that day, unknown to his partner, Bill S returned to the boat, sailing out to where their pots were located. On reaching the position, he carefully steered a compass course north east for about a mile. Here, he deployed a buoy with line and an anchor, a spare which they carried in their boat, then returned to harbour.

Next day when they'd finished hauling their pots, Bill S looked to the north east, took off his cap, scratched his head, then said, "there's a buoy out there, I can jus' make it out, it might be one of ours."

Bill C stared out to sea but could see nothing in the haze. Doubting his partner's vision he said, " y' mus' be dreamin' I can't see owt an' my eyes are better than yours."

Bill S was adamant, "there is a buoy there, I can see it. We should go an' 'ave a look." He was so insistent, that to humour his shipmate Bill C headed the boat out north easterly, in the direction of the pointed finger. They continued on this course for several minutes.

Bill C, mumbling, "I still can't see owt," was about to call off the wild goose chase, when through the gloom he saw the buoy. On reaching the surface marker and realising it was indeed one of their buoys, he helped his partner to retrieve it, stowing the float back on board where it had previously been, its disappearance having gone unnoticed. Bill C was totally perplexed. "Ow the 'ell did that get there? Some bugger's playin' tricks on us, an' 'ow come you could see it when I couldn't."

Bill S just shrugged and said, "dunno." He found it very difficult to keep a straight face, "mebbe me eyes aren't as bad as y' think." It was a long time before his partner commented on Bill's poor eyesight again.

Jitta lived with his wife Julie, who was opposite to him in every way. He was a tall, thin, quick speaking, rough and ready Yorkshireman. Julie was a small, plump, very slow speaking and meticulous Northumberland girl. Her dressmaking, alterations and repairing skills were used by many in the area. Sadly they had no children of their own.

One Sunday, shortly after noon when the boats were in harbour due to poor weather, Ernie 'Soapy' Williamson, a friend of Bills, knocked on his door, then entered the house, as he always did. Like Bill, Ernie was a coble fisherman; they had much in common, though Ernie was a confirmed bachelor, living with his mother. The two had arranged to visit the 'Leeds Arms' together for a few beers. This was a custom every Sunday when they were not at sea.

The 'Leeds Arms' was an old fashioned pub, situated on a narrow cobblestoned hill, close to the harbour. It had a unique atmosphere with a low oak beamed ceiling, covered by a model trawl net and walls adorned with nautical artefacts and photographs. It was more of a community centre than a public house. Many of the fishermen congregated in these pleasant surroundings to play dominoes, talk fishing or exchange jokes and tall stories.

Bill, at home, heard the front door open then close again. Looking at the kitchen clock to confirm his visitor's identity he called out, "I'm in t' kitchen Ernie. Julie's gone 'ome to see 'er family f' t' weekend so I'm fendin' f' meself." Ernie walked through the house to the steam-filled kitchen. A pan of potatoes bubbled on the stove. On the draining board by the sink, unmoving, a lobster awaited its fate. Bill, his head clouded in vapour, was standing by the stove. He turned as Soapy entered the room, "ow long does it tek t' boil taties Ern?" Bill asked of his pal.

"About twenty minutes," came the reply.

"Thought so. An' 'ow long does it tek t' boil lobsters?"

"About t' same, twenty minutes." Ernie replied.

"Oh, that's all right then, I'll put this lobster in wi' t' taties."

After assigning the crustacean to the pot, he picked up an oven tray containing a tender joint of beef, surrounded by scrubbed potatoes which he placed in the oven. Closing the door carefully, he turned to his pal again. "Ow many pints are we gonna 'ave in t' pub t' day Ernie?"

"Seven or eight I suppose," said Ernie, looking perplexed.

"Right oh, I'll set t' oven on number eight then," Bill said and off they went to the pub. Julie always got new pots and pans after a visit to her family.

I moved along the pier a few yards then looked down into the *Nellie*. This boat was operated by Alf Ward and his brother Robbie. They too had finished gutting their catch and were about to begin landing. Alf was ascending the iron ladder to the pier, a cigarette hanging from his lips. He was skipper of the *Nellie* and was a continual chain smoker; each new cigarette was lit from the embers of the previous one. Alf didn't have a watch or clock on board his boat. He calculated the passage of time and distance at sea when steering a course, by the number of cigarettes he'd smoked.

I looked up from the happenings on board *Nellie* to the outer pier wall. There were two distinct clouds of gulls moving slowly to the west beyond it, heading towards the harbour entrance. This signalled that there were two more boats making for home. These would be the first of the three-man cobles. My Dad was on one of these. Would this be him returning to port? My eyes followed the cloud of gulls as they travelled around the pier end before doubling back through the harbour entrance.

Into the harbour, shrouded by screaming gulls, came a large black coble with a narrow yellow stripe running from stem to stern. She had a single central mast, with a tanned mizzen sail loosely furled and hitched to the boom, which protruded aft from it. This was the *Betty*, owned by the Dalton family. Three brothers operated the boat and a fourth brother, Dick, was shore man in the baiting shed. Jack Dalton stood at the stern, steering with the heavy tiller while his brothers, Eric and Tom, were gutting fish.

Close behind the *Betty* came the *Rosemary*, also enveloped in a cloud of gulls. She was a similar craft but painted royal blue, topped with a bright red band. I could see my Dad, wearing his distinctive black beret. He was standing alongside Jack Rowley; they too were gutting fish. Jack's brother Tom was skipper and was steering the boat. Tom and Dad were partners in the *Rosemary*. They'd bought the vessel between them several years ago for seven hundred pounds. This was a major investment for Dad. As the boat came alongside the pier, I quickly descended the iron ladder, jumping into the boat at the first opportunity. More than half of the catch was already gutted and lay spread in the boat's bottom. The remainder was still in the 'crib', a deep, three feet wide storage section, which ran across the width of the boat. Fish were deposited into the 'crib' as they were taken from the hooks. It had capacity for about one hundred and fifty stones of fish when full.

When the boat was secured to the pier, Tom came for'ard to help with the gutting. Wanting to help, I picked up a spare knife. I couldn't easily gain access to the fish; I was only getting in the way and was told so by the skipper but Dad threw a few smaller fish onto the deck in my direction, so I could help. I opened the gills, inserting the sharp blade in the cold, slippery fish's throat with difficulty. My hands were soon cold and red again from the still biting wind. It was unheard of to use gloves when gutting fish. I slit open the belly of the dead fish, pulling out the liver and abdomen. I could never get it all out in one piece as others did, mine was always a messy operation. It was clear there would never be a career in surgery for me. Dad, who was gutting six fish in the time I took to do one encouraged me saying, "it'll come wi' practice son, y'll get the 'ang of it soon enough."

The catch of about one hundred and twenty stones of mostly large and medium sized cod, mixed with a few shiny silver haddocks, was soon gutted and I climbed back up the freezing ladder while Dad and Jack washed the fish.

Tom had also climbed to the pier and having located a portable weighing scale, wheeled it into position by the crane, appointing me to operate the capstan winch. This was an easy job and one which I liked. When the fish were washed Dad came up the ladders, leaving Jack in the boat to fill the baskets. Billy 'Blondie' Wood was standing close by, so Tom asked Bill if he would weigh the fish while he and Dad carried each 'weigh' the few yards to the fish market. Blondie would keep a couple of fish of his choice for his trouble.

Billy Wood was a small rotund man with fair hair. He owned a motor boat called *Venture*, on which he took passengers for trips around the bay each summer. He was a habitual smoker, though no one could recall ever seeing him buy a packet. "Gi' us cig," was his frequent saying. Blondie's sea gear was often in a state of disrepair and he'd wear seaboots discarded by other fishermen. It was said around the harbour, that if ever Billy Wood was out of work, he could get a job weighing snuff in a tobacconists, his accuracy with the scales was so precise.

Bill wasn't a greedy man but he could exist on less than most others. Stories of his meanness, mostly untrue, were exaggerated greatly when repeated. He enjoyed the legend created around him. It was said he could peel an orange in his pocket or he would climb to the top of Scarborough Castle before taking a pack of cigarettes from his pocket. He was renowned for having short arms and deep pockets. He would say, "never refuse owt that anybody gives ya, even if it's rubbish. Y' can always throw it away." Blondie would pick up any piece of twine or old rope lying around the harbour. He could always be found close by when any of the keelboats or trawlers were being painted. He would ask for the dregs remaining in the paint tin to paint parts of his own boat with.

As Jack filled each basket, he 'hooked' the iron hooks on the landing rope, into the basket handles. At the other end of the line, I passed three turns of rope around the capstan drum then hauled the fish from the boat. When the basket was level with the pier, Tom pulled the crane arm gently, pivoting it inwards to the pier. I lowered the basket of fish gently onto the scales. It was bad practice to drop it onto the scales and having had more than one bollocking for this malpractice, I'd swiftly learned the correct procedure.

After dropping empty baskets down into the boat for re-filling, I swivelled the crane out again, lowering the hooks back to the boat while Blondie weighed the basket of fish. It was quite a precise task. By taking a big fish from the basket, replacing it with a smaller one or exchanging three lighter fish with two heavier ones, the exact weight of five stones was reached, allowing seven pounds for the weight of the basket. Sometimes when the exact weight couldn't be reached, one or two pounds overweight would have to be sacrificed. This was never done willingly, though vessels that constantly gave below the required amount gained a bad reputation. This was reflected in the price received at auction.

Dad and Tom carried each basket to the market, where it was tipped onto the smooth, sloping, concrete floor. The fish were laid in neat rows, their heads in line, facing up the slope of the market. The end fish of each row was reversed denoting each five stone lot. The smallest sized codlings and the haddocks were tipped in neat piles. The fish market looked spectacular when filled from end to end with shiny, glistening rows of fish.

When the catch had been landed Jack sent up the used lines on the crane, two at a time. Dad and Tom stacked them none too carefully on a handcart. Each boat had its own. Soon all fourteen lines were piled upon the barrow and were wheeled the short distance from the fish market to the bait shed where they were stacked outside, next to the sacks of mussels. The skeining ladies had all retired to their homes, their work finished for the day. The baiting team remained, the required number of lines only recently completed.

Eight of the new baited lines were carefully loaded and delivered back to the pier by return. These were handled much more gently; the rows of baited hooks, though secured tightly on the skep, were disturbed as little as possible. A repeat journey for the remaining six lines was necessary, while I gingerly lowered these fresh lines into the boat. Jack, having swilled the vessel clean, removing the evidence of the day's catch, was pumping red bilge water from the boat into the harbour. He ceased this task, pleased to have a break from his exertions, to receive the baited lines, which he quickly covered with a large canvas sheet. This not only protected them from the elements until required, it also shielded them from scavenging gulls which would strip the hooks clean in minutes, given chance.

It was late afternoon now and almost dark. Boats that had finished their landing operations had moved further up the harbour. The cobles were tied side by side, sometimes as many as eight abreast. The keelboats were arriving back in port now, some waiting to discharge their catches. These bigger 'decked' boats, using more lines, had four crew, spent longer at sea, worked in worse weather and invariably caught more fish than the cobles, though were faced with greater overheads.

Dad and his shipmates tied the *Rosemary* on the outside of a row of boats, then trudged up the hill together to their homes and well-earned dinners. They still wore their long rubber seaboots, now folded down at the knee. Each carried his yellow oilskin, rolled tightly under an arm, encircling an empty sandwich tin and thermos flask. The oilskins and seaboots would be dried at home overnight in a kitchen or by a friendly fireplace. There was no heating or dry parts on cobles during the winter months, the vessels were constantly cold and wet.

Each man would be in bed by nine o'clock and would be ready to sail again in the early hours of the following morning, repeating the whole process again. It was gruelling work. 'Bad weather' was the only respite from the strength-sapping toil. On stormy days, when the skipper considered the weather too bad to sail, Dad and

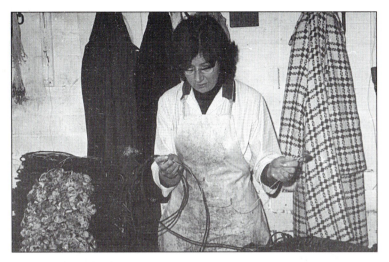

Rose Sheader baiting a line for the coble Hilda,
skippered by her husband Harry. Photo Ken Wigg

Dad at the harbourside with freshly baited lines. Note the used lines on
the barrow. In the background is the sailing ship Hispaniola,
used as a floating aquarium, circa 1953. Photo unknown

Coble Betty Sheader, a good catch of cod and haddock being gutted in the harbour. Photo Ken Wigg

The coble Betty owned by the Dalton family, circa 1953. Photo unknown

Jack would walk to the homes of the baiters and skeiners putting a note through the letter box of each, which simply said 'bad weather'. This saved the shore staff a wasted journey to the pier. The boat's crew would then return home for a few hours. There was still work to be found at the harbour, servicing fishing equipment, boat engines and a hundred other less essential but necessary jobs during the day ashore.

I remained on the pier and was able to help the crew of the *Osprey* to land their catch. Willing assistance was never refused and was usually rewarded with a couple of shillings or a fish. Tom Pashby, skipper of the *Osprey* was always kind and friendly to me. He was a very good fisherman though superstitious and quite eccentric. These were pre-requisites for command I later discovered. Most skippers were a little nuts and though I wasn't really superstitious, I never flaunted it or tempted fate.

Many people in the community were superstitious. Apart from the usual, not walking under ladders or touching wood, there were other taboos to be observed. Some skippers wouldn't sail on a Friday. There were fishermen's wives who refused to wash laundry on the day their husbands sailed. The women believed they would be washing their man away.

Whistling was frowned on; it was said to be 'whistling for wind'. When encountering poor fishing, men had been known to throw coins into the sea saying, if they couldn't catch fish they would buy it. Some would not take money to sea at all; many a child had the good fortune to encounter a crewman on his way to sea and be given the change from his pocket. It never amounted to much, there was seldom enough to meet the needs of most people. One trawler skipper, if encountering a priest, nun or a cross-eyed woman on his way to the harbour, would turn around and walk home again, preferring not to sail that day.

Tom Pashby believed all these superstitions and had others of his own. In his presence it was unlucky to mention pigs; they were referred to as curlytails. Rats were longtails, rabbits became bobtails or fluffytails and salmon, silverfish. A brush was only used sparingly on his boat and was never put on the lines or nets. It swept the luck away.

For a young person, not aware of this mumbo jumbo, offences against elders' beliefs were frequent though accidental, but as I grew older and less sensitive, the opportunities of upsetting some of the less popular or grumpier people were many.

Leaving the pier, I made my way home again. It was dark now and almost teatime. Sunday tea was usually a treat with trifle or sweet cakes. There were times when I'd have preferred to stay at the harbour, as some other lads did rather than go home for each meal. I could have bought a cup of tea and a sandwich at Harry's tea shack but Mum was insistent that I went home for all my meals, unless I was going out on a fishing boat. It was her way of knowing where I was at regular intervals, though she had long since stopped compelling me go to Sunday School.

That had been a major victory for me, but only after many rows, abscondings and forged attendance cards. My sisters were regular attendees, so it was easy for Mum to compare the little ink star in their attendance book with the attempted effort that I drew in mine. I conveniently lost the 'star card' when this ruse was discovered. There were too many distractions around me to be forced to attend school on weekends.

After tea I went to the back of the house to collect my barrow from the shed. This vehicle, a large wooden fish box in a former life, now had two pram wheels attached and timber handles 'borrowed' from the boat builder's yard. I climbed the drain pipe to the little balcony on the first floor at the rear of the house, tied a rope around the sack of empty mussel shells which Mum had skeined that morning, then lowered the sack from the balcony to the cart. Sliding back down the drainpipe, a much quicker exit than the front door, I untied the rope and threw it back onto the balcony. Dad would often lower the shells down for me if he was available. This refuse weighed about four stones, half the weight of a sack of live mussels.

I wheeled the barrow to the top of the street, then turned east along the road towards the sea, passing Maggie Bean's bakery. Maggie, a small, plump, cheerful lady with a flowery pinny, made wonderful morning rolls, 'hotcakes', which Mum gave us some mornings with butter and jam or treacle. When I was younger my pals and I collected brambles each autumn for Mrs Bean from the countryside. My pal John frequently got confused saying, "we've brought you some beans Mrs Bramble." She was a very generous lady often giving cakes to the children in the area.

En route, I called at two more houses collecting a sack of shells at each. The second sack fitted into the barrow but the third had to be stacked on top. I often spilled shells from the top sack onto the road. Controlling three sacks on a barrow going downhill isn't easy when they weigh more that you. Reaching the harbour road at the bottom of the hill was always a relief. It was even worse if I had to take full sacks up the hill from the bait shed. I could only manage one at a time. Fortunately this didn't happen often. Usually the delivery lorry dropped the full sacks at each house.

As I pushed my unwanted cargo of shells along the seafront towards the Marine Drive, I recalled how I was once sent to a house to collect a full sack of mussels to be returned to the bait shed. I was informed that Renee had that very day produced a baby, her eighth or ninth. "She won't be able t' skein mussels for a few days yet. Bring 'em back down 'ere," Micky Scales instructed me. Up the hill I went with my trusty barrow. When I arrived, a bag of empty shells stood outside the door. Next to it was a bucket of skeined mussels. Renee must have had her baby, then skeined the mussels.

I was heading in the opposite direction from my bike ride earlier in the day when I'd been flithering. Fortunately I only had to reach the beginning of the Marine Drive, not travel the mile or so that I'd ridden earlier. The wind had dropped so there were no big waves splashing up the wall from the sea but the night was pitch black. The few gas lamps in the ill-lit area sustained so much damage from the sea, they were in a state of disrepair every winter.

I approached the three-barred railings at the edge of the pavement, beyond which was a twenty foot drop to the sea. Though my eyes were accustomed to the gloom, I could see little more than an occasional splash of white, as waves broke with a crash on the rocks below. I picked up the top sack and threw it over the top bar into the blackness below. Tipping the barrow forward the other two sacks spilled out onto the ground. These were manoeuvred, one at a time, between the bottom two rails, helped with a hefty kick; then I was off like a shot from a gun, pushing my empty barrow back to the brighter street lighting of the harbour road. It was really scary in the dark on the Marine Drive, though I never told anyone.

There must have been millions of mussel shells dumped over the Marine Drive wall through the years. The sea dispersed them quickly; there never seemed to be a pile of shells at low water. I didn't always dump my shells over the Marine Drive. Sometimes, under the cover of darkness, I dropped them onto the deck of the harbour dredger when it was conveniently berthed. The crew would then have to dump them at sea when they sailed, along with spoil, taken from the harbour bottom.

Having returned my barrow to the shed, my final job for the day, following the evening shipping forecast, was to obtain Dad's sailing orders for the next morning. He gave me money for his supply of cigarettes; then I walked fifty yards to Jack's house. He too gave me money for cigarettes. It was only a few minutes walk to the skipper's house. Tom Rowley, having studied the shipping forecast would take into account where, if at all, it would be possible to fish on the following day. He'd consider how long it would take to get there and the state of the tide for the best fishing, then calculate the necessary departure time. It was always between two and six o'clock in the morning.

Furnished with this information, my next port of call was the Scarborough Castle, a pub on the way home. Here I'd purchase three or four packs of cigarettes and a packet of crisps for myself. Returning to Jack's house I delivered the cigarettes and sailing orders. These were usually received with cheerful thanks and a joke or good-humoured chat. Occasionally there would be threepence or sixpence for my trouble.

Minutes later, Dad would get the same information and supplies. When this daily errand was complete, I would usually go out to meet my pals, mostly the sons of fishermen. There was a fair chance that we'd return to the harbour again, it was like a magnet to us. If there was no vessel movements to observe or late workers in the bait sheds to help or hinder, we'd build dens in the piles of new wooden fish boxes, stacked behind the fishmarket doors. They were like giant building bricks. Constructing a den was easy and good fun. The lads that smoked would puff away out of sight of any adults. We'd use candles for lighting and spend hours talking and reading comics. Only once did we make a den from used fish boxes. They were dry and seemed fine to use but on returning home Mum's nose twitched and she said, "where've you been? You stink of fish." I probably did, but it was only when I arrived home that it was noticeable.

Sundays in winter were always hectic. The hours sped by; there was always something to do. The weekdays in comparison went at snail's pace. After school there were still shells to tip, cigarettes and sailing orders to get but it was the daily school attendance which dragged. It was school that kept me away from the harbour.

Although each day seemed endless, my school was a good one. Along with approximately a hundred other boys, I was fortunate to attend the Graham Sea Training School. These premises, including grounds, were given to the town for the training of boys for a life at sea, by the Graham family in 1916. This followed the death of this wealthy family's only son, killed in action in France. There were only five classes in the school, one for each yearly intake of twenty to twenty five boys.

As well as conventional lessons, we were taught seamanship, signals, chartwork, knots and splices and navigation. The headmaster, Mr Tribe was a retired Royal Navy Commander. He wore glasses but his alert eyes missed nothing. He was respected and his authority was never in doubt. If he used his cane, it was as a last resort and I'm sure he felt that he'd failed.

Our other nautical instructor was Mr. Herbert. During his sea career he'd been a First Officer, sailing the world in merchant ships. He had a thin, weathered, craggy face, dominated by a large pocked nose. His thinning straight hair was swept back tight to his head. Mr Herbert would stand no nonsense or suffer fools.

The first year teacher was Mr Grant. He was quite a big man with a round face, bushy eyebrows and straight greying hair. I and many other eleven-year-olds, had been clearly intimidated by him when first joining the school. A strict disciplinarian, he kept his short, thick cane in a cardboard tube, which he called his torpedo tube. When three or six strokes were required, he would count them out as if commanding a submarine, 'fire one, fire two, fire three.' He never spoke of his time spent at sea.

Bespectacled, silver-haired, small, red faced, slightly over weight and very unfit, Mr 'Harry' Casey was deputy head. He was also librarian, history and English teacher. A keen amateur dramatist, he seemed to be acting all day long. Everyone, including some of the staff, thought he was a little odd. He repeated stories of the children that he went to school with as a boy. The first few times these stories were amusing, but when the same stories were told time and time again through to the fifth year, everyone rolled their eyes and thought, "not again."

'Bruiser' Maine taught metalwork, geometry and technical drawing. Though smaller than some of the pupils, he was bald, fierce and violent. Muttering incoherently, his mouth half-filled with polo mints, he would throw anything close to hand, mostly chalk but also wooden blackboard dusters, at pupils not paying attention. Mr Maine was a very talented engineer, having made working models of steam engines but he was so difficult to understand, that I learned little in his class. In one exam under his tuition I scored a measly three out of a hundred. He said it was for spelling my name correctly. During a metalwork class, while attempting to construct a serviette ring, I made an error which could not be corrected. I requested to 'start again'. He said, "put it in the vice, file it away to nothing, then you can start again." It took me three lessons to reduce this failure to a pile of filings; I never did finish my serviette ring.

In a technical drawing class on the first day, we were given wooden drawing boards and T squares. Holding up a T-square he said, "these are not hammers, they are not to be used on drawing pins when attaching paper to your board". One boy thinking he was unobserved, did just that but was spotted. Bruiser stormed down the aisle between desks, snatched the T square from him and began hitting the unfortunate youngster over the head with it, ranting, "boy, how would you like to be a bloody drawing pin?"

The school possessed four boats; two small black painted cutters, *Dolphin* & *Tuna* and two varnished admiralty type whalers, *Maisie Graham* & *Hugh Graham*.. During the winter these craft were in the school's boatyard under canvas covers but in the summer, we rowed or fished with hand lines in the cutters and rowed or sailed in the whalers. In autumn, the boats were hauled out of the water from one of the harbour slipways, to be taken back to the boatyard. In the spring we cleaned, painted and varnished the boats before taking them back to the harbour, to their summer moorings. The maintenance sessions were occasionally an opportunity for mischief. Dressed in overalls, we often got as much paint on ourselves as on the boats.

It was no easy task taking the boats back to the school. The building was situated at the top of a very steep hill, overlooking the town. The boats were dragged up the cobblestoned street on gun carriages, hauled with ropes by half the boys from the school. It was very difficult to keep a straight face one day, when the Headmaster stepped backwards and fell in the harbour while organising the recovery of one of the boats. He surfaced, spluttering that no one should panic.

I enjoyed playing football, turning out for the school team throughout my time there. This wasn't a great achievement as there were so few boys in each year; it took the pick of the first and second years to make a second year team. This principle was followed in the third year too but the fourth year team did benefit from a few ringers in the fifth year. No other schools in the district had a fifth year. Now here I was back at school and Easter seemed an eternity away.

CHAPTER II

'FLOREAT'

The term dragged but eventually it was the week before Easter and the school was closed for the Easter holidays. I had two whole weeks to do as I pleased. My Uncle John, skipper of the keelboat *Floreat* had finished the winter line fishing and had changed the fishing gear on his boat to go trawling. Now he would be catching dover sole, plaice, dab, whiting, cod and haddock in a net. I was on my way to find him to request permission to sail with him the next morning. As I crossed the road to the harbour, I took in the scene at a glance; it was a hive of activity.

Along the seafront people were cleaning or painting shops. The crab stalls were being erected ready for the coming season. Amusement arcades were opening their doors to the early spring sunshine. It was as if everything had been in hibernation and was re-emerging. Across the road on Sandgate slipway, some of the small passenger motor boats and rowing boats were being scrubbed, cleaned and painted by their owners. Others were already gleaming with new colours and awaiting passengers.

I saw old Walter 'Pellet' Eves with Harry 'Pinner' Wray as they stopped for a yarn and a cigarette. I couldn't resist a smile; here were two real characters. Pellet had a rowing boat called *Unexpected*. I thought this an appropriate name. Pinner operated a motor boat with an equally suitable name, *Happy Days*.

I paused for a while, recalling a few years ago, when I was nine or ten, crossing this very same road at the same time of year, a bag of broken chocolate Easter egg in my hand. Pinner shouted to me as I reached the other side, "Eh young Nommy, can y' sing?"

I was confused. "I can sing a bit, but not very well," I replied hesitantly.

"Well if y' can sing go an' get in my boat."

I was even more confused and looked down to where his boat was berthed at the bottom of the slipway. It was full with lots of other kids. There must have been fifteen or sixteen of them and I knew them all.

"We'll jus' get a few more an we'll be off," Pinner said, smiling as the situation dawned on my confused face. "But ya' not coming if ya' can't sing."

"I can sing," I hurriedly assured him and rushed down the slipway to join the unruly mob in the *Happy Days*. My bag of chocolate egg was snatched from my hand and quickly distributed as I piled into the throng. The memory was clear as day in my mind. The boat was licensed to carry eight passengers and contained twenty or more youngsters. We were singing 'I love to go a wandering' at the top of our voices, drowning out the noise of the engine. At the stern, holding the tiller stood Pinner grinning from ear to ear as he pointed the boat down the harbour towards the entrance.

"Louder!" he was shouting, "Louder, I can't 'ear ya'!" The harbour was ringing with the sound and many people stopped their work to watch the *Happy Days* on her first cruise of the year.

When the passenger trade was quiet Pinner fished with a few pots for crabs and lobsters to supplement his income. One day while hauling his pots, close to the pier wall, a corpse appeared, floating close alongside his boat. "Suicide job," he thought, "happening more often these days." He dragged the man's body into the boat, then propped it up at the stern. After putting its arm over the tiller and his sou'wester on its head, he continued to haul his pots.

Fishermen passing by, leaving or returning to the harbour, thought he'd acquired some assistance for the day. He re-laid his pots then headed back to port. Pinner carefully steered his boat slowly through the harbour mouth then walked for'ard leaving the dead body slumped at the helm. He turned facing his unseeing helmsman and was heard to shout, "if y' can't steer any straighter than that, don't bother comin' tomorro'."

Reaching the harbourside I approached the two men, asking if either of them had seen my Uncle John lately. Pellet pointed to the far side of the harbour where the *Floreat* was berthed. I could easily see my uncle working with the fishing gear on the boat's deck.

"Use yer eyes ya daft young bugger," he said gruffly but not unpleasantly. I thanked him and headed for the *Floreat* at a trot.

Pellet had spent a lifetime at sea. He was a master net maker and mender and could also bait and 'set' lines as good as anyone living. Now, in his old age he was taking passengers around the bay in his rowing boat. He'd always seemed a bit grumpy, so I could easily believe the story told to me relating to a couple of prospective passengers.

Pellet was already having a bad day when a rather stout, well-dressed, matronly lady walked down the slipway to where his boat was floating. Against her better judgement, it seemed she had been persuaded by her small, timid husband to take a boat trip. She stood with outstretched hand, waiting to be helped on board the little craft. He ignored the hand, pointing to one of the rowing seats at the front of the boat.

His gruff voice barked, "Sit yer arse down there missus."

She scowled at him retorting in a voice that was pure Queen's English, "won't I have to row if I sit there? I don't want to row, I want to sit at the back for a leisure cruise."

Pellet was unmoved. "If you ain't rowin' you ain't goin' missus, ah sit at t' back t' steer."

The large lady reacted with fury. "How dare you? I'll not be spoken to like that, certainly not by a man. Men are intolerable, insufferable, in fact they are the weaker sex."

She continued her tirade but Walter remained unmoved, he twisted his cap a little, and looked askew at the ranting woman,

*Walter 'Pellet' Eves. This photograph appeared in the Scarborough
Evening News advertising Moor & Robsons ales, circa 1959.
Photo Scarborough Evening News courtesy of the Eves family*

*John 'Johnny Nom' Normandale sitting on the Lancaster Flat.
Photo Scarborough Evening News*

*The Floreat rigged for herring drifting. Taken at the end of the
West Pier. Note the herring drifters in the background. Photo Ken Wigg*

*The Margaret Jane sailing on a trawling trip. Note the trawl boards
fore and aft in the gallows, circa 1958. Photo Ken Wigg*

still in full flow, "if men had to have babies there wouldn't be any babies, men just don't know what pain is!"

He lifted his cap, scratched his head and quietly replied, "well all ah kin say missus, is you've never 'ad a kick in t' knackers!"

Running along the pier, I arrived breathless at the point above where the *Floreat* was berthed. Looking down I could see the trawl net spread across the deck. The two heavy 'kite' like trawl boards were lying against the boat's port side bulwark, one for'ard and one aft. On the starboard side, near the wheelhouse, lashed against the boat's side was the 'sole tub'. In a previous life it had been half of a wooden beer barrel, now it was a fish washer. Stacked on their sides, for'ard of the tub, were numerous empty fish boxes. Hopefully these would be full of fish tomorrow.

The wheelhouse where Uncle John spent most of his day, when not helping to pull in the net, had at some time had its sides artistically grained, but multiple coats of varnish, flaking by varying degrees, eliminated the effect. The interior of the wheelhouse was basic. At the fore end was the steering wheel, about three feet in diameter, its spokes worn to half their original size with constant use. The brass rim and centre boss were green with verdigris. Equally green was the brass compass, mounted on the shelf above the wheel. At the edge of this shelf on the port side, screwed to the wall, a wooden box with a circle cut in the centre contained a battered, old, household alarm clock.

In contrast to the compass, the brass wheel at the rear of the wheelhouse, which engaged and disengaged the engine, was shiny through constant use. Above the control wheel was an ancient, pale blue radio with the words 'Marconi', on what had once been a polished chrome emblem. About twelve inches square, standing eight inches off the wall, this equipment was used to communicate with other skippers to compare their catches. As no one ever told the truth, I always thought this was a pointless exercise. In an emergency the radio could be used to summon assistance using the distress frequency. Most skippers also reported 'home' at least once each day. Wives on shore would tune their radios to the inter-ship 'trawler band' frequency at a regular time, listening to the familiar voices of their menfolk giving reassurance and probable time of return, in a one sided conversation.

Next to the radio was an echo (depth) sounder. Similar in size to the radio, this was a more recent addition, though rapidly showing signs of deterioration in this hostile environment. A swiftly revolving stylus behind the glass face, depicted the seabed as a consistent brown mark on the white, moist paper. A metal gauge, calibrated in fathoms, indicated the depth as the paper was automatically fed through the machine.

A wooden grating on the floor, plus an upturned fish box which doubled as a seat when the weather was fine, took up half the remaining space, leaving very little room for the skipper to manoeuvre in his domain.

In front of the wheelhouse was a shiny new green and yellow painted trawl winch. The two revolving drums each held more that a hundred fathoms of gleaming, half-inch diameter, steel wire. This was a major improvement to the *Floreat*. Prior to this installation, the trawl was towed with two thick ropes, hauled by hand with the aid of a capstan. These ropes were coiled on the deck in two large piles.

I quickly scrambled down the ladder to the boat's deck, turning to take in the scene. Uncle John, a small, slight man with dark wispy hair, twinkling eyes and a ready smile was watching the shipwright, Johnny Clark and the blacksmith, Bobby Goodall, as they fitted the final bedding bolts which were to fasten the new winch to the deck. The two craftsmen were spending more time admiring the pretty young ladies, strolling along the pier in the spring sunshine, than progressing with their work.

Bobby Goodall had made the eight large bedding bolts securing the winch, constructing them from steel rod in his workshop, situated across the road in Quay Street. The bolts were threaded at each end and fitted with double nuts. On completing the job he'd given them to his wife Harriet, instructing her to take them to the boat. Harriet was his only assistant and wore a boiler suit as any man would. I found this strange because I'd never encountered a woman doing men's work before.

Harriet crossed the road to the quayside, cradling the bolts in her arms. On reaching the boat she proceeded to throw them down to the boat's deck. Unfortunately, one of the precious bolts bounced awkwardly and fell into the harbour, splashing between the boat and the pier. Horrified, she returned to the workshop to face the wrath of her husband. Calling her a useless bugger, he stated that he had no intention of making another. Giving his wife a large magnet tied to a length of light twine, he sent her back to the boat saying, "go an' fish it out an' don't come back 'til you've got it." She left the workshop in tears but doggedly fished for the missing bolt for more that an hour until she recovered it.

Unlike most people involved in the fishing industry, Bob and Harriet lived on the outskirts of the town, driving to work each day in Bob's little Morris van. Their route took them down the Valley Road leading to the foreshore, passing under the high Valley Bridge, notorious for suicide jumps. On several occasions in the early mornings, they discovered the bodies of unfortunate people, unable to cope with life. This happened so often, the police began to suspect Bob of throwing them off.

I crossed the deck to watch Uncle Robbie at work. He was the boat's engineer. Of medium height, Robbie was thin with sharp features and sunken cheeks. A flat cap was pulled down over his forehead, almost hiding his eyes. He was occupied adjusting the tension of the winch drive belt.

"Now then young Freddy, where'd you spring from?"

I told him it was the school holidays and I was hoping to go to sea with them the following day.

"You'll 'ave to ask our kid, he said, nodding in the direction of his brother. "E's t' skipper, it's not ma place t' say owt."

Uncle John, his fate in the hands of the tradesmen, sat resigned on the boat's rail, a pot of tea in hand, waiting for the men to continue their project. They in turn were surreptitiously admiring the legs of a very pretty young lady in a flared summer dress, standing on the pier above, looking down at the boat.

"Nobody'll be goin' anywhere unless them two buggers get that job finished." He nodded his head in the direction of the two still ogling tradesmen. Completing his work with the drive belt, he made his way to the engine-room, down a small square hatch behind the wheelhouse. I quickly followed. The engine-room was very gloomy, lit only by two bare, dim bulbs. These were powered from a twelve-volt battery stored behind the access ladder. The battery was charged when the engine was running. It was obviously in need of charging. Even when the engine was operating the lights were barely sufficient. Years of spillages of fuel and oil, exhaust leaks and rubber particles from the drive belt had left every surface stained or streaked with grime. It had been many years since the engine-room had seen a paintbrush.

If the lighting was bad the stench was worse. The mixture of old oil and stagnant bilge water was all pervading. Half crouched, I made my way to the port side of the engine, treading carefully on the oil soaked boards surrounding the base of the machine. From this vantage point I could watch him start the engine without impeding the proceedings.

Uncle Rob didn't notice these surroundings as he crouched over the engine. He was quite used to them. The environment was tolerable while the boat was in harbour but I made a point of avoiding the engine-room hatch when at sea. The smell, plus the heat from the engine, added to the motion of the boat was a sure recipe for seasickness. I'd learned this from painful experiences in the past.

The engine, a three cylinder, petrol/diesel was one of a range of machines built by 'Kelvins' of Glasgow. Petrol was used to start the engine, then it was 'knocked over' to diesel when it was running steadily. The diesel fuel was stored in port and starboard fuel tanks, each holding about a hundred gallons. I'd often watched Uncle Rob start up the engine; it was a work of art demanding a feel for the machine.

He picked up a red petrol tin, which had been lashed to the base of the ladder. It was almost empty but the residue would be enough for his purpose. He poured the contents into a receptacle on the top of the engine, at the rear end. Next, he tightened three small compression 'T' screws, one on each cylinder on the starboard side of the motor. These were opened to stop the engine. Returning to the rear of the machine he took off his cap, wrapping it around the big shiny brass handle attached to the base of the engine. This handle was polished daily by his cap each time he started the engine.

Using both hands he freely rotated the handle until the cogs meshed, then with more effort continued to crank it slowly, until the handle reached the top of its pivot. Uncle Rob gave a grunt, then began turning the handle with all his might, building up speed as it revolved. After five or six revolutions the engine coughed, fired and began to pick up speed.

Uncle Rob wiped his brow with his multi-purpose cap then replaced it on his head. The engine was chugging away steadily. He shuffled back to the starboard side, reaching for a lever on top of the engine, which connected all three cylinders. He waited, listening carefully to the rhythm of the motor. It wouldn't run for long with the small quantity of petrol used. The throbbing of the machinery picked up marginally and he immediately threw the lever through 180 degrees. The effect was dramatic.

The engine noise and speed increased significantly. The dim lights brightened, though the effect was only to highlight the grime. Billowing grey smoke from the exhaust overboard came drifting down the hatch. The section of the harbour where *Floreat* was berthed was temporarily clouded in exhaust fumes. Uncle Rob grinned and gave me a thumbs up sign across the engine. He'd explained to me in the past, that the engine speeds up slightly when it has consumed the petrol and is running on the remaining vapour. That was the time to 'knock her over'. If the right time was missed, the engine would stop and the process would have to be repeated. He said it was harder on the second occasion due to flooding. I didn't know what that meant. Starting boats' engines was a constant headache. Spark plugs and an electric magneto were required for the petrol section of the engine. These were often unreliable. If the mag' or plugs were damp or the plugs worn, the engine would refuse to start.

If anyone accidentally touched the exposed spark plugs or leads on the top of the engine, the electric shock received was stunning. Soapy's father, Old Ernie, when he was skipper of the family boat, *Shirley Williamson*, was impervious to pain and immune to the electricity given off from the spark plugs. Ernie senior could hold the wire lead with the voltage passing though him without feeling any effects. Young Ernie's eyes rolled when he said, "it was all very well for 'im but it didn't 'alf 'urt when 'e 'eld the spark plug lead wi' one 'and and 'eld my ear wi' t' other."

I emerged from the engine-room hatch to see the sun creeping back through the thinning exhaust fumes. The pretty young lady had quickly moved on when the choking gas filled the atmosphere. The two craftsmen were now addressing the remaining winch bolt in a serious manner. Uncle John looked happier. Now would be a good time to ask if I could sail with him tomorrow. I made my way to where he sat on the boat's side. As always he was wearing a clean, pale blue fisherman's smock. His wife Margaret, a small red faced, fussy woman with a tight hair bun and little round glasses ensured he was presentable each day. Margaret was quick of movement and meticulous in all matters relating to cleanliness.

In her spotless pinny, she would even 'black lead' Uncle John's anchors at the end of each line-fishing season. Her dustbin was scrubbed weekly after being emptied. The red brick floor of their house shone from constant polishing and was so slippy as to be hazardous. Even the exterior drainpipes of the house were clean as far as could be reached by Margaret standing on a chair. It was said that her windows were so thin with continual cleaning that the glass bulged when it was polished.

"What time are y' sailin' in t' mornin' Uncle John?"

"Five o'clock, what d' ya' wanna know fo'?"

"I was 'oping I could come wi' ya," I replied quickly.

"I suppose so, you'll 'ave to ask y' Dad first, see if it's OK with 'im."

I knew Dad wouldn't mind. Though he was very particular who he'd allow me to go out to sea with, Dad knew I'd be safe with Uncle John. There had been occasions in the past when I'd been refused permission to go on certain boats, but this wouldn't be one of them. The remainder of the day was spent getting the *Floreat* ready for sea. I was despatched to the marine engineer's workshop with the empty petrol can for refilling. There'd been times when I was younger, when I'd been sent to the engineer's on silly errands. I'd previously been sent for a 'long stand', a 'sky hook' or 'red oil' for the port light but I hadn't been caught on fools' errands recently.

On returning from this mission, Joe, the third member of the crew gave me a short grub list to bring from the 'provisioners'. It consisted of bare essentials, tea, milk, sugar, bread, margarine, bacon, eggs and corned beef. There would be nothing to pay, an account would be sent to the vessel's 'fish-selling agent'. The agent auctioned the fish, supplied boxes for the catches, collected payments and generally settled the vessel's accounts. For this service a deduction from the vessel's grossing, usually between three and five per cent was made.

Early that evening, I found Dad, having completed his meal, braiding netting on a crab-pot frame, while watching television. A steaming mug of tea was in easy reach by the fireside; he seemed in good humour. I picked up one of the empty needles he was using and began refilling it from the football-sized ball of twine at his side. Giving a little cough to clear my throat I cautiously began, "is it OK if I go 'off' with Uncle John tomorra? 'E's got a new winch fitted and I want t' see it working."

Dad continued his net making and said nothing for a while, considering the aspects of my request. He would know I was on holiday from school. We were never allowed to take time off from school for any reason. He would be considering the weather and my safety close to the new machinery.

"Ave you asked Uncle John?" he said after a while.

My mind raced forward, I could go. "Yes, 'e said to ask you," I replied quickly.

"That's alright then," he said. "What time are y' goin'?" It was like one fisherman talking to another. I felt as big as a house.

"Five o'clock," I replied, hardly able to get the words out.

"I'll give y' a shout at 'alf past four, we're ordered for five as well."

We both knew he wouldn't have to. I'd be awake. I had my own alarm clock and could get up at any time, unless it was a school day. I slept fitfully, excited at the prospects of tomorrow.

Chapter III

Trawling

When the alarm rang I was quickly out of bed, reaching for the clock on the chest of drawers at the other side of the room. I never left it close by the bed for fear of turning it off while still asleep. I had to get out of bed to cancel it.

My clothes were in a pile on the floor by the bed. Jeans, shirt, gansey, smock, seaboot socks, plimsolls, then finally a muffler. This checked cotton square rolled and knotted tightly round the neck prevented abrasion from the stiff, oilskin collar and prevented water entering the top. Apart from the jeans it was mostly Dad's sea gear, a little on the large side, which I'd borrowed from the airing cupboard. I never knew if he was quietly pleased or just resigned to me using his gear, he never said.

My seaboots were wrapped tightly in my oilskin, a bundle that would fit under my arm. These were bought with money that I'd saved from my various jobs. I wouldn't need them until later in the day.

I quietly made my way downstairs to the kitchen, not wanting to wake Mum or my sisters. There were two mugs of steaming tea on the oilcloth-covered table. I sat at the table saying nothing. Dad was filling his thermos flask with more tea. His sandwich tin had been stocked the previous evening by Mum. There would be meat or corned beef sandwiches, home-made scones or buns, jam or lemon curd tarts, clapped together so they wouldn't stick to any of the other items.

Dad would eat these at brief intervals during the morning, between the various 'fleets' of pots which he and his shipmates would haul that day. They would be back in the harbour before midday.

I didn't need any provisions. There was food on board the *Floreat*. There would be plenty of time while towing the trawl to make pots of tea. Our drink finished, a nod, then we were on our way to the harbour; Dad, wearing his seaboots, carrying his flask and 'packing-out' wrapped in his oilskin. My arm enclosed my 'oilly' and boots. It seemed strange that the streets were empty even though it was daylight.

"Not a bad mornin', we should get t' off side pots for some crabs today." I liked it when Dad spoke of fishing matters, it gave me a feeling of being grown up, accepted as equal, one fisherman to another.

I said something about the new winch on the *Floreat*.

"Keep out o' t' way when t' wires are runnin' out, an' watch out when t' codend swings in."

There were several other 'bewares' and 'don'ts' all of which I'd heard before, and that I would hear again from Uncle John, then again from Uncle Rob. When all this had been repeated, they'd probably let me operate the winch under supervision anyway.

The streets may have been empty but the harbour was a hive of activity. Keelboats were manoeuvring towards the harbour entrance or taking fuel from the bunkering tanks. Like the *Floreat* all these vessels were engaged in trawling during the summer months. Several coblemen were lowering boxes of bait into their boats with the pier cranes. Pot bait was always in short supply, it was a constant chore for these men to find sufficient bait for their requirements each day.

Fish which had no commercial value were saved by the trawlermen to supply the potters' needs. This bait changed hands for two or three pounds a box and was a useful supplement to the trawlermen's wages. The trawlermen would also save undersized fish for bait. These were fish below the minimum legal landing size and should have been returned to the sea. Hardly anyone did, there was no point in throwing dead fish back when they could be sold. Any live fish were returned, mostly codlings and flatfish which survived better out of water. The bait money, known as 'stocker' or 'wrangem' was the crew's perk. There was no share for the boat owner and usually nothing for the taxman out of this extra cash. When there were no fresh supplies the coblemen used anything available, including offal from the bins on the fish market.

Lobsters preferred gurnard, horse mackerel or flounder, known locally as 'mudbuts'. With harder skin, this fish would remain in the bait-band longer. Small whitings, haddock and codling were soon torn from the central position in the pot, to be devoured by greedy crustaceans. Crabs were very particular, they would only eat fresh bait. If it was even slightly off, they wouldn't enter a pot. Lobsters on the other hand would take the bait, even if it was rotten.

"See ya later." Dad stopped at the tier of boats which included the *Rosemary*, and carefully put his oilskin on the ground. If he broke his flask now it would be a dry day; it had happened before. His shipmates, expected on the pier in the next few minutes, would share theirs but there would be less for all. It was unusual for fishermen to 'sleep in' though one or two were renowned for it. These men would only be tolerated when good crew were not available. The top skippers never carried crew that were unreliable.

I walked a little further along the pier. A shout from the deck of the *Margaret Jane* as I passed brought me to a halt. It was my pal Tom. He'd left school only a few weeks earlier. "Now then Nommy, what are you doin' up at this time of o' mornin'? 'Ave y' pissed t' bed?"

I would have loved to reply with some equally smart quip and would think of one later, but a weak "very funny" was all that came to mind. It was pleasing to hear his skipper shout, "stop fuckin' about an' pull that bloody 'ead rope in, an' stow it, like y' were shown."

I envied Tom. He was only a year older than me but had left school and was 'shipped up' on one of the top boats. I had at least another year to do at school and even then Dad didn't want me to go fishing. He said fishing was 'finished' and that I should join the

Merchant or Royal Navy. He said I could be an officer if I stayed at school and worked hard. I resented still being at school when all my friends were on the boats. I was the youngest of the crowd of lads who haunted the harbour. They were all sons of fishermen and constantly reminded me that I was the runt of the pack.

Though the youngest, I didn't always follow their examples. One day, with four or five other lads, I was sitting at the pier end, our legs dangling over the side. We were watching the small boats passing in and out through the harbour mouth, taking visitors on their pleasure trips. As usual we were jeering at the visitors in the boats or shouting suggestive remarks to any girls on board. Some of the boat owners would reply with witty comments of their own. Others, the more grumpy ones would say things like, "isn't it time you bloody lot grew up?" or "pity y've nowt better t' do."

All the lads were smoking. I'd never bothered with cigarettes before but Mick thought I should have one. I placed the fag in my mouth and he lit it for me. There was nothing to it. I put the cig in and out of my mouth, puffing out the smoke each time I withdrew it. "You're not doin' it right," Mick insisted. "You've got t' really inhale it." He took a deep drag on his cigarette to demonstrate the art.

"OK," I said taking a large lungful. Immediately I began to cough and splutter, I felt sick and dizzy. My eyes streamed with tears. Now the harbour traffic was forgotten, I was the centre of unwanted attention, the butt of quips and jokes.

"Y'll soon get used to it," one them said, "we all did."

"Get used to it! If that's fun y' can 'ave my share," I spluttered and never smoked another cigarette.

I stood for while on the pier, watching the *Margaret Jane* pass through the narrow harbour entrance. Her skipper, Tom 'Denk' Mainprize was one of the pioneers of trawling with keelboats. New, light, synthetic materials were becoming increasingly available. Trawls could now be made of thin, strong, buoyant twine, offering much less resistance when towed through the water.

I could recall, just a few years ago, only large, purpose built, coal-burning, steam trawlers with nine crew used this method of fishing and now these were obsolete. Coal had become too expensive as a fuel. The last two steam trawlers in Scarborough were soon for the breaker's yard. Both the *Emulator* and *Reformo* were built before 1900 and were worn out. This was the end of an era. Prior to the Second World War, dozens of 'steam trawlers' sailed from Scarborough. During the First World War, seven of the Scarborough fleet were sunk by a German submarine in one day.

Throughout both World Wars is was not uncommon for fishing boats to encounter mines during the course of their work at sea. On one occasion a Scarborough steam trawler caught a mine in its net. The skipper involved was foolish enough to bring it close inshore, dropping it on the beach at high water. When the tide ebbed it was left high and dry. This created quite a panic in the town until the bomb disposal squad arrived, and removed the detonator from the weapon. The mine, now safe, was left in situ for later removal.

A few men from around the harbour decided that as it had no detonator it was completely safe, (though very heavy). The men loaded it on a handcart, taking it to a scrap metal merchant in the middle of the town. It took them about half an hour to get it to his premises, up the hills and through the streets. When the scrap man 'explained' what he would do to them if it wasn't removed immediately, it took them about three minutes to get the object back to the beach.

Sadly, a small schoolboy also thought it was safe and lit a fire inside it while it was still on the beach. It exploded.

Uncle John walked along the pier with his brother Rob; Joe arrived a few minutes later. Most of the fleet had already sailed. I waved to Dad as the *Rosemary* cruised past, running down the harbour towards the entrance. He was busy cutting up the bait into tempting pieces but waved back, clasping his knife aloft.

There was a banging and clattering from below, followed by the usual cloud of grey fumes filling the air as Uncle Rob started the engine. This soon thinned and we were ready to sail. Our skipper yelled, "chuck us off," to the duty berthing officer, 'Pudding' Appleby, who promptly unfastened our ropes from the mooring bollards. I coiled the head rope loosely around the stock of our anchor, lashed securely in the stem. Joe coiled the stern rope neatly, then hitched it to the back of the wheelhouse with a short strop. He then disappeared down the cabin ladders with a bundle of kindling to light the cabin fire. He'd smashed a previously-broken fish box into small pieces on his arrival at the harbour. There would be no tea for anyone until the stove top was glowing.

Uncle John skilfully manoeuvred the *Floreat* away from the pierside, thrusting the engine ahead and astern, while spinning the steering wheel hard to port and starboard. Two minutes later we were steaming through the harbour entrance. Uncle Rob emerged from the engine-room in time to exchange a wave and shout a brief "mornin'," to the tidal officer standing on the pier as we passed the lighthouse to port, before Robbie too disappeared down into the cabin.

When we were clear of the rocks, close to the pier end, Uncle John turned the boat ninety degrees to port, steering south east, parallel to the coast. Smoke began to billow from the cabin funnel which passed through the deck, immediately above the stove. A gentle breeze blowing from the land directed it out to sea, away from where I was standing.

The funnel, a six foot metal tube, five inches in diameter was blackened at the top and had little of the original material remaining. Many repairs had previously been effected using baked bean tins, hammered flat, then fastened in place with thin wire. Before too long it would collapse entirely. My eyes followed the direction of the smoke to the horizon, where numerous ships could be seen. There was never a time when the skyline was empty. Colliers, deeply laden, headed south to the Thames, where their cargoes were consumed in the Capital's power stations. Others, north bound, were empty, riding high in the water as they returned to the Tyne for more coal from the Durham coalfields in a never ending cycle. I could also identify a couple of Arctic bound trawlers, recent sailings from one of the busy Humber ports. Most skippers gave these ships a wide berth when outward bound, as their courses were occasionally erratic. The wild crews on these fine ships would be in various states of inebriation, after their all too brief visit home.

There was little to do for the next hour or so. It was six miles along the coast to 'Filey Tow' our chosen fishing grounds, three miles offshore from the notorious 'Filey Brigg', a long, low spit of reef, jutting out to sea. The sun was already high in the sky on the port bow. I leaned against the side of the wheelhouse, talking to my uncle through the open window. He pointed out the various landmarks along the coast and their names. As he spoke he steered the *Floreat*, subconsciously countering any deviation from his course before it happened. This never ceased to amaze me. I'd tried to steer the boat several times before, managing to travel in the general direction but when looking astern at the wake, it seemed as if a snake was following.

The six miles of coastline varied dramatically, from sandy beach to towering cliffs with rock strewn base. It was so deceptive. Today the sea was calm, the air warm, yet history told of many lives lost from the dozens of ships which foundered along this short length of coastline. Nothing manmade remained as evidence; constant winter gales pounding the shore with awesome power had destroyed all signs of shipwreck.

We passed close to a red painted coble where two men were busy hauling pots. "I wonder whose pots them two are 'aulin'," Uncle John said, pointing to the little craft. "Proper thievin' buggers they are. They don't just 'aul their own gear, they'll 'aul anybody's. They came unstuck though. They came across a pot buoy in t' fog one day. Instead of leaving it alone the buggers picked it up an' began 'aulin' t' pots. When they'd 'auled about twenty, another boat came out o' fog towards 'em. It was t' *Betty*, who t' pots belonged t'. T'*Betty's* crew were 'aulin' 'em from t' other end. There was bloody 'ell on. T' Dalton lads couldn't prove 'owt, but they med sure everybody knew about it."

It wasn't long before an arm emerged from the cabin hatch, placing two pint pots of tea on the deck. Free of his cargo, Joe climbed the cabin ladder to the deck, cigarette glowing between closed lips. Picking up the mugs again, one in each hand he ambled aft, his legs clad in thigh boots, folded at the knees. He handed one pot to me, the other to the skipper.

A large dollop of ash fell from the cigarette, which had never left his mouth, narrowly missing the second mug. He mumbled something indecipherable through a cloud of smoke, coughed, then without waiting for comment, turned to make his way for'ard again.

During the war, like most other fishermen, Joe had served in the 'Patrol Service', spending a considerable period of time overseas, 'out foreign'. During this extended stay he suffered the terrible embarrassment of contracting a mild venereal disease. Joe made the fatal mistake when writing to his wife, of reporting that he'd got the VD. The embarrassment for his wife Dora, who was not particularly bright, was even greater. She thought this was a medal that Joe had been awarded. Everyone she met throughout that day was informed, "my man's been given the VD."

Ship's tea was terrible. The taste was nothing like the tea at home. It was made with tea leaves, in a teapot and with boiling water but then evaporated milk and sugar were added to the brew. Throughout the day the pot was continually 'topped up' as required.

The cracked, pint mug, three-quarters full, had once been white. Large mugs were used so they wouldn't topple over when the boat rolled. They were seldom filled more than three-quarters full to prevent spillage. Though not full, there was far more here than I was prepared to drink. The weather was fine, I hoped not to be seasick today but if I drank this quantity I most certainly would be. After wetting my lips with the dreadful brew I placed the mug on the deck, where it would be forgotten until we arrived at the fishing grounds. I'd then swill the tea overboard before taking the two empty mugs back to the cabin.

When we reached the northern end of the fishing ground, Uncle John pulled back on the throttle then turned the brass wheel to neutral. As the boat slowed he put the wheel over, laying the boat across the wind. This was important. The net was always cast on the 'weather side' into the wind, allowing the gear to stream clear, as the vessel drifted down wind. The smoke from the cabin funnel indicated the wind direction. Boats with gas stoves used a small flag or ribbon attached to a stay to find the slightest breeze.

I took the now empty mugs to the cabin, where I swapped my plimsolls for seaboots. Oilskins were not required yet as the fishing gear was dry. The thigh length boots would act as protection, keeping my trousers clean.

The fishing ground was an area of flat, soft sand, several miles long, though less than a mile wide. To the west and south was impassable rock. At the east and north were numerous wrecks, victims of a First World War German minefield. The area chosen was popular with the 'keelboat' trawlers; several had arrived before us and were already towing their nets. The expected catch was mixed but plaice and sole were the higher value, main target species.

The trawl, a large conical-shaped string bag was a simple affair. At the mouth of the net along the top, a series of ball shaped, aluminium floats held the net up. Along the bottom, to keep the net down, forty feet of heavy chain was fastened. As the net was dragged along the seabed, the chain dug into the sand, disturbing the flatfish, forcing them from the bottom where they were scooped up by the net.

At each side, the net was held open by the trawl boards or 'doors'. This matching pair were constructed of heavy wooden planking, shod with iron at the base. These shoes became highly polished with the abrasive ground contact during the process of 'trawling'. The steel wire cable on the new trawl winch linked the doors to the boat.

The *Floreat* was rolling gently across the slight swell, which had grown with the breeze. The skipper tied the complicated 'codline' knot at the end of the trawl, where the fish gathered as the net moved through the water. When the bag of fish was hauled on board, this knot was easily untied, releasing the catch from the net, allowing it to spill to the deck.

I helped to lift the heavy trawl boards over the rail ready for use. They were slung to the boat's side fore and aft with short rope strops. I stood clear as the three crew carefully streamed the trawl out over the boat's side. When the net was in the water alongside, it was lowered down below the surface. Four, five-fathom bridles attached it to the doors.

Great care was taken to ensure the net went over correctly. There was no way of checking if it was 'fouled' below the surface. Only when hauled would mistakes be discovered. This would be vital 'fishing time' lost. If no fish were caught there was no pay for the crew, as all fishermen were paid on a share basis only. There were no wages or salary. The voyage expenses, which consisted of fuel, food, insurance, harbour dues, agents commission etc. were deducted from each week's gross fish sales. Appropriately named, the 'net' sum was divided into two parts. Half would go to the owner of the boat and gear, the remainder to the crew. Each man, including the skipper, received an equal share. My pal Tom on the *Margaret Jane* was on a 'half share' of a man's wage. If the gear was owned by the skipper he would take ten or fifteen per cent of the boat and gear money. If he owned the boat and was successful, he would earn a substantial amount, though would have to meet bank repayments, repairs, renewals and equipment replacements from this share.

The share system was the only concept of pay which I understood. I had an uncle who was a bus driver and for some time I thought he was paid a 'share' of the fares taken by his conductor.

Uncle John returned to the wheelhouse, turned the steering wheel hard to port then engaged the engine in head gear. Tension was taken up on the two wire warps, each shackled to a trawl door. "Leggo o' t' door strops, young Fred," he yelled. These were easily unfastened as their weight was now held by the wires from the winch. The vessel was now turning in a circle to port, the net streaming out on the port quarter. Uncle John was monitoring his compass. When the *Floreat* was on a southerly heading, he yelled, "leggo together."

Robbie and Joe, standing behind the winch, released their respective brake wheels, allowing the trawl boards and net to sink into the water. The boat, picking up speed, was now on the south easterly course anticipated. The warps, marked every ten fathoms, snaked across the deck, passing through 'fair-leads', then out over the side. The trawl was lowered to the seabed, astern of the boat. The depth of water was a little more than thirty fathoms. A ratio of about three times warp to water depth was needed to obtain the best seabed contact with the gear.

"Keep some weight on 'em, check 'em at ninety," the skipper bawled above the din of the revolving drums. The wires snapped taut as the required amount was reached. Both brakes were screwed down tightly. The helm was put hard over to starboard, bringing the rigid wires close to the port side. Robbie, now free of winch duty, wrapped a short length of chain, shackled close to the stern, around both wires, drawing them together. He secured the chain tightly around the mooring cleat, neatly harnessing the warps.

The *Floreat*, now labouring, moved slowly through the water dragging the gear along the seabed. Unless the net fouled a subsea obstruction, Uncle John would guide her up and down this stretch of ground for three hours until 'hauling time'. It wasn't uncommon for the trawl to snag 'fasteners'. The east coast of England between the Tyne and Thames is strewn with wrecks and debris. Colliers and fishing vessels have traversed this area for centuries. Severe storms and two world wars have left countless hundreds of ships sunk. Old, rusting anchors lost from sailing ships attempting to anchor when driven shorewards by gales, were occasionally caught and recovered. Large and small rocks, plus all manner of ordinance, mines, bombs, torpedoes and depth charges were caught in trawl nets.

Uncle John kept a constant watch on the land. The boat had no navigation equipment other than a compass and depth sounder. As the boat moved along the compass course, he used various landmarks in transit to inform him of his position on the grounds. At the southern end he turned the boat when a fissure in the cliff lined up with a distant farmhouse. To continue beyond this point would mean a badly damaged or lost net. A knowledge of the tidal movements was essential. Though only three miles from the nearest land, the tide continued to run here for three hours after slack water ashore. Allowance had to be made when towing a trawl before a strong tide, as it was impossible to turn the vessel quickly.

There were several vessels trawling this stretch of ground, we were passing them constantly. None had hauled their nets yet, so there was no indication of what catches were likely to be. We'd be the last boat to haul, as we were the last boat to arrive.

As we towed south east we passed close by the green hulled, *Margaret Jane*, which was now heading north west. There was no sign of any crew on deck, they'd be having breakfast or catching a brief nap below prior to hauling. Denk gave a friendly wave from the wheelhouse as we passed. Denk was married to Maggie, Margaret Jane, a large, formidable lady who during the summer months, assisted by her daughter Rachel and other family members, operated several of the open fronted shellfish stalls on the promenade. The stalls, in a line under a single corrugated iron construction, were old and quite primitive. All were supported on trestles, with white painted sloping surfaces to display the wares. A large name board at the front denoted the owner of the stall and hid the trestles. It was a major improvement to the quality of life on the stalls, when a communal electric point was installed, enabling all the stallholders access to a kettle.

Unfortunately, due to faulty installation, the corrugated iron wall on which the plug was mounted was live, as Paddy, the family's dog discovered when it cocked a leg against the wall. The hound, not known for speed, bolted and wasn't found for three days.

I occasionally worked for Mag on these stalls after school and at weekends. The jobs varied daily. On Saturday mornings there were whelks to be extracted from their shells. These were delivered pre-cooked in sacks. It was not unusual to see eight or ten youngsters sitting at the back of the stalls 'picking' whelks. The pay was good; one shilling and sixpence for each gallon or 'wash' of whelk meat produced. Four 'wash' was an average morning's work but six or seven could be achieved, though this quantity made for very sore hands.

On Sunday mornings I would boil two, five-stone baskets of crabs. These were drowned first in fresh water, which usually took up to two hours. This could be speeded up if the water was slightly warmer, though if it was too warm the crabs would 'cast off' their claws. When dead, each crab was scrubbed to remove sand and dirt from the exterior, then cooked for about fifteen minutes, in old washing coppers. The cooked crabs were then rinsed to remove residue from the boiling process. There was usually a few left over 'cast off' claws for me.

After school and late afternoons during school holidays there were kippers to post. The stallholders took orders from holidaying visitors for two or three pairs of kippers, to be sent to relatives or friends. An hour or two before the final post these orders were processed. The kippers were wrapped in greaseproof paper, then enclosed in a purpose-designed cardboard box labelled, 'Fresh kippers, a present from Scarborough'. Each was tied with parcel twine. Some days my box barrow was piled high with kippers to dispatch at the nearby Post Office. Each box required stamps; the licking and sticking left a foul taste for ages after.

As Denk was passing, I recalled a conversation which I'd heard on the radio on a previous trip on the *Floreat*. The crew of the *Margaret Jane* had hauled their trawl, only to discover it was severely damaged. It would need taking ashore for major repairs. Denk reported this on the radio to the other vessels in the area. An anonymous voice on the same frequency suggested that he should try towing a pair of his wife's drawers. Equal to this, Denk replied that he didn't think his boat had enough power to tow them. No one ever dared to report this to Maggie.

Midway through the watch, the 'arm' appeared from the cabin hatch again, placing a pot of tea, then a bread bag on the deck. Up came the cigarette, followed by Joe. The pot of tea and a bacon sandwich wrapped in the bread wrapper, were brought aft and handed through the window to Uncle John. Turning, coughing but still puffing on his cig, he said mine was down below in the cabin. I followed him for'ard, asking him to pass it up. It would be too hot in the cabin at present and there was no way of discarding the dreadful tea if I was below. Carrying my breakfast along the deck, I resumed my place at the wheelhouse side. The sandwich was good, made with thick bread, a heavy helping of margarine, plus several rashers of bacon topped with an egg. The tea was sipped sparingly to wet my mouth, most of it was swilled over the side.

A flock of gulls was gathering around the *Optimistic* about a mile ahead, on our starboard bow. This was a sure indication that she was hauling her trawl. The gulls have an unerring ability to know when food is available. *Optimistic* was owned and skippered by Tom 'Sonny' Williamson, brother of Ernie. Herby was one of his crew, his bulky shape unmistakable, pulling on the tight netting.

As we drew closer more and more gulls were arriving. I wondered how they knew when and where to come. There were few around while the boat was trawling but immediately the hauling process commenced, they arrived from all directions. The 'codend' was hauled from the water up the boat's side as we passed. It looked a good haul but there would be much debris to be jettisoned before the fish were sorted from it.

Finishing my sandwich, I sat on the deck with my back to the boat's side. The sun was warm and the boat rolling gently. It was very pleasant. "Give 'em a shout y' Freddy, it's 'aulin' time." It was the skipper calling to me from the open window. I'd dozed off. Getting up I headed towards the cabin hatch, staggering a little as the gentle roll of the vessel unbalanced me. Descending into the gloom of the cabin from the bright sunshine, I could see only a shaft of light, fighting its way though the grime on the skylight glass.

My eyes began to adjust to the poor light. I could see a dull glow and feel the heat from the stove on my left. Its fire had been allowed to die down a little and was no longer a threat to my disposition. A slight vapour of steam emitted from the kettle, perched securely on top. There was also a whiff of stewed tea from the dreaded teapot at its side. I wondered why they bothered with the kettle at all. Why not bring the water to the boil in the teapot, the resulting brew couldn't be worse. I didn't suggest it. I avoided looking at the other side of the ladder, where the 'gash' bucket was fixed. This was the refuse bin, formerly a five-gallon oil drum. It was emptied over the side when full.

Uncle Rob sat wedged in the apex of the triangular cabin, where the seat lockers met. His discarded seaboots lay close to his feet. Thick, grey, woollen socks encased his trouser legs to above his knees. The versatile cap, lying inverted on the locker at his side, contained his muffler, a packet of cigs and a box of matches. He was engrossed in a paperback book and hadn't realised I was there.

My eyes now adjusted, I looked around for Joe. A crumpled mound of blanket in the port-side, bottom bunk indicated his presence. "It's 'aulin' time," I said, "we'll be back at t' north end soon, 'e wants to 'aul before we get there." This information was the sum total of my knowledge of these grounds, but I thought it sounded professional.

Rob folded a corner of his page to mark his place, then threw it casually into the bunk at his side. He began pulling his boots on over the grey socks. Joe rolled from his bunk, scratched his head for a few seconds, then reached for his cigs and matches. Having lit up, he took down four mugs which were gently swinging from hooks screwed into a deck beam and placed them on the cabin floor. As he reached for the teapot, I did a quick calculation and realised that one was intended for me. I hurriedly said, "don't bother wi' one for me, I'm OK jus' now." I grabbed the nearest empty mug, and placed it back on a hook.

Uncle Rob removed the lid from the stove-top using his cap for insulation, then threw a couple of small shovels of coal into the void from the coal bunker under the nearest seat locker. He replaced the stove lid quickly, as smoke began to rise from the orifice.

Joe, having dispensed the evil brew which he called tea, was refilling the kettle from the single cold water tap, protruding from the bulkhead at knee height, next to the stove. The water was delivered from a tank, fixed behind the bulkhead in the fishroom. This tank was filled weekly from the pier hose-pipe.

My pals and me had great fun with the pier hoses, which had tremendous force. The pipes were regularly used to wash down the fishmarket following each day's landings and were often left connected to the taps, strategically placed in each section of the market. This mischief was usually followed by a drenching and bollocking from the duty pierman for 'pissing about'.

Mug in one hand, I climbed two rungs of the cabin ladder, using the other hand to place the mug on the deck above. Unencumbered, I climbed to the deck to take the skipper his next delivery of tea. Fifteen minutes later, I was clad in seaboots, muffler and a full-length oilskin frock which reached below the knees. I was ready to haul.

Rob and Joe engaged the winch clutches, enabling the drums of wire to revolve as the winch turned. The brake wheels, on their respective sides were released, then Uncle John eased back the throttle to half speed. The noise of the motor died to a dull throb.

On a nod from the skipper, I released the chain at the stern which secured the warps, then Rob turned the wheel engaging the winch. There was a screech from below as the rubber belt protested, then the winch began to turn, winding back the ninety fathoms of cable paid out earlier.

The trawl was coming up. Water ran from the wires as they crossed the deck, passing through fair leads directing them onto the winch. The two crewmen were now guiding the wires evenly back and forth onto the drums, using shoulder-length pieces of scaffolding pipe as levers. This was dangerous work, one of Dad's, 'don'ts'. Many injuries and fatalities have occurred while 'guiding on'.

Rob and Joe were standing in front of revolving machinery, on a wet, sometimes rolling deck. It would be impossible to stop the winch in time if anyone was to slip and fall. They'd be pulled into the winch, then wrapped with wire. I was told to stand by the tension wheel in case of accidents.

The last mark on the wire came inboard denoting ten fathoms of warp to come. The engine was eased to dead slow and Robbie, who had now taken control of the tension wheel, spun it quickly, stopping the winch, while Joe engaged the brakes. The trawl doors and trawl were now below the boat but clear of the propeller. Uncle John manoeuvred the *Floreat* in a semicircle until she was once more across the wind, then gave the engine a quick burst astern, taking the forward movement from the vessel.

Now across the breeze, the two trawl warps led down into the water, slightly off the boat's side. Uncle Rob gently applied tension to the belt drive, easing the doors from the water. Joe fastened the for'ard one, while the skipper, no longer required in the wheelhouse, secured the after one. Robbie disengaged the clutches then restarted the winch.

A rope, fastened to the after door was passed to Robbie, who took a couple of turns around the revolving winch barrel and began to heave. Over the boat's side appeared the bottom of the trawl, the attached chain now highly polished from its contact with the seabed. The winchman held the weight while we pulled the remaining section of the trawl's mouth on board. When this was achieved, Robbie cast off his rope, joining us at the boat's side.

The sock like 'belly' of the net, with the catch now trapped within, streamed out of sight, down into the sea. A few small fishes escaped through the mesh but were quickly picked up and devoured by the flock of gulls now surrounding us, their noise drowning the sound from the engine and winch.

The four of us now began to haul the net by hand, using the motion of the waves. We pulled in the slack net as the vessel rolled to port, jamming it between our knees and the ship's side as she rolled back to starboard. Uncle John began to call out, "together lads, on the roll, pull now." We scrambled at the slack net before us. A few seconds later he yelled, "jam it now lads, 'old on." Again we pushed our knees tightly against the ship's side, trapping the net. We could feel the drag from overboard, as the long stocking tried to run back, but our combined weight held it. Several more rolls and the catch was held tightly in the codend alongside. Joe passed a rope strop, an eye spliced in each end, several times around the net. Uncle Rob, now back at the winch, hauled half a ton of dripping mass from the water and over the rail, with a block and tackle fixed at the mast top.

We stood clear as the catch swung in, thudding against the wheelhouse side. On the inside of the 'bag' I could see whitings and codlings. Sticking out through the meshes were the heads of dover soles and dabs, unable to escape though the mesh. As the codend was held suspended against the wheelhouse, Joe bent down, reaching beneath the bulging bag to unfasten the 'codline'.

Released from its confinement, the catch spilled out across the deck. Fish of all types wriggled and flapped amid a pile of sand and shells. Countless five fingered starfish, some the size of dinner plates lay immobile, helpless out of water.

While the empty net was still suspended, Joe, Uncle John and I shook it roughly with heads averted, eyes closed, loosening most of the 'stickers' trapped by their gills. These fell out of the net onto the pile. The few remaining fish were pushed back or pulled through the mesh. Later in the year there would be jellyfish in the trawl too, which were extremely painful if splashed in one's eyes.

Now on deck, the catch was ignored. The priority was to get the net back into the sea; time was pressing. There was only time for three hauls. Uncle John tied the codline again and the trawl was lowered back over the side, repeating the 'shooting' process.

Once fishing we addressed the catch, which was now mostly dead. Soles, plaice and other flatfish lived longer out of water, 'round' fish; cod, whiting, and haddock died quickly. With the skipper back in his 'shed', Joe brought a stack of empty baskets from for'ard and the three of us gathered round the pile, on our knees, to sort fish from rubbish. Round fish and flatfish were thrown in separate baskets. Soles, by far the most valuable of the species were kept separate. All the undersized fish, long dead, were thrown into a box, to be saved for the potting boats. The residue was shovelled unceremoniously back over the side. Two and a half-baskets of mixed round fish, a basket of flats and twenty 'pair' of soles was the catch for that haul. Soles were traditionally counted in twos, forty soles were twenty pair.

Once picked up, we began gutting the catch. The gulls, immediately aware, commenced swooping for the food. They could catch the offal in mid-air, long before it hit the water. Plaice, with their familiar red spots, were slimy, making them difficult to hold when gutting. Their intestines, located on the right, close to the head were tiny. It required only a small slit to facilitate removal. Gutting soles was even more difficult, especially when still alive. They wriggled like eels and were almost impossible to hold.

As the catch was gutted, it was sorted into species and graded into two or three sizes. Next the baskets of fish were dragged to the 'sole tub' to be washed. I was given the 'draw bucket' and instructed to fill the tub. It was a galvanised bucket with a fathom of rope spliced around the handle. A large knot in the other end of the rope prevented it from slipping through my hand if the bucket filled suddenly. I began to draw water from over the side, which was a precarious task. There was quite a drag from the bucket as the boat moved through the water. The bulwark rail at the side of the vessel was little more than a foot high. It would be easy to overbalance, and fall into the sea.

While I was filling the tub, Joe and Robbie were dunking half-filled baskets of fish into it, swirling them too and fro vigorously.

This very quickly rinsed the fish, washing the blood and sand from them. It was essential to keep fresh water flowing into the tub, as it quickly became discoloured. As each half-basket was washed, it was tipped into the fish boxes stowed beyond the tub. The fish were arranged tidily fore and aft, then the boxes were covered by a canvas sheet; protection from the elements and predatory gulls.

When the washing process was completed, Uncle Rob shed his oilskin, dropping it to the deck, then disappeared down into the engine-room to survey his domain. Addressing the engine, he withdrew the dipstick, checked the lubricating oil level and replaced any shortfall from a five-gallon drum. Satisfied that there was no excess water sloshing in the bilge, he returned to the deck. Bilge water was ejected by a hand pump fixed into the deck, a job allocated to me when required.

Picking up his oilskin, he made his way to the cabin, where Joe was dispensing the most recent batch of the endless supply of tea. I was despatched to the wheelhouse again with a mug and a doorstep-sized corned beef sandwich. Returning, I kicked off my boots. Conditions in the cabin were not too bad now. After finishing my sandwich and sipping at the tea, I managed, unnoticed, to dump the remainder in the 'gash' bucket before climbing into the spare bunk. It would be two hours yet before we hauled again.

The next two hauls yielded similar results, though a big turbot in the last haul of the day boosted the value of the catch. This large flatfish, similar in size to a dustbin lid, would weigh at least a stone. Like the soles, it would be sold by the pound on the market.

Now we were on our way back to harbour with several boats ahead of us. All were shrouded with gulls. We hurried to get the catch gutted, washed and stowed in the boxes before docking. Time spent gutting in harbour was time lost. As we passed between the piers, I looking up to St Mary's Church, the magnificent building overlooking the town. Its clock indicated that it was already past six o'clock; the day had sped by. The pierman took our ropes, then chalked 'Floreat' on a blackboard, prominent at the back of the market. All boats' names were added as they arrived in port. This was the rotation in which the catches would be auctioned tomorrow.

There was congestion at the fish market as boats waited in turn to land their catches. We could go ahead of any which were still gutting or washing their fish. Sometimes, if a boat had a big catch of whitings, the crew would be gutting and landing the catch until late in the evening but would still sail again in the early hours of the following day.

We didn't have long to wait before a landing berth became available. There were lots of people milling round on the pier. Some were visitors, curious, wanting to see fish that were not encased in batter or accompanied by chips. There were coblemen hoping for bait from the trawlers. Others were looking to earn fish, by helping to land the boats' catches but there were also scroungers. The same faces were present each day, people who thought fish was free. "Can I 'ave a couple o' small 'addocks?" was a frequent request, which was difficult to refuse without offence. It was annoying when the person asking then took four or five medium sized fish.

Uncle John would mutter under his breath, "a couple was two when I went t' school," then "they wouldn't go in t' butchers an' say can I 'ave 'alf a dozen sausages," but he never refused anyone. It was common to see men carrying a bag of fish in each hand, the accumulated collection scrounged from several boats. In most cases it wasn't taken home to feed hungry families, but sold in pubs. One individual carried so much fish from the pier he was universally known as 'seagull'.

We were assisted in landing the catch by Albert, an elderly man with a brown craggy face. His few remaining blackened teeth were obvious when he spoke, which was not often. He wore an old, torn, stained jacket, which at some point had been part of a suit, though not his. His grey, crumpled trousers were hardened with dried fish juice. The short rubber seaboots he wore constantly, were no longer waterproof.

Albert wasn't very bright, but willing to work for his fish. He'd been ship's cook in one of the old steam trawlers in his younger days. This wasn't a position bestowed for of any culinary expertise that he possessed, though he could boil a kettle. He could also fry, bake or boil fish and was able to make steamed suet duffs and 'elastic' stew, which stretched for the duration of the voyage. The skipper reasoned that if Albert was in the galley, he wouldn't be impeding work on the deck.

It was part of the cook's job to visit the butcher's and grocer's shop, arranging for provisions to be delivered to the vessel, in readiness for the next voyage. Albert called at the grocer's on his way home from the Dolphin pub one afternoon, a little worse for being on the wrong side of six pints. Although he'd never been able to read or write, he was able to indicate to the assistant his requirements, simply by looking round the shop.

At sea, during the next trip, the hungry crew left the deck after stowing the catch below, to find a huge, steaming meat and potato pie standing in the middle of the cabin table. They sat around with eager anticipation. Albert sliced into the pie, dispensing it to the waiting men who tucked in with relish. One by one they looked up, faces contorted. "This bloody meat's off," croaked one of the crew.

"It shouldn't be," replied Albert, reaching into the slop bucket. "It's just come out o' these tins." He held aloft an empty 'cat food' tin.

Albert had never mastered the art of baking bread. All his previous attempts had been fraught with disaster, as he explained to any of the deck-hands prepared to listen. His bread would never rise. The consensus of opinion was that he wasn't using enough yeast and that he'd only been kneading the dough half heartedly; he should put more effort into it. He set about a new batch of baking with renewed vigour, adding extra yeast and then some more. He pounded it, thumped it, elbowed it; he did everything but jump on it, until he was quite exhausted. Recovering, he cut it into lengths, placed it in the coal fired oven, then went confidently onto the deck to inform the crew of his latest attempt.

Following half an hour of banter and a few rude jokes, several of the deck-hands accompanied him to the galley to observe his latest effort. Low and behold the bread had risen beyond his greatest hopes. Unfortunately the oven door had to be dismantled to get it out.

Our catch was soon landed, weighed, then laid out under the fish market ready for the morning sale. Albert, rewarded for his labours with a couple of codlings and a large plaice, shuffled from the pier contented. Uncle Rob brought two boxes of ice on a barrow from the ice plant near the pier entrance. He spread this across the boxes of fish, which were covered with a canvas sheet overnight to retain the ice. It would also be protection from scavengers, feathered and human. Pilfering was a common occurrence.

Joe and I used the barrow to bring empty boxes to the boat, replacing those which had been landed. These were passed down to Uncle John who was keen to move from the landing berth. Others were waiting to land and tempers were short with anyone dallying. Everyone was keen to get home. With one exception, me, they would all be sailing again in the morning. I had other plans.

It was a good feeling coming ashore with my two uncles after a day at sea, though there was an underlying feeling of being a fraud. They'd be back again at five o'clock, ready for another day at sea and though I'm sure I was of some assistance, they'd manage perfectly well without me. They almost always did. I parted company with the crew across the road from the harbour. They opted for a brief diversion to the 'Newcastle Packet', another favourite watering hole for fishermen. They'd talk, exchanging fishing reports and discuss potential for the morrow over a couple of pints.

I reversed my earlier route, back up the hill in the direction of home. Was it only this morning? It seemed ages ago. The contrast was stark. The previously empty roads now thronged with people, mostly holidaymakers. There were a dozen or more kids, my sisters among them, playing a game in the street as I neared the house, but I ignored them. Entering the warm room, a feeling of weariness began to creep up on me.

Mum and Dad were sitting either side of the unlit fireplace, like a pair of bookends; Dad with the daily crab-pot under construction between his knees, Mum, knitting needles flashing, a cardigan nearing completion in her lap. After the greetings Mum insisted that I, "Get rid of those stinking clothes into the wash tub, an' get a bath, while I get your dinner ready." I couldn't smell anything unpleasant.

Dad conducted an investigation into my day before I went to the bathroom. "Did y' catch owt? 'Ow did t' new winch go? Did y' keep out o' t' way? 'Ad you any spare bait?" Having satisfied his curiosity, I took a hurried bath, returning in clean clothes to a man-sized steaming plateful of Sunday dinner.

A long day at sea, a hot bath, then one of Mum's dinners was more than enough for me. I retired to bed unbidden. My final thought was that the weather forecast for the following day was warm and sunny. There'd be thousands of holidaymakers in town, a good day for a curio stall.

CHAPTER IV

THE CURIO STALL

Next day, fully recharged and following a hurried bowl of cereal, I took off for the harbour again. It was mid-morning, the weather as predicted. The small passenger boats were already busy plying their trade. The old steam trawlers, *Reformo* and *Emulator*, were tied up in their customary berths near to the harbour entrance, having landed their unprofitable catches overnight. There were a few other boats in port for repairs or painting but most of the fleet were at sea.

I walked along the fish market, where the auctions were coming to an end. The previous day's catches had almost disappeared, only two or three 'shots' of fish remained to be sold. Stopping close by, I watched the sale in progress. The auctioneer, standing on the boxes of fish, was plucking bids from the crowd of merchants surrounding him, in a garbled and what appeared to be foreign language. The bidders were undetectable to all but the trained eye of the salesman. Some buyers were wholesale merchants, with a staff of fish filleters. Their companies dispatched fish every evening to the inland markets of Billingsgate, Sheffield, Manchester and Birmingham. Other buyers were local retail fishmongers and fish and chip shop proprietors, buying their produce first hand. One merchant was renowned for buying only cheap or damaged fish, which when battered and cooked was undetectable. No one from the harbour bought fish and chips at his shop.

There was great resentment and distrust between fishermen and fish merchants. All fishermen considered the merchants to be robbers, who, though not seeming to want fish, never left any unsold on the market. Dad collectively called them 'the forty thieves' though I was never sure which was 'Ali Baba'. The merchants always accused the fishermen of giving short weight or 'dressing', putting the best fish on the tops of boxes and the poorer specimens underneath. It was a strange relationship. The two factions had no love for each other but couldn't live without each other.

Some merchants were honest and fair, others would steal fish by changing the labels which were placed on each box to identify the purchaser. They would also alter the tallies, which denoted the weight in each box. The fishermen never won in this scenario; they lost misappropriated fish and were paid less for short weight. I heard a disgruntled fisherman watching his catch being sold mutter, "at least Dick Turpin wore a mask when 'e robbed people."

I could see George and Tommy among the throng of fish merchants. Both were quite elderly but had been rum characters through the years. During the depression of the 1930s when the steam trawlers were tied up, both fishermen and merchants were temporarily unemployed.

Early one bitterly cold day, when snow lay thick on the ground, these two friends decided to try their luck shooting game in the nearby countryside. They'd walked to the moors beyond the town, where rabbits, hares, pheasants and grouse could usually be found in abundance. The pair trudged across field after field for miles with borrowed shotguns, unused, as they hunted 'something for the pot', to feed their families. It was late afternoon, the watery sun sinking when Tommy turned to George saying, "I'll tell y' what Georgy, I'll carry anythin' you shoot today."

"Right oh!" said George, and promptly shot a cow. "Carry that bugger!" They were each fined five shillings at the next Quarter Sessions of the Scarborough Court.

Leaving the sales behind, I wandered round the harbour looking for my friends. Coming towards me, pushing a handcart almost as big as himself, was 'Billy Aye Aye'. Bill was bound for Sandgate slipway, his cart laden with seven or eight, five-gallon drums of fuel for the motor boats. Billy was my Dad's uncle. He was about fifty years old, less than five feet tall and weighing no more than six stone. His wizen face, resembling a retired jockey, was old before its time. The inevitable cigarette in his mouth, from a distance, appeared to support his cap, which threatened to envelope his head.

His shock of tussled, greying hair hidden, Bill wore bib and brace overalls, shirt and an old fisherman's gansey even on the hottest days. On Sundays he wore a dark blue suit and his best gansey. The workload for one so small was stamina-sapping. Billy distributed hundreds of gallons of fuel and lubricating oil around the harbour each week on his cart. Not only delivering but gathering the empties and refilling them, from a large storage tank in the engineer's workshop.

He lived with his widowed sister Nan, in a small, ancient house overlooking the harbour. I remembered with great affection the visits to their house with my Dad. I would stand in the window, watching the traffic coming and going in the harbour entrance. Nan, whose husband was killed in a winch accident on a trawler, and only child, a daughter, had died in her teens, was very kind to all the youngsters in our family. A large part of her meagre income was spent on fruit and sweets. She was affronted at any suggestion that she mustn't waste her money.

As the distance between us narrowed I said, "Hiya Bill."

His reply was predictable, "aye aye," hence his name. Billy never had time to stop, or perhaps his barrow took such effort to shove that he was reluctant to stop, knowing he would have to gather momentum again.

On round the piers I wandered until I saw Dougie & Brian, digging for worms in the harbour-bottom where the tide had receded. I yelled, "Hiya, are y' gettin' any?" then clambered down the iron ladders to join them, without waiting for a reply. The duo had a large tin, more than half-full. The graving fork, which they took turns to use, was similar to a garden fork but with wider prongs.

As the tide retreated, the worms could be found below the surface, buried in the sand and mud. A small worm shaped 'cast' identified the presence of the creature, which would be somewhere below, twelve to eighteen inches down. The trick was to start digging beyond the cast, working deeper towards it. The digger must work quickly, the worms move fast in the soft sand and the hole quickly fills with water from the surrounding watertable, as the sea was only a few yards away. The success rate of capture varied, I only managed about fifty per cent, some people would get almost every worm they pursued.

"D' ya wan' a hand an' d' ya fancy makin' a curio stall later on. There's loads o' folks about. We could make some money an' 'ave a bit o' fun." They were digging worms to sell to the fishing tackle shop for bait. Soon the tide would advance again, cutting off this source of income, which was never very lucrative. The man in the tackle shop would only pay two bob a hundred for the worms but would then sell them to the anglers at a shilling a dozen.

They refused my offer of help with the worming, as they had already put considerable effort into the project and there would be little enough for two to share. We agreed to meet at one o'clock at the back of the fish market, where our stall was to be erected. I padded back to the ladder, leaving deep footprints from my plastic sandals in the soft sand. My footwear during the summer consisted of plimsolls, borrowed from school or plastic sandals. The latter were ideal in or near the sea. They were impervious to salt water, sand, rock pools, engine oil and the hundreds of other contaminants which I came in contact with. On the down side, they were hopeless for exploring the castle hill, due to the abundance of nettles. My feet were permanently striped from sunburn.

On the nearby 'Golden Ball' flat, which took its name from the adjacent pub, stood the *Courage*. She was a lovely, well kept, fifty four foot, blue keelboat; the pride of the fleet. The *Courage* was on the 'hard' for some general maintenance work following the winter cod-fishing, before setting off for Grimsby, where she would be based for the summer, catching dogfish. Her skipper owner, Will Pashby and his crew had put the boat on the flat, leaning against the harbour wall, at high water. Now the tide was out, the boat was high and dry on the flat concrete surface and the crew were busy painting her bottom with maroon 'antifouling' paint. This special paint contained copper, which inhibited marine growth on the underwater part of the craft.

During the war, Will and a crew, aboard an earlier *Courage*, were hauling lines before daylight, when they were attacked by a German aeroplane. The pilot had mistaken the lights on the boat and a light on a marker buoy close by, as the navigation lights of a larger vessel. The pilot, strafing between the two sets of lights, narrowly missed the fishing vessel with accurate shooting.

On another occasion, the four-man crew of this craft were hauling their lines, when out of the gloom, a mine drifted close to the boat. Will, standing at the vessel's side called out over his shoulder to one of his crew, "Dan get a boat-'ook, don't let t' bloody think touch t' boat's side." There was no response from Dan. Will turned from the floating menace, looking in vain for the missing crewman. He called out again louder, "Dan where the 'ell are ya'? Get a boat-'ook."

The absent deck-hand, hearing his name, looked out from his place of shelter behind the wheelhouse, shouting to his shipmates, "come behind 'ere wi' me lads, if that bugger goes off somebody'll get 'urt."

Will was brother to Tom, skipper of the *Osprey*, yet sadly they never spoke. A family quarrel many years before had become a permanent impasse. He was the best fisherman in the port. Whichever fishing Will Pashby pursued, he was almost always 'top ship'. His lines or nets were always of the finest quality and he always used the best baits. One of the hardest skippers on the coast, he would drive himself and his crew, including his two sons, mercilessly.

Fishing with 'long lines' for dogfish was especially gruelling. If one skipper was using ten score of hooks on each of his lines, Will would use twelve. When others worked twenty lines, he would use twenty five. Some stopped to give their crews a brief rest, Will's men remained on the deck working the lines. As each line was hauled, it was re-baited with mackerel or herring strips. When all the lines were re-baited, they were 'shot' back into the sea again.

It wasn't unusual for him and his crew to work forty eight hours at a stretch, stopping only for brief meals.

One day during a particularly hard stint, his son Tom was standing at the rail, hauling the line, hand over hand and was totally exhausted. The line fell from his hands and began to run out again. Tom wasn't aware of this, his eyes were closed. He was asleep but his arms were still moving, as if hauling the line.

On another occasion, Will collapsed on the deck, probably a blackout due to fatigue. When he came too and thinking he was dying, he told his sons that when he'd 'gone' they were to put him on ice and carry on fishing.

It wasn't quite dinner time, so I stood talking to the crew while watching them work. Had there been a spare brush, I'd have joined in, no doubt getting more paint on myself than on the boat. It was a pleasant feeling of security, to be known and be able to talk to almost anyone working around the harbour. Wally Johnson asked why I wasn't at school. I replied that it was school holidays. He asked after Mum and my sisters.

Wally was a lovely man with the clearest, kindest, pale blue eyes I'd ever seen. He was tallish with a rugged, weathered face. He invariably had two or three days' growth of salt-and-pepper-stubble, unless he was 'dressed up'. Then he wore a mid-grey suit, with huge, baggy 'bell-bottoms' and a white shirt and tie. Unusually, Wally seldom wore a cap. He was about Dad's age and had never married. He lived at home with his parents. Everyone thought well of Wally, he was a free spirit. At the end of the summer fishing, Wally would come home with a pocketful of money and his delight would be to collect all the youngsters he knew and treat them to the best of the ice cream parlours and fairground rides along the seafront. All parents felt complete trust when their kids were with him. Wally was like a rich uncle to dozens of children and clearly derived a great deal of pleasure from his generosity.

Robert, much younger than Wally, was another of the *Courage's* crew. He was tall and thin with a heavily pock-marked face. He too was single. Robert enjoyed a good time when he was ashore. He'd spend his money on drink and lavish presents on the girls he fancied; none of which he seemed to attract for any length of

*Bill Sheader and Bill Cammish hauling pots to the
north of Scarborough in their coble Constance.
Photo Dennis Dobson courtesy of the Cammish family*

*The coble Constance entering Scarborough Harbour.
Unknown passenger on board. Photo Bill Cammish Junior*

The keelboat Courage approaching the harbour on a fresh winter afternoon, circa 1962. Photo Scarborough Evening News

The steam trawler Emulator making for home in poor weather. Photo Scarborough Evening News

time. He couldn't save his money, no matter how much he earned. A few days ashore and 'nights on the town' and he'd blown it all. The problem was, as a share fisherman, he collected his wages, gross pay. There was nothing deducted for income tax. He was liable to pay this every six months from any savings. After several missed payments and even more demands, he was summoned to visit the 'Collector of Taxes'.

The taxman, a severe gentleman with no apparent sense of humour said, "Well Robert, you've earned all this money in the past two years yet you inform me you can't pay all your Income Tax. Just how much can you pay me?"

He'd caught Robert at a particularly bad time, following a spell of poor fishing and a good night out. "Well sir, I'm afraid I've been a very silly boy," he said producing his last ten-shilling note.

The taxman was almost speechless but was able to splutter, "if that's all you've got left from the hundreds you've earned, you haven't been a silly boy you've been a fucking idiot!"

The youngest member of the crew was Jimmy. When fishing from Grimsby, after landing the catch, Jimmy was dispatched along the dock to the provisions store to order supplies for the next trip. Unlike the steam trawlers, keelboats didn't carry a permanent cook, the duty usually fell to the junior crew member, who was also a deck-hand. One day, while in the shop, Jimmy noticed a special offer available. On collecting six coupons from a well-known brand of breakfast cereal, he could be the proud owner of a dessert knife. Visions of scimitars, flashing blades, flowing robes, stallions galloping across sand dunes sprang to his fertile imagination. He wanted that knife.

The problem was that the crew back on the boat expected huge traditional English meals or fish for their breakfast. He took a packet of the cereals to seek their reaction. The response was predictable. "Who's goin' t' eat that crap? We want proper grub," plus various other negative, unhelpful comments. Jimmy ate most of the packet himself during the course of the trip. On his next visit to the grocers the offer was still on. He longed for that knife. He ordered another packet of the dreadful stuff. It took Jimmy longer to eat the second packet; some of it was secretly dumped at sea. All through the summer he continued eating mush for breakfast, while the other lads were tucking in with relish. He'd show them. Just wait till he got his knife, they'd be so envious.

When he finally purchased the sixth packet of the dreadful food, he tore off the coupon, presenting it with the other five to the grocer, who in return gave him a small package, no more than six inches long. Jimmy looked dismayed as he opened the little box. Inside was a small, imitation-pearl handled table knife.

"What's this?" he challenged the grocer, "I want the desert knife."

"That is the dessert knife," came the reply. Spelling never was Jimmy's strong point.

Following a hurried dinner, I left home for my rendezvous with Dougie and Brian. Before leaving I collected a large scallop shell from the balcony, a remnant from the winter fishing. They were good bait. The shell, about six inches in diameter, was similar to the 'Shell' logo, though cup shaped. I also took a large piece of coal from the coalhouse.

Meeting my pals near Sandgate Corner, we made our way along the pier past the bait sheds. They were unoccupied now, long lining was a winter job. The skeiners who didn't work on the crab stalls mostly took seasonal work in the many seafront cafes. Mrs Wright took in visitors.

Many people from Leeds, Bradford and other northern towns and cities took their holidays at the seaside. The guest houses and hotels were full to capacity throughout the season. Several people in our street, all living in council houses, took guests throughout the summer.

We assembled half a dozen wooden fish boxes into a makeshift stall at the rear of the fish market. Holidaymakers passing looked perplexed. After concealing my scallop shell and coal within the construction, the three of us scattered purposefully to the tiers of boats, to forage for curios. We scoured the decks, nets and scuppers of all the vessels in the harbour. Anything animal, vegetable or mineral would do, small fish, shells, sea urchins, bits of twine or netting. I found a small lemon sole, a gurnard and a horse mackerel on board the *Emulator* before returning. Dougie had 'borrowed' a crab-pot, one of a fleet, stacked on the harbourside ready for deploying.

Brian returned triumphant. He had a dogfish and several small rays, held by their tails, in his left hand. In his right, its tail dragging on the ground, was a large monkfish weighing at least a stone. An extremely ugly fish, with a huge head and mouth to match, it had a brown back and a white under side. On top of its head, between the bulging eyes, was a small luminous rod which attracted its prey. All types of fish were lured to the glowing little fishing rod, to be snapped up by the gaping mouth with its deadly, needle-sharp teeth.

All these creatures were valueless to the fishermen, but collectively, they were the means to a few bob and some fun. I retrieved the coal and shell from their hiding place and we quickly arranged our collection on top of the box stall. I cut a small hole in the lower jaw of the monkfish, while Dougie hid under the stall holding a short stick, awaiting his cue. I too had a stick.

Brian stood at my side with the crab-pot, mounted on top of two more fish boxes. I began to shout at the already gathering crowd. "Come and see the curios of the deep." In no time at all a large crowd had gathered. "Come and see the curios of the deep," I shouted again needlessly.

I was centre stage, the spectators hanging on my every word. "Ello everybody. We 'ave 'ere today a collection of curios t' show y' that 'as been gathered from all around t' North Sea, but first my friend Brian will show y' a crab-pot an' 'ow it works."

Brian gave a mock bow then took up the story in an attempted posh voice. "Here his a crab-pot, the same pot his also used to catch lobsters. Hit's only the harea where you put 'em that makes t' difference." His accent slipped but he recovered. "Sometimes both hare caught hat the same time." He went on to describe how the creatures were lured through the spouts by the bait secured in the bait band. Next he explained how the fishermen took the catch from the pot via the door, which was hitched closed but easily opened.

"My good friend Frederick will now show you hour hother curios," he ended his spiel, waving a theatrical arm in my direction.

I took up the story, pointing with my stick, "ere we 'ave a lemon sole, feel 'ow smooth its skin is." I invited those at the front to touch it. "This is a dab, feel its skin, it's rough." I pointed to the dogfish, explaining that just like a dover sole, its skin was like sandpaper when rubbed from tail to head, but like silk from head to tail.

"Mind y' don't touch its poisonous spikes," I stated dramatically, highlighting the two unpleasant spurs hidden close to the fins on its back. I continued my role centre stage, "this is a gurnard, it's got poisonous spikes as well." I picked it up, fanning its dorsal fin to reveal the needles protruding from it. One or two people were beginning to drift away so I quickly moved on. "This is an 'orse mackerel."

Pointing to the coal, I swore it was a genuine piece of coal from the cargo of the collier, *Betty Hindley*, which sank in Scarborough Bay in 1947, after hitting a stray mine from the recent war. I stated that this piece of coal had been trawled up by one of the local boats. This raised a few eyebrows and an exclamation of, "I bet it didn't, it's still got dust on it," from a man at the back.

I hurried through the remaining exhibits until only two items remained. I pointed to the big monkfish. "This is a monk," I lifted its fishing rod, dangling it in front of the massive closed mouth, then gave Dougie, who had waited so long for his cue that he was nearly asleep, a nudge with my toe. He began to jerk his stick up and down through a gap in the stall top. His stick was also through the hole in the lower jaw of the fish, which I'd made earlier. The monkfish began to open and close its huge mouth with no assistance from me.

"Oh it's alive," a woman at the front squealed, stepping back. Most of our audience stepped back, which was counter productive, as the last item on the stall was the shell.

"This is a scallop shell, scallops are good bait f' cod. They're also good to eat, an' t' empty shells make nice ashtrays. This one also doubles as our collection box, an' all donations are gratefully received."

Most of the crowd, already distant, moved off at this point but some entered into the spirit of the show, giving us loose change from their pockets and purses. Brian called after those moving off, "I've got a wife an' three kids t' keep y' know." As he was only fifteen this was highly implausible and made no impression on the disappearing backs.

After a brief interval we exchanged roles, beginning again with a fresh group of visitors. We were careful not to frighten the next crowd away with the monk. After a while the duty pierman came along, telling us to "clear off!" He always did.

As we walked from the pier, pockets jangling, Brian said, "ow could all them people think that monk was still alive? It stunk to 'igh 'eaven. It 'ad been on t' boat's deck fo' two days. The' must all be daft in t' Wes' Ridin'." Infectious laughter burst out among us, until tears were streaming down our faces.

We had only reached Sandgate Corner when a voice said, "Eh young Nommy, I'm 'aulin' me pots at six o'clock if y' wan' t' come." It was Blondie Wood; he was leaning on the railings awaiting likely candidates for a bay trip.

"I'll be there." His invitation was accepted, I liked Blondie. Though he'd an exaggerated reputation for being frugal, he also had an immense knowledge of the local coastline and a fund of stories of times and characters past which he shared. He was also head launcher of the lifeboat.

I spent the remainder of the afternoon with my pals then, after tea, turned up promptly at six o'clock to sail on the *Venture*. I didn't need permission for trips of this nature. We'd only be at sea about two hours and would never be more than a mile or two from the harbour, close to the shore. I stood aft, holding the tiller and was allowed to steer the boat out of the harbour, keeping to the right as we entered the narrow entrance. If any vessels were encountered coming in, we'd pass port to port. Blondie kept a close eye on me while preparing to haul his gear. On the starboard side of the thwart seat, he placed a box of bait ready to re-bait the pots as he hauled them. Under the thwart he placed a cane basket, half-filled with old hessian sacks, soaked in seawater. The basket had probably been 'lost' from one of the trawlers.

"'Ead f' White Nab!" he shouted, pointing to the nearest promontory. "T' first fleet's jus' t' south side of it." He reached into his pocket, taking out his elusive cigarette tin. Most fishermen kept their cigs in tins or under the brim of their caps to keep them dry and prevent damage. Few had seen Blondie's cigarette tin. He invariably smoked other peoples, though he offered one to me, knowing I didn't smoke.

It took about twenty minutes to reach the first fleet of pots. As we approached a buoy Blondie pulled up his seaboots, clambered into his oilskin frock then wrapped a vinyl apron round it. It was a miracle his boots stayed up, as they were past their best when he'd acquired them. The holes in the apron were placed strategically to avoid the holes in the oilskin; so he was waterproof. Sea gear was expensive, but not to Blondie.

"Tides flowin' so go t' south end o' this fleet, that way we'll be able to 'aul into it," he yelled as I drew close to the marker. I altered away from my target, steering for the buoy at the other end of the fleet. "Go past it, then turn back north west, in t' tide." Following his instructions, I turned the boat into the tide, bringing her alongside the southern most buoy, then pulled the engine lever into neutral. Blondie plucked the buoy from the water, quickly ascertained that the rope was leading away from the propeller, then shouted, "come 'ead, straight at that."

The tide was pushing the *Venture* back from the line of pots, so Blondie frequently called, "come 'ead and to it." In answer, I engaged the engine ahead and steered towards the direction of the rope. He'd call "ead an' off it," if the line was leading under the boat. I understood why Blondie asked me along. It would be much harder to work the boat on his own, though he did so daily, sometimes hauling his three fleets of pots, three times a day.

As he hauled on the rope, hand over hand, the pots began to appear over the boat's side at regular intervals. Each was quickly lifted aboard, emptied, re-baited and stacked in the boat, in sequence, ready for shooting again. I craned my neck to look inside each pot as it was lifted in. Sometimes there'd be a lobster. "There 'e wags," Blondie would shout, as the creature flapped its tail helplessly, attempting to swim in thin air.

Occasionally a pot would contain dozens of small green crabs which everyone called 'doggies'. Lobsters seldom entered a pot that was inhabited by large numbers of crabs. Blondie would curse loudly. "Bloody doggy crabs, if y' could sell 'em y' wouldn't be able t' catch em." Sometimes there'd be two lobsters in a pot and he would cheer. The ones which were clearly undersized were immediately thrown back, but those which were doubtful required measuring and were retained until he had time to check them.

As he emptied each pot, he carefully placed the lobsters into the cane basket at his feet. Avoiding the snapping claws, he quickly covered them with sacking. The lobsters were quick and quite fierce. Unless kept apart they'd fight, easily breaking each other's claws and shells. There were only twenty pots in Blondie's fleets, so it wasn't long before we arrived at the other end. He looked at the land to ascertain his position, then directed me to steer to an area a few hundred yards away, where we could re-lay this fleet before going to the next. Though he'd no navigation equipment other than a compass, which was only required in fog, I'm sure this man knew every stone, gully, ledge and patch of sand for at least three miles north and south of the harbour.

I steered the boat, going with the tide as Blondie began to shoot his pots back into the sea. The gear would remain tight on the seabed and was less likely to become fouled on an obstruction, if shot 'with the tide'. He dropped each pot in turn over the side, as the main rope snaked overboard, quickly reaching for the next in the sequence. It was vital to take the pots in the correct order. It was not unknown for pots to fly through the air if they were not in position at the boat's side, ready to be released as required.

It was equally important to keep one's feet away from the pile of rope in the bottom of the boat. If the cable became tangled round a leg it could have serious repercussions. It was difficult to stop a boat when travelling with the tide. Even without engine power a vessel would continue making way with tidal assistance. Fishermen have been dragged overboard when grabbed by the main rope. A quick thinker would allow his seaboot to slip off, to be taken by the rope. This would be expensive for the fisherman involved, not in Blondie's case of course, but could possibly save his life.

Having shot the first fleet back, the exercise was repeated twice more. As he threw the finishing buoy over the side, (it was unlucky to use the word 'last') he yelled, "point 'er for t' lighthouse," then indicated needlessly with an arm. When the magic cigarette tin had put in a brief appearance, its owner sat on the seat, puffing contentedly. As we proceeded towards the harbour he inspected and measured the catch contained in the basket. The minimum legal landing size for lobsters was ten inches overall length. For crabs it was four and a half inches across the widest part of the back. This was rigorously enforced by a 'Fisheries Inspector' known universally as 'Crab Jack'. Anyone caught with undersized shellfish was prosecuted in the law court. Some people were prepared to take the risk but Blondie wasn't one of these, though he could stretch a lobster tail, making it fit the measure when most would deem it undersized.

He measured each lobster carefully. If it was undersized it was reluctantly thrown back. If legal, each claw in turn was held firmly between his knees while he deftly tied the other tightly closed, using old snoods stripped from the previous winter long lines. Nothing was wasted. The catch of fifteen lobsters was good. It might not seem much but Blondie hauled his pots two or three times every day, which gave a good aggregate each week during the summer. He also carried anglers and trippers too, so during the season his small boat, with minimal expense for fuel and bait, made him a good living.

On arriving at the harbour, our catch was placed in a small weighted box then hung overboard. This container was tied to the boat with enough line to suspend the box inches below the surface. Lobsters must be kept alive to have a value. In the morning they'd be sold to the dealer, along with the results of the next haul of the pots.

The holiday was fast drawing to a close, Easter had gone. Soon it would be time for school again. I'd spent each day totally engrossed with boats, fishing gear or around the harbour and it was idyllic. There were so many people willing to spend time encouraging, instructing or allowing me to help that I was learning a trade without realising it. Sometimes I learned how 'not' to do things.

On the day before I was due back at school, I went with my Uncle Walt, one of Mother's brothers, in the *Golden Crest* helping him to haul his pots, as I'd done many times before. His was a small craft, similar to Blondie's, though Uncle Walt wasn't as experienced as Blondie. He had a short temper though was never unpleasant to me. He'd once thrown the starting-handle into the harbour when unable to start the engine.

The weather had changed. The wind had turned to the east and was blowing from the sea. Though only moderate, it was creating a swell, which was breaking on the shore. If the wind freshened, his pots would be in danger of being smashed in heavy seas. It was important to retrieve them; to keep them on the boat until the weather improved.

We steamed south east, not far from the position I'd been the previous week with Blondie. We were quite close inshore, only a hundred yards or so from the surf breaking on the rocks. With the gear recovered, the boat was stacked with pots and was rolling quite heavily in the swell and I sensed Uncle Walt wasn't happy. Catches were poor and it had been a hard, awkward task to retrieve the gear with the wind blowing across the tide.

A bucket, containing snoods and short ends of twine was sliding from side to side across the boat, as she rolled. This erratically moving object was clearly irritating him but rather than stow it securely, he kicked out at it, spilling its contents into the bilges. These were instantly grabbed by the propeller shaft coupling and spun, immediately catching other obstacles. The engine stopped dead and the *Golden Crest* began to drift towards the shore.

Uncle Walt quickly recovered his composure, reached for a sharp knife, which was kept close to hand for emergencies, and began to chop at the twine. It was a race against time. We were only a few minutes from a soaking or worse. Deploying an anchor was pointless, we'd be ashore before we could pay sufficient cable out for it to hold. Walt was strong as an ox and hacked at the offending material in a frenzy. The *Golden Crest* was only yards from the rocks when he managed to clear it. The starting handle was shipped and fortunately the engine fired first time, seconds before the boat hit the rocks. Had it not done so her fragile, clinker-built hull, constructed of only half-inch overlapping planking, would have been smashed to pieces in minutes.

I was pleased when the little craft, piled high with pots, arrived back in the harbour. I never told my Dad about the incident on board the *Golden Crest*. He would have been furious. For a brief while I was even pleased to return to school. We'd be putting the boats back in the water during the next term.

CHAPTER V

SUMMER

Each Wednesday evening my friends went to a dance at the Olympia Ballroom. The lads mostly worked on boats which landed daily, so were free each evening. Pop music had arrived; everyone was swept up in the new sound. The 'Beatles', 'Stones' and 'Kinks' were constantly topping the charts. Local groups with catchy names, 'Jonty and the Strangers', 'The Moonshots' and 'The Panthers' hammered out the latest hits.

When I went with the group for the first time, it was as if a veil had been lifted from my eyes. There was another aspect to life apart from school and the harbour. We'd arranged to meet at seven thirty, on Sandgate Corner. To be sure of not missing them I arrived ten minutes early, dressed in my only suit, a smart but old-fashioned one, produced for weddings and funerals. The sleeves and legs were too short and it was tight under the arms. My school tie, my only tie, was reversed so the thin part was at the front. School shoes were the only clean footwear I possessed, so these too were worn for the occasion. Mum said I looked very smart as I tried to escape from the house without being seen.

I hovered around the rendezvous, trying to look inconspicuous but standing out like a sore thumb. Two or three of the critics were looking in my direction. I began to wish I hadn't been so early, hoping reinforcements would arrive soon. They did arrive, but were reinforcements for the critics. My pals were all wearing the latest trendy gear, jackets with no collars, narrow trousers with no turn-ups and winklepicker shoes. I felt very square and fought hard to resist the urge to run away.

"Where'd y' get t' suit from Nommy, t' undertakers?"

If y' ask t' 'arbour master 'e'll give yer a licence f' t' shoes, y' could tek passengers in 'em!" They soon tired of making fun and it wasn't malicious so I was content to tag along.

"Shall we 'ave one in t' 'Ding Dong' before we go?" Tom suggested. Baz and Mick agreed, I nodded but hadn't a clue what they were talking about.

The 'ne'er do wells' on critics corner were having a field day discussing these 'four clever buggers wi' more money than sense' when Mick turned in their direction and shouted, "piss off y' silly old twats!" I was horrified, I knew them all, and they knew my Dad. I felt sure I'd be implicated in this heinous act.

We walked along the foreshore road next to the beach, heading towards the Olympia. The discussion was of the latest Mersey groups and their records. I listened intently on the fringe, hoping no one would engage me in direct conversation. I need not have worried. We crossed the road, fifty yards before the dance hall and began to ascend the steep hill, heading into the town centre. I was puzzled but kept mum. Close to the top, off to the left, was an old coaching inn, 'The Bell Hotel'. Ah, 'ding dong', now I knew. We were going to a pub.

Baz pulled me to one side as we entered, "give me y' money an' keep at t' back, I'll get you a pint." He was eighteen and was the oldest of the group. The dingy pub wasn't very busy, eight or nine other lads all of a similar age were preparing to play darts. The elderly landlord seemed glad of the trade so apart from saying, "keep the noise down lads," didn't question my age, though I felt he was looking in my direction. I avoided eye contact. Baz handed me the beer and I took a big gulp. It was by no means my first beer. On the previous two Christmas Days I'd done a tour of fishermen's houses with these same pals. Drink was liberally dispensed.

"Put our names down t' play Georgy," Tom shouted to the thin, pock-marked lad who was chalking names by the dartboard. "Me, Mike, Baz and Nommy."

"It's a shillin' a game," Georgy replied seriously. This was dismissed as peanuts by Tom, who was earning pots of money in one of the top boats. The game was called 'killer'. Each player was allocated a number, then given three stripes, 'lives', by his name on the blackboard. The object was to remain in the game as long as possible. Playing in rotation, each player had to hit his own number in the double section. There were no trebles on the board. He could then choose any other player's double. A life was taken whenever this was achieved. The last one in the game won the money.

There was much rivalry and mock anger as contestants lost lives. Threats of revenge and worse were hinted at, as each player stepped up to the oche. Some of the competitors were quite big and unknown to me, so I was relieved to be among the first out, even though it cost me a shilling. The darts match concluded when Georgy won, though he was greatly dismayed when unnoticed, a female Salvation Army collector gratefully put the twelve shillings in her tin.

We four supped our remaining beer with a flourish and left the 'Ding Dong' for the Olympia. The band belting out 'Love me do' could be heard from the foyer. The Olympia was an extensive, old, grey-painted, wooden building with a large dance floor. Its upstairs balcony on three sides, was perfect for spectators to watch the dancing. The building, now a little jaded, must have been superb in its heyday.

As we entered, I could see the band on stage, bathed in spotlights at the far end of the hall. Three guitarists and a drummer wore identical outfits, the guitarists stepping together in a well-rehearsed routine. The atmosphere was electric, there were two or three hundred people attending the venue and I felt part of it. This was a totally different world from anything I'd ever experienced before, though the pint of beer may have helped colour these feelings.

I followed the lads round to the left of the room, midway between the entrance and stage. My eyes were scanning the whole room in the dim light, watching the band, the dancers, mostly girls and the dozens of teenagers, mostly boys, leaning over the balconies. I recognised several people from years past in junior school. Everyone looked so relaxed, confident and 'with it'.

At this point I realised we were standing with a group of girls, that my pals were talking to them as friends and must have met them before. I sensed the girls looking at me and I felt myself going red and feeling very conspicuous. "It's Nommy," Tom shouted above the music to the group of girls, "he's one o' t' lads," for which I was grateful. It felt very uncomfortable being scrutinised by these girls. They were looking at my attire and I heard the words, shoes and suit mentioned. It was a strange feeling. The only other young females I'd ever come into close contact with were my sisters. I didn't know these girls, but cared what they thought. I promised myself that next week I'd be dressed in the latest fashion, giving no one the opportunity to laugh at me.

The young ladies were all good looking and quite friendly once my garb had been dismissed. Sylvia said she worked in a clothes factory and asked where I worked. I just couldn't say I was still at school so I said I worked for Tom Pashby on the *Osprey*. I reasoned that if Tom worked on the *Osprey* and I made crab-pots for him during summer and baited lines in winter after school, then I worked for him. I hated telling lies, knowing I'd be found out but I just couldn't say I was still at school. I became even more determined to leave as soon as possible.

Standing alone, I watched Tom dancing with a girl called Lindy, while Baz danced with Sylvia. Mike had wandered off somewhere. I was joined by two more pals, Herby and Ray. Ray was an apprentice plumber, though his Dad was a fisherman. Like me, Ray wanted to go fishing but his Dad had made him 'get a trade'. The three of us stood for a while, talking fishing when the music allowed. It was a topic which I felt comfortable with. The band retired for the interval and our two rock and rollers rejoined us, accompanied by Mike. The girls had departed to the cafeteria for a cold fizzy pop.

Herby addressed the group, "are we gettin' a pass out an' goin' f' one?"

There was unanimous agreement, even I, quick to catch on, was in favour. It was decided that we'd go to the Dolphin. "Watch y' change wi' this lan'lord," Herby warned, "e's a right robbin' bastard."

A five minute walk towards the harbour brought us to the entrance of the Dolphin Hotel. I glanced across the road before entering, the critics had gone home and the piers were in darkness. The walls of the busy pub were adorned with nautical artefacts and photographs of boats, which I found fascinating. Most of the customers were fishermen, all of who we were familiar with. There were several calls in our direction, all good-humoured. as we gathered near the bar.

"There's a fine body o' men."

"Where've you lot come from, Burton's window?"

"Bet y' dads don't know you lot are loose on t' town."

There were several others, but I kept my head down while Baz bought the booze. Again I was worried I'd be asked to leave, but it seemed this landlord was so greedy, he'd serve anyone.

I heard Herby say to him, "I gave you a quid, y've only gi' me change f' ten bob." I looked up to see the bald, bespectacled host mutter something, then pass him a ten-shilling note. We formed a rough circle in the middle of the room, talking to each other and to several fishermen close by. "I'll get that bugger back before we go," Herby muttered quietly to our group.

Ernie 'Soapy' Williamson who was sitting close by, rose to go to the toilet. "Now then lads, 'ow are y' all doin', I'm just off for a piss. Last time I left a pint o' beer in 'ere, it disappeared, some bugger nicked it. It won't 'appen this time." So saying, he removed his false teeth, plopping them into his remaining beer. This caused great hilarity among our group but there were calls of "y' mucky bugger" from the next table.

We'd finished our beer and were making ready to leave but Herby said, "'ang on a minute an' back me up." Returning to the bar he ordered a pint, tendering a ten-shilling note. When he'd obtained his beer and his change he began heading back to our party, then looked at the change in his hand. "Just a minute lan'lord, I gave you a quid an' you've gi' me change f' ten bob. That's twice y've done that t' me an' I've on'y been 'ere ten minutes."

All eyes turned on the publican as he attempted to argue, but no one in the premises believed him. There were shouts of "robbin' bugger," and "shame on ya," from close by and "fiddlin' prat," from Mike. The landlord, protesting vigorously, his face very red, handed over a ten-shilling note to Herby, who was having difficulty suppressing a grin. We jubilantly returned to the dance hall, where the tale was related with much embellishment to our female friends.

I spent some of my savings kitting myself out with acceptable clothing during the following week. Dad tutted when he saw my 'winklepicker' shoes. "You wore plastic sandals fo' picking winkles until now," he said mirthlessly, but I didn't care, I was 'with it'. From then on I hardly missed a Wednesday at the Olympia, sometimes going to school, a problem yet to be addressed, with a slight hangover. It was months before I plucked up the courage to dance with anyone and then I thought everyone in the place was watching me. One exception was when I found a few spots on my chin which seemed like volcanoes. I decided to stay at home. Mum said I was stupid and that no one would notice or even care, but I hated the thought of being spotty so opted not to go. I stayed at home, sulking and feeling sorry for myself.

The Whitsun holiday finally arrived bringing me more time to haunt the harbour. There'd be another trip on the *Floreat* and several potting excursions with Blondie. There'd be no curio stall though. Each year at Whitsun the 'Tunny Hut' was erected. This was a professional curio stall with real exhibits, though no less smelly.

In the 1930s there were large numbers of 'blue fin tuna' known locally as tunny fish, to be found offshore from Scarborough and neighbouring Whitby. These fish, which grew to many hundreds of pounds, followed and fed from the huge shoals of herrings that gathered off the Yorkshire coast each year to spawn. Scarborough became a centre for big game fishing. Some local keelboats and even cobles were chartered by 'well-to-do' visitors, wishing to participate in this new sport. An elite club, 'The Tunny Club' was formed and until the early fifties, tunny were caught in abundance on rod and line. The biggest of these fish were exhibited in a hut on the pier, 'The Tunny Hut'. The record fish weighed more than nine hundred pounds.

During the early fifties, for no apparent reason, perhaps due to changing migration patterns or water temperature, the tunny failed to appear. The 'Tunny Hut' became obsolete and was then used to exhibit curios. For a small admission fee, unusual specimens caught in the region could be viewed. These creatures were displayed on a bed of ice, replenished each morning from the 'Icehouse'. On hot, sunny days the ice would be mostly melted by evening and the exhibits soon began to smell. The stink from the shed was all pervading.

During this holiday, Brian, Dougie and me planned to gather sea urchins from the rocks at Jackson's Bay. These colourful creatures, a variety of brown, red and purple, a little bigger than tennis balls, were completely covered in brittle, white spikes. When cleaned, we'd sell these urchins to the visitors for a shilling each. The collection site was along the coast, on the north side of town. We'd bike as far as the roads and paths would allow, then walk around the headland into the next bay.

It was the final period of spring tides for several months. We'd consulted the tide book, checking the time of low water, which was approximately midday. During the spring tides, which perversely also occur in autumn, the tide rises higher and ebbs lower than normal. These big ebbs exposed the sea urchins near the water's edge, among the long streamers of brown kelp. I'd explained to Mum before leaving that it was essential we were there for low water and I was excused from dinner.

We left our bikes at the end of the North Bay promenade with an hour of ebb still to run. Each carrying a hessian sack, Dougie and I crossed the small beck on uneven stepping-stones while Brian, wearing seaboots, forded at the shallowest point, the water hardly reaching above his knees. Dougie and I had decided earlier that we'd prefer to wear swimming costumes for the collecting and were wearing them under our jeans. I wore my usual versatile plastic sandals while Dougie's feet were clad in a pair of sacrificial plimsolls, nicked from school.

It was impossible to travel quickly over the slippery, seaweed-strewn rocks and though we were constantly looking ahead for the easiest path, it took half an hour of gingerly stepping, leaping and paddling before we encountered our first urchin. The purple coloured 'hedgehog' was stuck on the side of a large rock, a few feet from the gently breaking swell. From this point we found more, liberally strewn though not always easily accessible.

Dougie and I removed our jeans, placing them on top of a prominent dry rock, set back from the water's edge. The three of us then paddled or waded, dragging our sacks behind, collecting dozens of these spiny shellfish. My catch was steadily increasing as I plotted my way to each urchin. Suddenly a loud curse drowned the background noise of sea on the shore. Brian had slipped and was standing waist deep in a rock pool, brown bands of kelp hiding his lower body. "I'm fuckin' wet through," he gasped as the cold water took his breath. "'Elp me out!"

We scrambled to his assistance, laughing loudly at his unhappy situation. This didn't help his demeanour and he began to curse again. He used words Dougie and I had never heard before, but we weren't surprised. Both Brian's parents swore like troopers. His thigh-length boots were full of water and he was stuck in the kelp. It would have been easy for him to slip off the boots, but he wouldn't hear of it when it was suggested. First we asked him for his sack of urchins, which made him swear once more. The pool was deep but not very wide. At arm's length I took the bag of produce from him placing it to one side. Then with a hand each, we hauled our wet, vocal friend from his predicament. He must have curled his toes, for the long rubber boots were still attached to his legs, even though they now contained a large amount of water.

Brian sat on the nearest rock, water spilling from his boot-tops. As if rehearsed, Dougie and I grabbed a boot each, hauling them from his legs and together, inverting them. A torrent of seawater poured forth, followed by wet socks. We couldn't help laughing again. "You're both a couple o' clever prats," said our glum friend. No 'thanks lads' or 'it's a good job y' were there mates'.

We left him sulking, drying off as best he could while we continued to harvest the sea urchins. It was a warm day so he wouldn't freeze. My sack was beginning to get heavy now and Dougie had a similar volume in his. Brian cheered up as he warmed and was soon putting his wet boots on again to recommence his collecting. Fifteen minutes later we called a halt to the proceedings. The tide was flowing, our dripping sacks were heavy and it was quite a distance to the bikes. We agreed it was time to head back.

After collecting and donning my jeans from the big rock, now being lapped by the sea, I tied the neck of my bag with a bit of twine then slung it over my shoulder. I immediately regretted this hasty action, as dozens of needles pricked my skin through my thin shirt. I winced, then cursed. This was a mistake as it gave Brian some ammunition for retaliation. It was my turn to be on the receiving end of the witty comments. "I bet you felt a real prick just then," Brian chuckled, pleased to be giving the stick rather than taking it. I grinned but said nothing, knowing any reply would be used against me.

It took ages to get back to our bikes. We were forced to take frequent stops, putting down our burdens, but couldn't rest long, the tide was flowing fast. It was a relief to round the headland and breathless, we arrived back at the promenade where we sat for a while to recover. Soon we were discussing cleaning and where to sell our urchins. Several options were suggested including our present location, but we finally decided that the West Pier, where we'd operated the curio stall, was the best site.

We would acquire empty tins from the crab stalls that had previously contained bulk prawns. They were ideal for rinsing and cleaning the urchins, which was a messy job. First we'd scrape the spines from the delicate globes with our pocket knives. Next the interiors would be cleaned, accessed through a small, soft, circular cavity in the bottom of the shell with knife point. With this section withdrawn, the intestines and other contents, mainly seawater could be removed. Dougie suddenly said, "aren't we daft!" Brian looked at me then we both looked at Dougie. "We've jus' carried that bloody lot for an hour. We're knackered, an' most of t' weight's water. If we'd emptied 'em before we set off it would 'ave been dead easy." He was right. We'd carried fifty or sixty urchins each, less in Brian's case, but they were heavy, yet quite delicate creatures. Had we drained them, they would have been much lighter and fewer would have broken in transit.

"Why didn't y' suggest it earlier?" I groaned. We balanced the sacks on the crossbars of our bikes and were able to ride with knees spread. Occasionally a knee would knock against a sack causing the injured party to curse. On arrival back at the harbour we were pleased to see plenty of visitors strolling the piers. We immediately organised ourselves to take full advantage of the opportunity. I began to build the stall, Brian quickly rounded up a couple of empty prawn tins, while Dougie dashed to the nearest shop for a bottle of Domestos. The stall was assembled and I was arranging several urchins on top when Brian returned with the tins. We half filled them with water from the nearby tap then began scraping the first of the urchins.

We used one tin for washing the severed spikes from the shell, the other remained unused. Immediately we were surrounded by a crowd. "What are they? What are you doing? What are they for? Can you eat them?" The questions came thick and fast, as we knew they would. We kept the interest aroused as we scraped away the spines, exposing the contrasting colours of our subjects. "They're sea urchins, they make really good ornaments, and can be used f' lampshades too. They make unusual presents, souvenirs of Scarborough. Sometimes y' can get a matching pair."

I whipped the innards from my specimen expertly and the people watching, in unison, said "yeuck!" I inserted my forefinger inside, loosening the organs and various bits of gunge.

In a thick West Yorkshire twang, the nearest woman to me said, "they're no bloody good f' ornaments, they'll stink t' 'ouse out in no time." As if on cue, Dougie arrived breathless, carrying the bleach. I snatched it from his hands.

"No they won't Missus, 'cos we clean 'em wi' this."

I poured about a quarter of the contents of the bottle into the tin of clean water then immersed my urchin until it filled then sank. Dougie was concerned that he'd had to pay for the bleach but was assured he'd be repaid from the day's proceeds. We continued to scrape and clean the urchins. The concentration of bleach was such that a few minutes steeping was sufficient to cleanse the empty shell totally. If left too long they would disintegrate.

We did a brisk trade, selling most of our stock in a couple of hours but then to my surprise, a group of pretty girls came walking along the pier. I recognised two of them immediately, Sylvia and Lindy from the Olympia Dance Hall. They spotted the gathered crowd and naturally approached to see what was happening. I felt my face redden and was terribly embarrassed as they saw me. They thought what we were doing was amusing and very profitable, but it had spoiled my day. I wanted them to think of me as a fisherman not as a school kid messing about during the holidays.

When they'd gone I made the excuse that I was bored with it all. I think Dougie and Brian must have had similar feelings, for no one disagreed when I suggested we quit. We shared the proceeds equally following a reminder from Dougie that he was owed for his outlay. We gave the remainder of our stock to some smaller boys, who'd been watching our enterprise. These budding young proteges jumped at the chance of making a few bob and promptly entered into our roles with flair and enthusiasm. With the spoils divided, we collected our bikes, each going our separate ways, but not before agreeing to meet the following day. I felt subdued, yet it had been great fun until the girls came along.

Why did breaks from school go so fast? The holidays were almost over again. They always passed quickly. Tomorrow I would be captive again until the summer recess. Would I ever leave school? I was standing on the pier close to two keelboats, their crews were assembling, preparing for sea. Three more were berthed nearby, but these crews from nearby Filey would never sail on a Sunday. The decks of all these vessels, forward of the wheelhouse, were piled high with dark brown, fine-meshed, cotton drift nets. Around their sterns on each side were fifteen to twenty huge baskets, each filled with line. Hundreds of large hooks, much bigger than those used for the winter fishing, were attached by thick snoods then 'hooked' round the rim of each basket.

The 'basket liners' were hunting for large cod and turbot. These giants were to be found thirty to fifty miles offshore, in and around a fifty fathoms deep subterranean trench called 'Bayman's Hole'. These vessels would fish during the night with their drift nets for herring. This catch would be used to bait the big hooks, a whole fish on each hook if sufficient herring were caught. Herring were available in small quantities early in the year but the main season wasn't until August and early September, when the harbour was full of Scottish, English and occasionally Dutch drifters. I looked forward eagerly to the herring season.

The lines were hauled with a petrol-driven hauler. As it broke the surface, each fish was 'gaffed' by a crewman armed with a long pole with a large unbarbed hook secured at the end. This ensured the fish was caught, even if it wriggled off the hook as it was hauled up the boat's side. The fish was assisted on board by the 'gaffer'. I was dismayed to hear that when turbot were hauled to the surface, they were occasionally followed by their mate, swimming free. The fish on the hook was left in the water until its mate was gaffed.

Occasionally, the mechanical line hauler would be temperamental, refusing to start. For these occasions the skipper carried a bottle of ether, easily obtained from the chemist's shop. This highly combustible fuel, a well-known anaesthetic, was liberally sprinkled on a piece of rag then tied to the hauler, close to the air intake. The correct length of line ensured the rag wouldn't be sucked into the engine, blocking the intake. This liquid almost always exploded the machine into use. Mischievous young crewmen were known to surreptitiously splash a little of the mixture on the peaks of older hands' caps. The anaesthetic qualities would cause them to stagger around the deck as if drunk. I don't think anyone ever fell overboard but it was a dangerous prank.

Colin 'Dilt' Jenkinson was a deckie on the *F & S Colling*, waiting to sail. I'd known Colin since I was small, often talking to him around the harbour. He had ambitions of being a successful skipper. On this particular day he must have been feeling particularly sensitive or had something on his mind. I was cheeky or said something which upset him for he made a lunge to grab me, but I managed to dodge him. He yelled words to the effect that he was going to throw me in the harbour. I don't think he would have harmed me, however I was taking no chances. He began to chase me but would never catch me. I couldn't fight much but I was a good runner. I kept a reasonable distance from him as he pursued me, knowing he'd never reach. Without warning, he grabbed a monkfish head weighing at least half a stone, from a nearby offal bin. Without breaking step, he, hurled it in my direction.

It hit me between the shoulder blades and I was bowled over. He had no trouble catching me then but was so helpless with laughter he could do no more. I slunk from the pier blathered in slime, stinking of bad fish and feeling very sorry for myself. At least I'd brightened his day.

It was impossible to pass Sandgate Corner without some comment from the 'standing committee'. A voice from the group said, "what a bloody stink o' rotten fish, young Nommy, wait till y' get 'ome, y' mother'll go mad." It was Alan, the fishermen's representative on the Harbour Committee at the Town Hall.

Another voice responded to his comment saying, "you'll know all about bad fish Alan, weren't it you that stood up in t' Council Chamber durin' war an' said, "we need fish an' we need it bad." A burst of laughter echoed from all present and I was able to slip past without further comment.

Two things happened during the next school term which detracted from the desire to leave. First we moved house from Friargate to Cooks Row. It was still a council house, but it was more modern and it was nearer the harbour. The second event was even stranger. I'd been back at school for only two weeks when Dad's skipper and partner, Tom, was taken ill with flu. Tom's brother Jack had left the boat previously and was operating his own small boat for the summer. Lobsters were scarce; they were hidden at this time of year, moulting to grow bigger shells. The *Rosemary* was temporarily rigged for trawling, using rope warps.

On arriving home from school, Dad met me as I walked into the room. "You're not goin' t' school tomorro' son. Tom's badly, so you'll 'ave t' come t' sea wi' me." I couldn't believe my ears. We were never allowed to be absent from school, yet here was Dad instructing me to take time off. What was even better, I was taking time off to go to sea. Not as a supernumerary but as indispensable crew.

We sailed at five o'clock the following morning on a lovely fine day. After stowing the head rope, I turned the calor gas bottle to 'on', then bent down entering the little 'cuddy' cabin in the bow of the boat to light the stove. The cabin was only big enough to access on hands and knees, through a small entrance with sliding doors.

It contained spare fishing gear, a two-ringed gas stove, a kettle and teapot, a five-gallon drum of fresh water and a small wooden box containing packets of tea, sugar and sweet tinned milk. An old tobacco tin contained matches.

The gas bottle was kept outside the cuddy to minimise the risk of explosion. Several fishing vessels have been wrecked by gas explosions. Harry on board the *Rachel*, the *Rosemary's* sister ship had a fortunate escape when lighting the stove at sea one day. Harry lit the match, unaware of a gas leak. The subsequent explosion blew the top completely off the cabin. The cuddy top, of strong construction was fastened with four-inch nails. Had it been bolted in place, the vessel would undoubtedly have sunk. Harry was left shocked, singed but otherwise unscathed in the centre of the explosion, still holding the match.

The *Grateful* a fifty five foot keelboat was a total loss in the harbour when a gas explosion occurred. One of the crew was painting on the vessel and went below to brew a pot of tea. He struck a match and his next recollection was of being rescued from the harbour, as the boat sank beneath him. The vessel's entire bow section had blown apart leaving him injured but alive.

The fetid air in the *Rosemary's* cuddy was heavy with stale gas, mould and bilge, a lethal mixture for anyone with a sensitive stomach. Trying to breathe as little as possible, I quickly filled the kettle from the big drum, spilling quite a lot onto the bottom boards in the process. This didn't matter too much, it would find its way to the bilges. With the stove lit and kettle in place, I made an exit back to the deck, taking with me the two mugs which I washed in seawater from the 'draw bucket'.

The freshly brewed tea with just a little sweetened milk was palatable, though there was scarcely time to down it before we arrived at the location to commence fishing. Dad eased back the throttle, stopping the boat across the slight breeze. At first the procedure was similar to that on the *Floreat*, only on a smaller scale. The *Rosemary* had only half the horsepower of Uncle John's boat so couldn't physically pull a net and boards so big. Unlike the *Floreat*, the *Rosemary* didn't have a dedicated trawl winch, only a single twelve inch diameter capstan, mostly used for hauling pots.

The warps were two inch circumference ropes, neatly coiled for'ard and aft.

Dad came for'ard and together we lifted the doors outboard on the starboard 'weather' side, where they hung on stubby 'samson posts'. Next we fed the net overboard between the doors, Dad instructing me and making sure everything was going clear. As the net sank, its weight was taken by the bridles which attached it to the doors.

Climbing back over to the steering position, Dad re-engaged the engine and the trawl began to stream away astern. "Get ready!" he yelled holding the wheel with one hand and the warp, three turns passed around the samson post, in the other. I loosened the hitches holding the for'ard door, until I too had three turns around the post. I could feel the strain being exerted as the boat moved through the water. "Check it when I shout, an' keep plenty o' weight on it." He glanced at the land, waiting for his required course as the boat circled, then yelled, "Leggo".

I let the rope snake through my hands as it flowed from the coil at my feet, round the post, then out over the side. The wooden post was soon smoking with friction, as the taught rope whizzed round it. "Check!" Dad yelled. We both grasped our rope tightly, preventing the flow. The effect was dramatic; the boat was reined like a fleeing horse, slowing instantly.

Dad looked astern to ensure the trawl was open, that the doors were spreading, then called, "OK". The rope and boat began to run again. At sixty fathoms we checked again, then tied off with the marks level at the stern. He put the wheel hard to port, bringing my warp alongside. Deftly he passed a short end of rope around my warp, binding it securely. The two warps, fastened side by side were leading down into the water astern, at an angle of about thirty degrees.

Now we were 'shot' there was little to do; we'd trawl for at least three hours. I put the kettle on again, then went aft to talk to Dad. Suddenly a large porpoise swam alongside the boat, snorting air from its blowhole as it broke the surface. Next it swam down the warps and must have bounced on them, for they trembled violently. This lovely creature stayed with us for fifteen or twenty minutes, circling, diving and on several occasions jumping completely out of the water. It was wonderful, a private show, with just Dad and me to witness it. As quickly as it arrived, the star of the show swam off, leaving us in wonder at its performance.

I looked for'ard to see steam billowing from the cuddy door. I'd forgotten about the kettle, luckily it hadn't boiled dry and a fresh brew was soon forthcoming. We shot and hauled the trawl three times during the day. After each haul I sorted the catch into boxes and baskets, then shovelled the refuse overboard. Dad helped with gutting and washing the fish. He probably gutted most of it and was still able to steer the boat.

On arriving at the harbour that evening, we unloaded the catch together. Several people asked, "where's Tom?" To each Dad replied, "e's badly; me and t' lad 'ave been". I think he felt quite proud saying that. He didn't say as much, I just sensed it.

The week passed all too quickly and soon my brief deck-hand job ended. I received nine pounds in my pay packet but it was a million to me, because I'd been at sea to earn it. This feeling was reduced somewhat when it was suggested that I give Mum something towards my keep, but even with six pounds left, I was rich.

The following week I was back at school but I had tasted life beyond the classroom and felt even more restless. When I suggested to Dad that I'd be sixteen in September and perhaps I should leave school and get a job, he was most emphatic. "You're not goin' fishin'. I've told y' before, it's finished. You're clever enough t' go in t' Navy or t' Merchant Navy. Y' could be a Captain. Stay on at school an y' can go t' sea as an apprentice officer."

I knew this was true, certainly the apprentice part. I was half convinced. My school had an arrangement with the 'Bank Line', a company which operated general cargo vessels all over the world. Several former pupils had found successful careers in this way. He went on, "if y' joined t' Royal Navy an' signed on f' twenty two years, y' could come out wi' a pension an still be a young fella." I quickly added sixteen to twenty two and was horrified. Thirty eight! I'd nearly be dead by then. I wanted to go fishing.

CHAPTER VI

THE DRIFTERS

The summer holidays finally arrived heralding freedom for the foreseeable future. It was late into July; any day now the first of the drifters would arrive. The nomadic Scottish herring fishers left their sturdy, austere towns of Fraserburgh, Banff, Peterhead and the many villages along the Moray Firth in spring, pursuing the shoals of herring down the North Sea. The vast shoals, sometimes miles long, contained countless millions of fish. The herring migrated annually, to a predictable timetable, pursued by the fleets of many nations, but more recently only Scots, English and Dutch.

The drifters fished in Scottish waters in the early part of the year. In June and July they could be found off the Northumberland coast, landing into North Shields each day. August and most of September were spent fishing from Scarborough or Whitby before they moved south again to Grimsby, then finally Yarmouth or Lowestoft. In December they would sail the length of the North Sea to be home for Christmas.

These vessels were bigger than our local boats, ranging from sixty to seventy five feet in length. Each carried a proud meaningful name, *By Dand*, *The Way*, *Fisher Queen*, *Forethought*, *Prevail* and scores of other romantic or emotive titles. They were sleek, immaculately painted craft, predominantly black, though one or two were green. All were festooned with the scales from the myriad of herring caught nightly. These scales with their peculiar adhesive quality were ever present.

The fleet of up to fifty boats would sail from each of the ports before dark, with the exception of Sunday, which was religiously observed. Their quarry spent the daylight hours on or close to the seabed, unassailable, but swam close to the surface at night, with a tendency for deeper water in bright moonlight. Seen from shore on a clear night, the combined fleets resembled a brightly-lit town on the horizon.

Each vessel carried a crew of ten and many of these nomadic fishermen made local friends, friendships which lasted a lifetime. There were difficulties on occasions, understanding the broad, North East Scottish dialect, which was so strong, it was almost a foreign tongue, though the international language of drunk is universal. Local men occasionally worked as crew on the drifters. In a fleet so large there were often vacancies due to illness, injury, problems at home or conflict with the skipper or crew.

George was one such 'chance shotter'. A swarthy character, whose dark colour appeared to be more from lack of soap than nature, he had a reputation as shady person. Aptly nicknamed 'Tarrar', he was a locally-born man though was a 'sea gypsy'. He'd probably spent time in most of the ports surrounding the North Sea on his travels, getting into untold scrapes. During one of his short visits home, he was engaged as temporary cook on the drifter, *Loyal Friend*. One day while in harbour, he made the cook's cardinal sin of allowing the fire in the coal-burning stove to die. The crew were demanding a pot of tea.

As a boy of ten or eleven, I had the misfortune to be stepping across this vessel on my way from the *Floreat*, which was berthed close by. George stuck his head out from the galley, and confronted me as I passed, saying, "'Ere young un, can y' do a little job f' me."

I stopped warily, knowing George's reputation, wanting to go on but not daring to. "Good lad, tek this teapot over t' 'arbour Bar an' ask t' lady t' fill it up. Tell 'er it's fo' George. It'll be alright." He passed me a huge soot-blackened, battered teapot, lagged with rough twine around the handle and spout for insulation. He removed the lid, decanting half a packet of tea into the pot before replacing it. I didn't want to go on this errand, but there was no way out of it. Being of a tender age, I felt I couldn't say no to this grown up.

Very reluctantly, I crossed the road from the quayside to my destination, hating the situation I'd been placed in through no fault of my own. The Harbour Bar was a large ice-cream parlour that also served hundreds of cups of coffee daily. It was thronging with visitors throughout the season. The standard of cleanliness within the premises was exceptional. Eight or ten ladies dressed in immaculate matching overalls, were constantly cleaning and wiping every available surface, when not serving customers.

I entered the opened glass doors, dreading the encounter, trying to look inconspicuous. A large steaming, stainless steel boiler gleamed behind the counter at one end. Deliberately going to this position, trying to shield the utensil from the dozens of customers with my body, I quietly said to the nearest counter assistant, "excuse me, George says can y' fill this, 'e knows the lady in charge."

I cringed as a look of horror came to her face. She took the battered pot from me between the forefingers of both hands, holding it aloft. "Lucy," she called out loudly, in a posh voice, "can we fill this?" Time froze. Every eye in the place seemed to be focusing on the teapot and then on me. The proprietor hurried over, staring at the blackened object with distaste.

"Where's it come from? It's disgusting." Her eyes challenged mine in an uneven contest.

Looking down I muttered, "it's from an 'erring boat, an' their galley fire's gone out."

The disdain remained. "We'll fill it this time, but it's highly irregular, don't come again."

She took the offending article, placed it under the steaming urn, then opened the tap. The huge teapot disappeared in a cloud of vapour. It seemed to take an eternity to fill. I stood there looking at the tiled floor, hands in pockets, wishing I was at school. Finally the hissing, bubbling flow stopped. The lady, reappearing from the cloud, replaced the lid, then lifting the giant teapot with both hands, she carefully placed it on the counter. An assistant stood hovering, damp cloth at the ready, to confront the expected stain.

"That'll be two shillings," the proprietor said primly.

"I 'aven't any money," I replied in a whisper. If I'd had money of my own I'd willingly have paid it to extricate myself from the nightmare. "George said 'e knows y' an' it would be alright."

"George! George who? I don't know any Georges over there!" She waved her hand dismissively in the direction of the harbour. This was a poser for her, she clearly didn't want to keep the teapot, so had no choice but to let me go with it. "Take it away, take it away and don't ever come back!" I could feel the stares as I left the premises. My face felt like a beacon as I laboured with the scalding load, manoeuvring it towards the doors. I was almost knocked down by a car as I crossed the busy road, in my haste to escape with the precarious cargo.

"Good lad, com' an' see me at t' weekend, an' I'll treat ya," said a relieved George, as I hove into sight, struggling with my heavy load. I knew 'the weekend' meant 'never' but didn't care, I just wanted to get away from the horrendous scenario. It was weeks before I dare go anywhere near the Harbour Bar again, even then I kept my head down.

Dad was temporarily fishing on a herring boat from Scarborough when I was very young. One evening when the weather was poor, the skipper decided not to sail until he'd heard the midnight shipping forecast. He informed Dad that if he was required, following the bulletin, one of the crew would knock on the door at home.

The following morning when Dad arose from bed at seven thirty, Mum asked him where he was going so early. He said he was going down to help land the catch. "But you haven't been to sea," Mum said, confused.

He had been to sea. Following the forecast, he'd been summoned to sail. Once at sea, the skipper had located a shoal of herring only a few miles from harbour and had quickly returned with a catch. Dad was back home again at five in the morning and after a wash, had gone back to bed. Although they slept in the same bed, Dad had got up on hearing the knock, gone to the harbour, sailed, caught fish, returned and got back into bed again, yet Mum hadn't noticed he'd gone.

I first sailed on a drifter when only ten years old. After much pleading, Dad had arranged a trip for me on one of these fine vessels. Her crew of middle aged, mostly religious men, were annual visitors to the town and well-known to the locals.

As the sun dropped low in the sky, I stood proudly on the deck of the *Northern Light* as she sailed through the harbour entrance. She was one of forty boats leaving port that evening, to seek the massive shoals. Others would be leaving Whitby. These vessels would join the Dutchmen, who stayed at sea for several days, preferring to preserve their catch in barrels of salt rather than land them fresh.

I walked to stern and looked into the galley at the glowing stove. This black, cast-iron range was Doddie the cook's pride and joy. The oven adjoining the fire would produce wonderful roasts, crispy duffs or superbly baked fish. The range top held the usual, permanently-steaming kettle. At his invitation, I followed the crew into the galley, then down the ladder to the cabin, leaving the skipper in his wheelhouse to locate the herring. Entering the dimly-lit cabin I looked around. Compared with the accommodation on the *Floreat*, this seemed huge. It was panelled throughout in dark, varnished wood. A table filled three-quarters of the available space. I counted ten bunks, five on each side, two lower and three upper. The extra top bunks almost met, tucked inaccessibly at the after end of the cabin. The narrow boxed section separating them, contained the rudder shaft. The younger, more agile crew, were assigned to these berths.

The men, seated comfortably around the table, each had a piping hot mug filled from the ubiquitous teapot and were helping themselves to oatcakes, bread, cheese, pickles, jam and other sandwich snacks placed in the centre of the table. Given a mug of tea, I was invited to join in the meal, but unusually for me, I wasn't hungry. It was a wonderful experience sitting around the cabin table with all these big men, in their ganseys and smocks. I wanted to stay, but the heat in the confined space and the motion of the boat compelled me to make for the deck. I needed fresh air urgently. I felt more comfortable but still queasy standing on the deck, in reach of, but not too close to, the galley door; a position I kept as darkness fell.

Overhead, thousands of stars gave a spectacular show against a black back drop. On the surface, in every direction were the navigation lights of scores of boats, heading on all points of the compass, their echo sounders pulsing, searching for the elusive shoals. I wondered why there were no collisions. Suddenly a boat close on our port side was illuminated as her deck lights were switched on; a sure sign she'd located a 'mark'. Within minutes her crew were paying out a wall of nets. A row of corks at the top and weights at the bottom ensured it would hang like a curtain in the water. Spaced at intervals, attached by ropes, were coloured 'pellets', inflated vinyl buoys which floated on the surface, supporting and marking the position of the nets below. The *Northern Light's* head swung round, as did many other vessels', heading in the direction of the unknown, brightly lit craft. Our deck lights too were switched on and the engine eased. The crew scrambled from the cabin, eager to shoot the gear. Speed was essential if they were to get a good position among this shoal.

The *Northern Light* weaved too and fro, zigzagging as the skipper located the herring under his boat. His men, poised at the ship's side, were ready to commence shooting the nets. When the skipper was satisfied that his boat was in position, he bawled from the open wheelhouse window, "haway ma lads, let 'em go, set 'em at ten fathoms." The individual nets, joined together to form a wall, were pelted overboard at a tremendous rate as the *Northern Light* cruised across the wind. They would hang at sixty feet below the surface, the depth at which the shoal had been located. The skipper occasionally growled further instructions to his men, but these were indecipherable to me. When all the sixty nets were shot,(some boats carried more) not only the lights, even the engine was switched off so the quarry wouldn't be diverted away from our gear. Now we were 'drifting'. With no power the rolling of the boat was enhanced significantly, causing me to hold onto the galley side, my stomach churning.

Only three white lights in a triangular shape at the masthead, indicated our presence. This was an international signal, informing other mariners that a vessel was engaged in fishing. There were dozens of triangles to be seen in the vicinity, each one a drifter tending her nets. It was now late in the evening. The crew had returned below, some to sit at the table, others to doze in their bunks until the skipper called them back on deck. He would remain vigilant in his wheelhouse, reluctantly flashing the boat's searchlight in the direction of his gear, warning off approaching shipping. He would attempt to talk to his fellow skippers on the radio, but this was an almost impossible task, as almost all fishing vessels used the same frequency.

For the next hour I sat in darkness near the stern, in the lee of the ship's small boat. All the drifters carried a boat, though there was no obvious means of launching them. They were mostly used for storing vegetables and spare fishing gear. I moved only to spew over the low rail of the rolling boat. Even when there was nothing more to come up, the retching continued. The skipper kindly brought me a mug of water and some dry toast, saying I should keep something in my stomach. There wasn't much chance of that. Above my head the creaking and flapping of the tan coloured mizzen sail was exaggerated in the still night. This had been set by the crew when they came aft, to keep the boat head to wind.

Dozing and curled in a ball for warmth under the boat, I was eventually roused by the deep throb of the engine starting below. The lights came on again and the crew trooped from the galley in their oilskins and sou'westers. Several had encouraging remarks for me as they observed my pathetic state. I felt a little better when the yellow clad figures began to haul the nets. The skipper came out to where I was sitting and suggested that I went for'ard to watch. He dressed me in an old oilskin, which engulfed me and I staggered forward, holding onto the handrail. The men, standing shoulder to shoulder, fore and aft in the centre of the vessel, were hauling the huge sheet of net, slowly over the port side, in harmony with the motion of the boat. When she rolled to port they took up the slack, leaning back together holding onto their gain when she went the other way. At first there were no fish to be seen and their mood was glum, but this quickly changed when the first of the herring began to appear from over the side, meshed by their gills in the fine netting. Soon herring were in abundance.

Fish and scales were flying through the air in all directions as they were shaken or 'shigged' from the net, as a housewife shakes a carpet. The men averted their eyes as they shook the wriggling fish out. Most dropped to the deck, where they quickly died, but occasionally a fish flew back overboard to a lucky escape. The crew, now positively jovial, their oilskins and sou'westers coated in glistening fish-scales, were standing on the pile of net which they'd recovered. Despite the efforts of their labour they shouted encouragement to the fish still in the sea. "Haway noo, swim up, ye lovely critters," or "come aboard ye silver darlin's." As the fish began to accumulate, a hatch in the deck under the incoming nets was opened, allowing the catch to spill into the fish hold below.

It was now well past midnight. There was miles of net still to be hauled; it would be hours yet before it was all recovered. I felt totally exhausted and though still feeling seasick, discarded the oilskin, creeping below to the cabin, where I climbed into the nearest bunk, not caring whose it was. I fell asleep immediately and slept solidly. I woke to the sound of the engine easing down as the boat entered the harbour. I'd been asleep for about five hours. Standing on the pier, where I thought I'd feel better, I began to feel sick again. I was still rolling with the motion of the boat and the land was stationary. I stood wobbling, by the top of the ladder, feeling very sorry for myself, intending to leave quietly, unnoticed, when the skipper called out, "that's ye finished wi' the sea then, young Freddy. Ye'll be a farrmer noo." I might never have gone to sea again but for this calculated remark.

"No I won't, I'll be back, I'll come again," I was able to reply weakly, though unconvincingly. It was the following year before I felt up to sailing on a drifter once more and I'm sure it was this shout which challenged me to return. I was seasick many times subsequently, but never as bad as on that occasion.

The local butcher asked if I was interested in the job of 'ships runner' for his shop, obtaining the fleet's meat requirements each day. For the next six weeks there would be hundreds of hungry men to supply. I didn't know anything about butchering. I was to relay the orders back to the shop, where they'd be prepared by him and his assistant for my delivery. His only instruction was "ignore requests for 'legs' of liver and 'fathoms' of sausages."

My pay was to be half a crown for each boat that used his services during the season, plus a five per cent commission on the total amount spent. It sounded complicated and there was no mention of a wage, but as I virtually haunted the pier and enjoyed going on board the Scotsmen's boats, I decided to take the job. I was aware of what was entailed, having seen the butcher and grocer boys working in previous years. There would be competition, there were other butchers interested in trading with the herring boats but I wasn't too worried about this. I would be at the harbour each morning at six o'clock with my notebook and pencil, meeting the boats as they arrived in port. The butcher's shop opened at eight and my deliveries would hopefully be completed by mid-morning, leaving lots of free time for other pursuits.

The *Watchful* was the first of the year to arrive, on the last day of July. I saw her distinctive drifter features the instant I turned the corner to view the harbour. An early morning arrival, moored alongside the pier, she dwarfed the cobles berthed next to her. The black hull with artistically painted registration number BF 107 on each bow, denoted her origins and individuality. Her raised wooden wheelhouse and adjoining galley were beautifully grained with rectangular boxed sections, each panel outlined in black to highlight the grain. All the drifters' deckhouses were decorated in this manner, an expensive, time-consuming process which underlined the fierce pride each skipper took in the presentation of his vessel. The port side, from the wheelhouse to the ship's side, was caged over, accessed via a net screen at the for'ard end. Within were stored scores of large yellow and orange vinyl pellets, approximately three feet in diameter.

The skipper of the *Watchful*, 'James Alec' was a large, rotund man with a red weathered face and tussled black hair. He was a previous winner of the trophy for the largest catch of the season; a beautiful silver model of a keelboat, which was presented at a ceremony annually by the Mayor. The award was kept by the winner for a year. The only rule was that to win the trophy, the skipper must have sailed from Scarborough the previous evening, before returning with his winning catch. This encouraged drifters to use the port, thereby adding to the harbour's revenue.

It was obvious that the crew of the *Watchful* were unloading their catch. The cran pole, a long wooden boom used solely to land the catch, was acutely angled from the base of the foremast. This pole was lowered with its tip resting on the top of the wheelhouse, firmly secured during fishing operations. The herrings bulked in the hold below were landed in stiff cane baskets, four baskets equalling a cran. Uniquely, this was a measure of volume not weight. A cran was historically deemed an average of one thousand herrings. Its weight, though not official, was about twenty eight stone. Each quarter cran basket was branded with the insignia of a crown, denoting a bona fide measure. A hundred cran was a huge catch, a talking point around the harbour. The lucky boat would sag in the water with the weight of fish. Twenty to forty cran was considered a good silver harvest.

I stood for a few minutes watching the crew discharging their catch, landed directly onto a lorry, its cab emblazoned with the logo 'Croan's Kippers' in red and gold. This vehicle would transport the cargo, in fresh condition, to the Edinburgh smoking kilns for processing. Two oilskin-clad figures stood waist-deep in herrings in the fish hold, scooping the catch into baskets, which were hoisted with the boom to the waiting truck. A winchman operated the fast revolving drum at the foot of the mast. Each basket was tipped into a waiting fish box on the lorry, with a minimum of effort, by two more crew men. As a youngster in junior school, I'd crouch with others precariously between pier and lorry, competing to snatch the herrings which spilled from the brimming baskets. When enough fish were acquired or we were encouraged to 'clear off,' we'd erect a box stall to display our wares.

"'Errings, fresh 'errings, a penny each," was the universal cry. The demand was good, especially on Saturdays when visitors were travelling back to their inland homes. The goods were wrapped in a supply of newspapers brought from home.

A movement at the stern of the vessel caught my eye. The cook was tipping a bucket of potato peelings into the harbour. Intent on catching his order, I clambered down the ladder to the midship section of deck, scrutinised and questioned wordlessly by James Alec, sitting on an inverted fish box, deftly mending a split in one of the fine cotton nets. "Butcher," I said quickly, grabbing the notebook and pencil from a back pocket, pointing to the cook. He nodded his approval, then still without a word, reached for the knife protruding blade first from under his cap and began trimming the edges of broken mesh, preparing it for stitching.

Herring drifters at the North Wharf in late summer, circa 1955.
Photo Ken Wigg

Herring drifters landing their catches. Note the basket of
herrings enroute to the shore. Photo Ken Wigg

Dicky Elliott and Ernie (Soapy) Williamson shooting pots in their coble, Who Cares. Photo Dennis Dobson courtesy of the Elliott and Williamson families

Aerial photo of Scarborough's West Pier in summer. Note the fish market with bait sheds and 'Harry's Tea-shop' at the rear of the buildings. Sandgate Corner and slipway are towards the top right. The Lighthouse is at the bottom left and the Lifeboat House at the extreme end of the beach. Photo Scarborough Public Library courtesy of Max Payne

After securing an order from the *Watchful's* cook I met the *Incentive* and *Silver Wave* as they tied up, all requiring provisions. More vessels would be arriving each day now, until it would be possible to cross the harbour from boat to boat.

The following week in company with twenty craft, the *Hazael III* arrived. I could recognise most of the boats but this vessel, painted in two colours was unfamiliar. She had the usual black bulwarks but the remainder of her hull was mid-grey, the contrast was striking. Most of the Scotsmen in the fleet were friendly, but Davy the skipper, George the mate and Jimmy the cook on the *Hazael III* seemed particularly so. I looked for her specifically each day and was happy to run errands, post letters, bring newspapers, cigarettes or lemonade for the crew. On a couple of occasions, following a chat between Dad and Davy, I was allowed to go sea with them.

Near the end of August, which had shot past in an instant, Jimmy the cook said they'd be going home for a long weekend. Four boats from the fleet were to sail from Scarborough on the coming Thursday evening. They'd land their catches into North Shields on Friday morning, then a coach was to take them home for the weekend, returning on Monday evening in time to sail. Jimmy said if it was OK with Davy and my Dad, I could go with them, staying in his home in Fraserburgh for the three nights.

Davy didn't mind, the coach had sufficient seating so I needed to persuade Dad that my welfare was in safe hands. He was surprisingly positive, saying I should go and that it was an opportunity to see new places. His main concern was that I shouldn't let the butcher down. Someone must take the meat orders. I was able to persuade Brian, who also spent every spare moment on the waterfront, to substitute for me.

I sailed on the *Hazael III* on Wednesday night, not waiting another twenty four hours, calculating that if the boats fished closer to Whitby during the night, Davy might opt to land his catch there and I'd miss my first visit to Scotland. We seemed to be positioned in the middle of the fleet, surrounded by lights when Davy called the crew to shoot the gear. I felt a little queasy but not nearly as bad as I was on my first drifting trip.

It was great fun watching the crew as they hauled in the nets. They were shouting and singing and being generally amusing as they pulled tirelessly at the laden nets, shigging rhythmically to release the trapped fish. I was given the easy job of pulling the pellets on board, unbending and returning them to the cage behind the net curtain. Occasionally the cry, "scalders," would be heard. This was a warning of jellyfish. The men would close their eyes or pull the peaks of their caps down tightly as the stinging tentacles of these worthless creatures were launched into the air with the shaking of the net. The stings created a constant irritation to the skin but were unbearable to the eyes.

The grey light of dawn was in the sky to the east when the last net was hauled in. Looking around the entire horizon, I could only see four boats. It's a strange phenomena that lights can be seen much further in the dark than the vessels which bear them in daylight. Davy set a westerly course and an hour later we were sailing between the twin piers of the old whaling port of Whitby, on the River Esk, overlooked by the ruined abbey on the East Cliff. We landed twenty cran of bonnie herring onto a busy pier.

Whitby was an adventure for me. I'd only been there once before, though it was only twenty miles from Scarborough. There was much exploring to do on both sides of the river during the morning. I discovered the lifeboat museum, full of photographs and stories of famous rescues. During the afternoon while the crew were asleep in their bunks, I slept comfortably on the wide seat locker.

Following another night of fishing north of Whitby, in company with the *Flourish, Argosy* and *Strathbeg* we sailed into the River Tyne. It was fascinating to enter such a busy waterway with ships of all types, tugs, ocean-going cargo vessels, trawlers and even warships plying their business. Our catch was poor, as was that of our consorts. Davy said he wasn't too surprised as the season had finished on this part of the coast. The herring were now further south between Whitby and Flamborough Head.

The coach was waiting by the quayside and the passengers, cleanly scrubbed, dressed in their best 'going ashore' gear were keen to be off. I was very surprised to see a familiar face waiting to board the bus. Dennis was in my class at school and was going to

Fraserburgh to stay with the cook of the *Argosy*. This was great news; it would be so much better having someone to share the adventure with. We sat together at the front of the bus watching the scenery ahead.

The journey north seemed endless. As we crossed the border at Coldstream, Davy tapped our shoulders saying, "you'rr in another country noo boys, y'll best behave yo'rrselves." We drove through Edinburgh, along Princes Street, viewing the famous castle, which wasn't a bit like the one back home. Edinburgh Castle seemed much more imposing and was intact. We had a mid-afternoon stop for a meal, which the skipper kindly paid for, then continued north. It was late evening when we arrived at our stop in Fraserburgh, having previously visited several strange sounding villages, St Combs, Inverallochy and Cairnbulg, allowing men to disembark close to their homes. The bus then continued for several more miles, offloading its passengers at Gardenstown, McDuff and Banff.

Dennis and I were both exhausted so took no persuading to have an early night. Our hosts lived in close proximity and we'd meet after breakfast the following morning. I followed Jimmy into the granite-built cottage. We hadn't seen a brick building for the last hundred miles or more. From the outside it looked drab but once through the door the contrast was unbelievable. I felt immediately at home in the cheerful, immaculate room where a fire roared in the hearth.

Jessie, Jimmy's wife, a small, rotund lady with specs, was wearing a flowery pinny and white turban-style headsquare. She'd newly arrived home from her work at the nearby fish-processing factory. The poor lady was in a dither as she attempted to air the spare bed with a stone water bottle, cook something for us, improve her appearance, mother me and at the same time scold Jimmy for not informing her that he was bringing a guest home. Jessie was speaking in a tongue that to me was totally incomprehensible. I thought the menfolk's accent was broad but I couldn't understand a word this lady said, though her smiles in my direction, which I returned each time, spoke a none-threatening body language.

In a very short time Jimmy and I were attempting to eat our way through a mountain of fish, chips and peas with enough bread and butter to make a staircase. Jessie said something to her husband then disappeared into an adjoining room. "She say's she's awa' tae mak her sel' mar presentable," chuckled Jimmy, "mon ther's nay enough time, werr on'y hame the twa days."

I slept as if unconscious. The last few days had been exciting but very tiring, so it was sheer luxury to sleep in a proper bed for a whole night. I didn't realise how tired I was. It was nine o'clock the following morning when I was wakened by Jimmy, tapping lightly on my opened door. "Yo'rr chum's here, seekin' ye, ar' ye goin' tae sleep a' day?" I probably would have, had he not roused me. Dressing quickly I made my way to the compact little kitchen where a pan of porridge was simmering gently on the stove. Dennis, his host busy with jobs at home, was seated at the table nursing a pot of tea. Jimmy was fussing with dishes for the breakfast. "Jessie's awa tae her worrk, I thought ahd com' wi' you loons tae the harrbour."

We didn't mind, we didn't know where the harbour was. The stories told by the Scotsmen of how big Fraserburgh Harbour was and all the facilities it offered, we'd heard many times, but it was going to be exciting seeing it all first hand. I spooned my porridge subconsciously, thinking of the day ahead, then exclaimed, "euk salt." The steaming meal was laced with it.

Jimmy laughed, "it's the on'y wa' tae tak' it. That's hoo the Scotsmen ha'e it," but then produced sugar and milk which I added liberally. It was a long walk from Jimmy's house to the harbour. As the first of the boats appeared in view down the road, Jimmy said, "ah'll nay be lang boys, ah'll catch ye up," then promptly disappeared into the 'Balaclava Bar' on the harbourside. We never saw him again for the remainder of the day.

For a while we expected him to rejoin us and loitered close to the immediate area, looking in all directions at boats. There were drifters, seiners and trawlers, all big boats which gleamed immaculately. We pointed various aspects to each other in a professional manner. In another section of the harbour were berthed dozens of little, ancient-looking craft that fished for mackerel with hand lines. Dennis noticed the lifeboat shed, where an open door beckoned us. We were drawn inside as if by a magnet. A 'Watson-Barnet' type lifeboat, much bigger than the vessel at home, was poised at the top of a ramp ready for instant release. The Scarborough boat took ages to launch with a tractor and trailer. The friendly mechanic took note of our interest, pausing from his maintenance schedule to give us a guided tour of the boat and station. We felt quite privileged to be given this special attention. We were quickly realising the hospitable nature of these folk. Nothing seemed to be too much trouble.

Dennis and I were not perturbed at Jimmy's non-appearance. He'd be 'takin' a wee dram' with his pals. We had the freedom to walk the many piers and different sections of harbour, which seemed to stretch for miles. The icehouse dispensed tons of ice, directly from an overhead gantry into the boats' fish holds. Back home it was supplied by the fish box full to the vessels, as they landed. If any quantity was required, it came on a five-ton truck from Hull and was shovelled onto the boat.

We strolled through the vast fish market, where remnants of the day's sale were stacked. This residue was more than a full week's supply in Scarborough. Not far from the fish market, five boats were standing completely erect on the slipway. They'd been pulled from the harbour by carriage, then 'side-slipped' for underwater repairs, propeller changes or painting. At home the boats relied on the 'Golden Ball' slip or the beach for this type of work, all of which must be completed while the tide was out. None of these boats would fit on the 'Golden Ball' slip. It was a long trek to the far end of the harbour where we could see a sign 'James Noble, Boatbuilder'. Denk's boat *Margaret Jane* had been built there in 1957.

Noble's yard was a hive of industry. We entered warily expecting to be ejected but were acknowledged with, "hullo boys" or "morrnin' boys" by the workers we met. Inside the shed the oak skeleton of what seemed an immense ship was on the stocks. The air was full of the smell of sawdust and new wood, giving a warm pleasant sensation. Incessant hammering drew our eyes to a team of two shipwrights perched on a raised, trestled platform, each wielding a heavy hammer. Alternately they were belting a huge, square-shanked, galvanised nail into place in a four inch wide plank. Their timing was 'split second' and they never missed. A matching team worked as a mirror image on the opposite side of the vessel. The ringing of their hammers echoed around the yard. Both pairs were in sight of each other through the ribs, but as the 'skin' grew on the bones, they'd become separated until the hull was intact.

Later, slight gaps between the planks would be caulked with oakum, a rope like substance, driven home with a hammer and chisel. This would swell amazingly when wet, making the vessel watertight. There were dozens of craftsmen working in harmony throughout the yard, giving life to this chrysalis. Horizontal sections of whole trees were being marked out and cut to the correct dimensions. These were planed by man and machine, then consigned to a 'steaming box', making them pliable. We were witnessing a creation and I was dumbstruck; my pal equally so. We walked very slowly, in awe, around this maternity unit. Eventually a living creature would emerge from this cocoon, down a greased way to enter its new world with a splash. It would be fitted out at the pier alongside the shed with engines, winches, a wheelhouse and all the other necessities required for it to become someone's beautiful baby. It was beyond even a dream to think that one day, these same craftsmen would build a boat for me.

It was late afternoon when we trekked back to our respective houses for tea. I entered the house to find Jimmy slumped in a chair, burbling incoherent apologies to a very vexed Jessie. She'd left early from her shift at the factory to prepare tea for her guest, which was unfortunate for Jimmy, who happened to stagger home at the same time. It was impossible to decipher a word this woman was saying, but I didn't need to know the language to get the message. Finally she slowed down, paused for breath, then apologised for her man's terrible behaviour in a more comprehensible tone.

All through the tea, which was every schoolboy's dream, consisting of buns, iced cakes, sandwiches and orange juice, Jessie alternately berated her hapless husband in a harsh growl, then cooed her regrets at what she perceived was Jimmy's negligence of me. I tried to shrug off the situation as of no consequence but she wouldn't let the matter rest. Jessie was still snarling at her husband, who was pretending to be asleep, when I went out again to meet Dennis. As I passed, Jimmy cautiously winked at me and gave a wry smile, as if to say, "I've heard it all before."

That evening we went to the only cinema in town to watch a second rate, instantly forgettable, black and white film. Fraserburgh may have a huge harbour but their picture house was hopeless. We had five of them in Scarborough, all bigger than this one.

If Saturday offered little entertainment to two lads from a holiday resort, then Sunday was dead. There was nothing to do. We walked to the harbour again but it was devoid of activity, though Jimmy, who never left our side, highlighted several interesting facets which we'd missed. He was excused, returning home, probably by a circuitous route when we took the bus to nearby Rosehearty, four miles to the west along the Moray Firth. We were assured there was a swimming pool in the village which would be open. Passing through the village of Sandhaven en route, we looked for the 'J & G Forbes' boatyard. Jimmy informed us earlier that Forbes built even bigger boats than Nobles and had double the workforce. All was quiet as we passed through the village, where someone's rather large, shiny, new, black 'baby' was on the stocks. This baby had been abandoned for the day.

At Rosehearty we were the only swimmers in the small, freezing, seawater pool. The two outdoor pools back home were much bigger than this, and one of them was heated. Staying only a short while, we quickly dressed and returned to Fraserburgh. In the afternoon, as pre-arranged, we visited three of the crew at their homes to meet their wives and families. At each we were compulsorily fed with the staple diet of cakes, biscuits and sandwiches until we couldn't eat another thing. The contrast of these men, in the domestic surroundings of their homes and families, with the hard drinking, wild weekends they spent in Scarborough was amusing. They were Jekyll and Hyde characters. One whispered, "dinna say onythin' tae the wifey aboot oor hijinx doon soouth."

Early Monday saw us back on the coach as it stopped outside the door, but not before I received a big hug to a more than ample chest and a, "y'll com' tae see us agin, will ye nay, ma loon?" I hastily promised I would, hoping no one would notice Jessie's motherly goodbye, but it was a forlorn hope. I was the centre of much ridicule from the men on the bus, even Dennis was smirking as I climbed the steps, red-faced. There was no stopping on the way back once all hands were aboard the coach. Shields was the first port of call. The shoals of herring were a long way south from there. For these men their break was over, they wouldn't see home again until December. I'd be home again in the morning, hopefully.

The little fleet sailed south east from the Tyne and working as a team, the skippers located a late swim of herring to the north east of Whitby. All four vessels landed between forty and sixty cran of good herring into Scarborough on Tuesday morning. My Scottish holiday was over. Summer was rolling on.

The herring season wasn't only a bonanza time for the drifters, it was a boom time for the local keelboats too. The billions of herring that congregated on the Yorkshire Coast came to spawn. Their eggs, in unbelievable numbers were strewn across the seabed over a wide area, attracting all manner of fish. One fish's young are another fish's meal. Cod, haddock and whiting gathered in abundance to gorge on this food mountain, until they too became prey to the combined trawling boats of Scarborough, Whitby and Bridlington. These vessels dragged their nets along the seabed where the spawn was laid, easily catching these bloated predators.

I could be found on the West Pier most evenings as the harbour emptied of drifters and the keelboats began arriving, their decks laden with fish. They could always use a willing hand. These vessels would sail again in the early hours of the morning as the drifters were returning. The Whitby boats landed to their home port but it was common for Bridlington fishermen to land their catches at Scarborough.

Joss and Alex successfully operated a boat from Bridlington with assistance from two crewmen. The brothers had graduated to this lovely vessel from a coble, which they'd worked together, inshore between Bridlington and the steep white cliffs at Flamborough Head. This headland, one of the most spectacular sites in the British Isles is a magnet to thousands of visitors, attracted to its rocky shores and caves. Gannets, puffins, guillemots and kittiwakes breed in huge numbers on its sheer walls, drawing many bird watchers during the breeding season.

One spring day, while hauling their pots close to the breakers at the foot of the cliff, the brothers heard a shout, "ahoy there! Help!" Stopping work they scanned the coastline. Alex pointed to a man, marooned thirty feet up the cliff face with no way up or down. The unfortunate chap had climbed the precarious wall to avoid the incoming tide and was now stranded.

Alex manoeuvred the coble close to the cliff, yelling to the man to jump into the sea and they'd pick him up from the water. Bawling back that he was a non-swimmer and afraid of the rocks below, the fellow declined this offer of assistance. It was impossible for a helicopter to fly this close to the cliff face and the lifeboat at the nearby North Landing would be unable to get any closer than the brothers in their small craft. How were they to get him down?

Joss picked up a coil of light rope, weighting the end with a small shackle, then threw this to the stranded man, who grabbed it gratefully. "Fasten it around ya waist," he shouted to the unsuspecting victim, who promptly obeyed the instruction. Joss fastened the other end to a strong point on the coble, then said to his brother, "'ead out t' sea, full speed!" His brother quickly followed these instructions and the poor unfortunate chap was plucked screaming from the cliff face, plummeting into the sea, from where he was hauled, spluttering, unceremoniously into the boat.

"'E never even thanked us, t' ungrateful sod," said Alex to his brother, as the man ran shivering up the shingle beach, the instant the boat touched at Flamborough Landing.

The brothers were good fishermen, respected by their contemporaries. They earned very good money for themselves and their crew, selling their catches through an agency operated and managed by Arnold. Though only small and slight, Arnold was an important, influential businessman, a university graduate well acquainted with life beyond the harbourside. He was involved in all aspects of fishing, from owning vessels, auctioning his and other boats' catches and retailing the end product.

In contrast, Joss and Alex, though excellent fishermen, with a fair degree of natural cunning, were not at all familiar with the ways of the world beyond their own locality. One day Arnold let it be known that he and his wife Helen were to visit London for a weekend break and were to stay in a top class hotel. "D'ya mind if me an' t' missus comes wi ya lad?" Joss said, when informed of the impending visit.

Clearly Arnold did mind, though when he weighed up the commission received from this client, against his reluctance, his business sense prevailed. Helen didn't see the situation in these terms and wanted to cancel the trip, but was persuaded by her husband that all would be well. It was agreed they would meet at the local railway station for this brief visit to the capital. Arnold, resplendent in light flannels, smartly-cut blazer and cravat; his wife decked in a light summer dress, short trimmed jacket with seasonal bonnet were there in good time. Their matching luggage was placed neatly to hand by the grateful porter, in receipt of a large tip.

Looking at his watch, the executive whispered to his wife, "perhaps they've changed their minds darling," but it was more in hope than belief.

Shortly before departure time, Joss and his missus arrived, perspiring and puffing onto the platform. Joss wore a pair of clean, but well-worn black, twill trousers and an ancient gansey, which had obviously been darned. The old shoes he wore were polished but battered, the laces long gone, replaced by black fishing twine. His crowning glory was his best new Sunday cap.

Joss's luggage consisted of his black, shiny tarpaulin kitbag, which he used each week for his sea gear, plus a dirty raffia bass with hessian handles frequently used for carrying fish and shellfish. His wife, red of face, hat and coat, clasped a battered suitcase under her arm, one side neatly hitched with the ubiquitous trawl twine. "Sorry we're late lad, we missed t' bus. Bloody fastener came off t' missus' case, I 'ad t' put a lashin' o' twine on it."

Arnold and his wife shuffled away but with their backs to the edge of the platform there was little room for escape. Fortunately, the timely arrival of the train prevented further embarrassment. They entered the first class compartment, adjacent to the restaurant car, where they took possession of the seats reserved for them by Arnold's secretary. Joss looked round at the plush carriage furniture in amazement. "Tha's done us proud 'ere lad," he growled, not knowing that his share of the costs would be debited directly from his next landing of fish.

"When we get beyond Doncaster, we shall take lunch," declared Arnold.

"No need lad, I thought o' that." Joss thrust his huge callused hand into the fish bag, pulling from it a rust-rimmed thermos flask. Plunging in again, he withdrew a greaseproof package previously containing sliced bread. Pulling the parcel apart with his massive hands, Joss revealed four full rounds of doorstep sized sandwiches. "Med 'em meself wi' a few crabs we got in t' trawl yesterday," he said, wiping his nose with the back of his hand.

Helen emitted a choking sound, leapt from her seat and was heard mumbling something about fresh air, as she dashed from the carriage. "Don't worry 'oney we'll save one f' ya," Joss yelled down the aisle at the fast disappearing back.

For Arnold, the remainder of the journey seemed endless. His supposed visits to the toilet when he pleaded with his wife, ensconced in the next compartment, to return to her seat were met with an icy glare. Words were neither spoken nor required to express her opinion of the situation.

"Is she feelin' any better? Poor lamb, is it women's trouble? Shall ah go an' sit wi' 'er?" Joss's wife said, sympathetically. Arnold assured the red lady that everything was fine, that his wife would return shortly. The situation had not improved when they arrived at the end of the line. A cab was hailed for their onward journey to the hotel. Throughout the taxi ride Arnold and his wife sat in silence, diametrically opposed, both their noses pinned to their respective windows. The silence was frequently broken with comments, "that statue 'as no clothes on, 'ort not t' be allowed."

"That's a bloody big 'ouse, wonder who lives there."

"Look at t' state o' them mucky buggers, 'ose-pipe an' scrubbin' brush is what they need."

At the hotel the two couples were given adjacent rooms, so it was impossible to avoid travelling in the elevator together, in company with two porters carrying the luggage. There seemed a distinct odour in the confined cabin, which was unnoticed by two of the occupants. The ceiling of the vehicle was examined minutely by the other four. Joss observed the dinner menu, framed on the wall of the lift. "Bloody 'ell Alice, me an' you could live for a month fo' that much, it's bloody robbery."

It was humiliating for Arnold and his wife, following immediately behind the leading trio, to observe the porter in front. He was attempting to hold a kitbag and fish bass disdainfully at arm's length, as he manoeuvred the long corridor. The final straw however, when the executive and his wife wished the floor would open and swallow them, came when the party stopped at their respective rooms, allowing the bearers to open the doors.

As he pulled some loose change from his pocket to tip his carrier, Arnold was horrified to see his associate's hand dive into his fish bag, to emerge with a large crab. Hand on mouth he watched, unbelieving, as Joss slapped the brown crustacean into the opened hand of his porter, and hear him say, "that's f' you lad. Don't worry, it's boiled, ah cooked it meself yesterday on t' boat."

The couples never met again during the entire weekend. Helen felt too ill to leave the room. Helen and Arnold travelled home on an earlier train than arranged, without informing their fellow travellers. Arnold never ever again, mentioned prospective holidays to anyone.

The summer holidays had flown by; school was again looming. I would be sixteen in a few days but was not allowed to leave. Half my class had left at the onset of the current holidays. The drifter numbers were decreasing as the shoals moved relentlessly, ever southward. For the next two weeks I'd still note the requirements of the remaining herring boats each morning, but would drop the note pad in the butcher's shop on my way to school. He'd deliver the orders himself or send his assistant. This plan worked well but required my going early to the harbour in my school uniform. Everyone could see I was still a schoolboy.

Chapter VII

CHRISTMAS

The drifters had gone, though the spawn fishing would continue for a little longer. I was paid admirably by the butcher, receiving the grand sum of fourteen pounds for my efforts, though Brian 'requested' two for his services while I was away in Scotland. I was back at school, the resentment becoming intense. Dad was now potting in the *Rosemary* but winter was approaching. New long line, hooks and twine for snoods began appearing around the house. Soon preparations for the coming winter fishing would begin in earnest.

Late one afternoon, following a miserable day at school, I went to the Labour Exchange to enquire about employment in the Merchant Navy. The clerk gave me several brochures and an application form. Subject to a satisfactory medical and eyesight examination, I'd be required to undertake a three month course at the Vindicatrix Training School at Sharpness, near Gloucester, where Stewards and deck personnel were trained. I took the information home to show Dad, explaining that I could leave school now and could join the Merchant Navy. The application form required his signature.

He read the document then explained that this would get me into the required service, but only as a Deck-Boy. My career moves would be, Ordinary Seaman then Able Seaman, at best Bo'sun. He said if it was what I wanted he'd sign, but said I was being daft, that if I'd only wait until the end of the Easter term I could go to sea as an apprentice Officer. I'd be nearly seventeen by then I calculated, incorrectly. I couldn't wait, so reluctantly he put his signature to the form and I quickly posted it.

My headmaster, Commander Tribe was extremely angry when informed that I'd applied for the Merchant Navy as a Deck-Boy. He said I'd wasted the last four years, learning chartwork, navigation, signals and a host of other subjects, which as a deck-hand I'd never get the opportunity to use. He said I'd spend my days cleaning the ship, chipping rust and painting. He asked why he'd not been consulted before this decision was made. I didn't answer, I couldn't tell him I just wanted to leave school.

A reply informing me of my acceptance arrived within days, but the next training course wouldn't commence until the second week in January. I was issued with a travel warrant, enabling me to take an eyesight test at the 'Shipping Office' in Middlesborough, a fifty mile rail journey, on the direct line from Scarborough. This test was easily passed and I was now eligible to join in the New Year. Meanwhile I had to remain a schoolboy until the Christmas break.

Christmas was very slow in coming. I did the usual things, baited lines, chipped flithers, tipped shells, went to dances, went to pubs, until the day finally arrived, I left school. All the masters said goodbye, wished me well, several said, "come back to see us, let us know how you get on." I said I would of course. It was a huge anticlimax, it didn't feel any different. It was, after all the Christmas holidays, everyone was off school, but at least I didn't have to go back.

The festive season was a time to look forward to; there were dances and parties to attend. The fishing fleet was tied up, most men had money in their pockets from the government subsidy, paid on every stone of fish landed. The selling agents banked this cash for the skippers and crews until the year end.

I arrived home on Christmas Eve afternoon, following a prolonged stay in the Dolphin with Tom and Herby to discover that we'd had a telephone installed. Feeling very mischievous I decided to test it. Jack Dalton, skipper of the *Betty* and his wife Peggy lived next door. They were a very nice couple, if a little serious. After checking their number in the directory, I called them on the phone, attempting to disguise my voice. "Is that Mrs Dalton?"

"Yes it is, who's that?"

"Mrs Dalton, we are doing a new scheme called, 'carols by phone', I'm going to sing you a Christmas carol over the telephone then I'll come around later to collect a donation." I began singing the first line, "Away in a mang...

"You bloody well are not," shot back the reply and the phone was slammed down.

Walking outside the house, I knocked on the adjacent door. The pinny-clad lady quickly opened it, confronting me. I said, "That wasn't a very nice thing t' do, Mrs Dalton, you were goin' t' be me first customer."

She rolled her eyes then looked to the sky in despair, "I should 'ave known it was you, y' daft bugger. When are you going t' grow up?"

My presents on Christmas Day were practical ones, a suitcase, shaving set and working clothes. Everyone knew I was preparing to leave home. There was fun to be had before I left though, tomorrow was Boxing Day, a very special day in the town. An annual football match, Fishermen v Firemen, was played on the beach, kicked off by the Mayor. Top hats were worn throughout the contest, fishermen in white, firemen in red. Free kicks were awarded if a player lost his hat. Though kick off wasn't until mid-morning, the players commenced 'training' several hours earlier, touring friendly homes and hostelries, fortifying themselves with strong drink for the fray ahead.

Though now a light-hearted affair, the origin of this traditional game, first played in 1893, was an extremely serious matter. A sailing smack *Evelyn & Maud*, fishing from Scarborough, was lost with all hands, probably during a gale on the 18th of November of that year. She was reported as 'missing presumed sunk' on 25th November. An official fund was opened throughout the town for the dependant wives and families of the five men lost in the tragedy.

The crews of the trawler fleet of the time, decided to play a charity football match to support this fund. The deck-hands 'fishermen' were to play the stokers 'firemen'. This was a challenge match, as there was no love lost between these factions. The deck-hands, exposed to the elements, thought the stokers had an easy job, down below in the warm stokehold, getting regular sleep. The stokers, working four hours on and four hours off, endlessly shovelling coal, thought the deck-hands were better off, out in the fresh air, only working when the trawl was hauled. In fact both groups toiled extremely hard, in an unforgiving environment, but the rivalry was ever present.

The first match, which the firemen won four goals to one, playing conventional football, was watched by about fifteen hundred spectators. Following the success of this contest, it was decided the match would become an annual event. The proceeds of the game in subsequent years going to widows with young families in the 'old town'. A tradition was born. The 'Fishermen and Firemen's Charity Fund Committee' was established to organise the match and allocate the funds each year. Down the years, the Boxing Day festivities expanded, it became a fun day; a tug of war, races and a comic band were included.

For many years sacks of coal were distributed liberally to the old and needy. Subsequently, with few homes burning solid fuel, a voucher system was introduced, giving a choice of goods from local shops, to more than a hundred recipients annually.

At eight thirty on a freezing cold Boxing Day morning, along with Tom, Baz, Ray, Brian and many others, I entered the Lord Nelson Hotel to collect a hat, shirt and any other garb available. With the development of diesel engines, firemen no longer existed in the fleet, almost all present were fishermen or their friends. The team captains were vainly attempting to divide those present into two teams. It was a pointless exercise, more would turn up later. It was impossible to assess numbers until minutes before the kick off. There could be anywhere between ten and fifteen aside. I grabbed a red painted topper, intending to be on the firemen's side. I'd played for them in my first ever game the previous year and felt an inexplicable loyalty to the reds.

As we dressed in our playing kit, a couple of crates of beer appeared, courtesy of the landlord. These were quickly dispatched by all present and the teams, suitably attired, left the alehouse to prepare for the ordeal ahead. The combatants split into small groups, going their separate ways around the harbourside streets. Most hosts welcomed a group of players, providing some liquid refreshment, but not many would wish to have twenty or more visitors tramping through their homes. Each band would visit several 'ports of call' before meeting again near the town centre, to march to the pitch. My pals and I visited four skippers' houses, where we were given a beer or a drop of rum, then wished a good game by the friendly inhabitants. We wished them success and happiness for the New Year. From our final call we made our way towards 'Boots Corner' in the Main Street. It seemed warmer.

We turned into the main thoroughfare to see a crowd gathering at the cross-roads, near the well-known chemist's. Music of a sort could be heard coming from the group. As we approached we could see the other footballers and many spectators being entertained by a 'rag tag' band. The performers, mostly unidentifiable in fancy dress, had clearly consumed their share of hospitality and were in, or full of high spirits. With the exception of a cornet player, there didn't appear to be any real musicians present, but what was lacking in talent was clearly made up in enthusiasm by the group.

A washboard was being battered by its holder, an elderly, plump man dressed in a school uniform of blazer, cap and short trousers. Each of his fingers was armed with metal thimbles. A clown, not much bigger than the base drum on his chest, was pounding beats, half-beats and mis-beats with gusto. Tambourines, castanets and kazoos were being played loudly by other members of the ensemble, adding to the discord. The leader of this comic band, a large, rotund man with thick-lensed spectacles was wearing a pair of pink, baggy bloomers. An off-white corset and long blond wig added no attraction to his appearance. Totally engrossed, he marched back and forth across the road, his booming voice bawling the words to 'McNamara's Band' as he went. His drum major's staff, which he spun, twirled and threw adeptly in the air, was a brush shaft with several hundred beer bottle tops, slotted on strings along its length.

It was ten fifteen, time to march to the beach for the big match. The comic band, its leader to the fore, closely followed by the teams, now equally divided, were in two parallel lines, white top hats on the left, red ones to the right. We stepped out down the road with the band playing, 'When the Saints go marching in'. Alternately the players would sing, "Oh when the reds," then, "Oh when the whites", as they marched, the mini crowd accompanying the ensemble along the way.

Collectors shaking tins flanked the procession; they also stopped any traffic. Motorists, willing or not, felt obliged to 'tip up' to the modern highwaymen, boosting the coffers of the worthy charity. They would also collect along the seafront and among the hundreds of spectators surrounding the pitch.

It was only a short distance, a ten minute march between the starting point and the beach but there are five pubs between the two points. Two thirds of the players went missing from the procession as it straggled slowly down town. Some players were consuming a final half-pint of beer, others just desperate for a pee before the challenge ahead. They would all catch up before play commenced.

The drum major, now breathless, was relieved to call a halt to the parade outside the Lifeboat House, at the edge of the beach. The Mayor and Mayoress, decked in their chains of office were present to greet the motley group. They shook hands with the team captains, both men in excess of fifty years, then met Harold the referee. Harold was well past sixty, having refereed the match for as long as anyone could remember. He wore a pair of football boots, an ancient, but well pressed brown lounge suit with matching tie, plus an exceedingly large, red and white checked top hat, with a price tag 10/6d attached. Around his middle, tied in place with thick rope, was a shiny brass alarm clock.

The band struck up 'The Saints' again, this being the most appropriate of their three-tune repertoire and with the Mayor leading, his wife wisely remaining in the safety of the boathouse, the entourage marched onto the sands to commence battle. The sloping pitch was roped off with crab-pot tow, hanging from iron stakes on three sides. The lower touch-line was only ten yards from the waters edge. This would be a problem later as the tide flowed. The top edge of the playing area was the promenade, two feet above the sand. Horizontal cast-iron railings protected pedestrians from the drop.

The uprights of the two wooden goals, none of which had seen a lick of paint for many a year, were standing in open-ended, fifty-gallon oil drums, filled with sand to hold them erect. The goalkeepers were warned not to swing on the crossbars as the entire construction was in danger of collapsing.

The teams, nudging and tripping each other, raring to get started, ringed the centre of the playing surface. Harold carefully lowered himself to his knees, then, scooping sand with both hands, built a sandcastle. With great ceremony he perched the battered old ball, lace uppermost, on his construction. The two captains grabbing an arm each, helped the official back to his feet. Next the referee made an exaggerated gesture of reaching into his trouser pocket, from where he drew an imaginary coin. Handing nothing to the perplexed Mayor, he invited him to toss the coin. "You call," the referee instructed the red-hatted captain.

"Heads," was the call. Both team leaders looked skywards then down as the imaginary coin was tossed, then caught by the dignitary who'd now grasped the situation and joined in the farce. The Mayor held out his opened palm for both players to scrutinise closely.

"Tails," said the Mayor.

"Bugger," said the red leader, "I've never won t' toss yet."

Harold took the Mayor to one side as he stepped back preparing to kick the ball. "My advice t' you Mr Mayor, when you've kicked off, is t' run like 'ell f' them railin's." Holding up his hand to show his whistle, he went on, "once this goes it's every man for 'imself. I'm not even blowin' fo' full time this year, 'til I get off these sands. Las' year t' rotten sods in t' losin' team threw me in t' sea."

He blew loudly on the whistle and the Mayor promptly booted the ball at least twenty yards in the direction of the firemen's goal, self-preservation adding distance to this huge kick. With play deflected from the immediate area and the dignity of office was forgotten as the Mayor hurried to the safety of the promenade.

He was grabbed by several spectators to be hauled unceremoniously over the top railing.

The match was in progress. Anyone with any sense passed the ball the moment it came close, but then, anyone with any sense wouldn't be participating in this debacle. Attempts at dribbling were met with flying lunges or crunching tackles. Any player brought down desperately attempted to retain his hat in position. A lost hat meant a free kick to the opposition. The referee was very strict on the lost hat rule. There were times when this seemed the only rule.

It's difficult to run on soft sand but it's even more difficult to play football on it. There were some very good footballers among the teams, players who competed at district level each week. There were also players who turned out once a year for this match only. Usually those that couldn't play, managed to stop those that could, though for days following, they found it difficult to walk. It wasn't just the bruises that hurt, leg muscles unused to such punishment, locked in protest.

Strangely, for all the hard, 'no holds barred' play, no one ever seemed to get seriously hurt. Perhaps it would be different if they were sober. Half-time came not a moment too soon, I was desperate for a pee. The fishermen's team were leading one-nil thanks to a brilliant header, all the more spectacular as the scorer never lost his hat. Both teams vacated the pitch, heading for the Lord Nelson across the road, to the applause of an appreciative crowd.

It was a difficult task for Harold, attempting to persuade the teams to return for the second half. Most had consumed one or more pints during the interval. He blew his whistle loudly, then alternately pleaded and cajoled. Our group were happy to continue playing, as eventually were most of the others but one or two gladiators could not be induced to leave the bar.

If possible, the second half was even more chaotic, resembling free for all rugby rather than soccer. The ball was occasionally lost in a melee of players, only to be discovered up the shirt of an offender. Wavelets were now lapping the lower section of the pitch, and spectators at the byline were driven by the advancing surges to dryer vantage points. Attempts to kick the ball, as it occasionally floated in a few inches of water, resulted in much splashing. Twenty minutes into the second half, with the lower rope underwater and the iron stakes just visible, the match degenerated into chaos.

I deliberately kept away from the play, choosing to remain higher up the beach as did the referee whose tenuous control had now evaporated completely. He blew a long, shrill blast, denoting that from his point of view, the match was over. Harold quickly turned and sprinted for the relative safety of the hostelry across the road, at a speed which belied his years.

On the beach behind him, struggling in vain, two first time participants were being carried by arms and legs, shoulder high, to be ducked in the sea. I shivered at the thought; it was only last year this happened to me. The victims, perspiring profusely were to be immersed in water, only a few degrees above freezing. I felt too vulnerable to assist the dunkers. Maybe they'd soak me again, forgetting I'd played last year.

With the initiation of new participants completed and the sobering effect of the cold water, a relative calm held sway. Next on the programme was the tug of war, contested between the two football teams. This too quickly degenerated into farce, with the firemen tying the end of the rope to the railings on the promenade and the fishermen, not aware of this skulduggery, enlisting half a dozen from the crowd, in a forlorn attempt to pull the railings down. The firemen were declared the winners when the exhausted opposition, unable to demolish the cast-iron structure, eventually tired and were an easy pull over.

The final event of the day was the flat races, each team in turn running the length of the pitch between the two goals, the winners and second placed receiving prizes. Again it was fixed, the young, fit runners were held or tripped at the start. The wily, older participants hid in the crowd, which now lined both sides of the track, emerging ahead of the field as the runners approached the finishing line. It really didn't matter who won, it was being a part of this wonderful spectacle that was important. All the players, wet and shivering, dry or semi-dry, in varying states of inebriation, converged on the Lifeboat House for the presentation of the cups and prizes. The Mayor, his dignity now restored, stood on the lifeboat's trailer, the boat's polished propellers and rudder at his back, as he faced the gathering crowd. Harold, wobbling precariously on a fish box at his side, was preparing to impart the relevant information to the beaming Mayor. The participants of the events flanked the pair on both sides.

First the 'Gold Cup' was presented to the captain of the winning team. This battered, gold-painted trophy was made from tin by the old harbour blacksmith, 'Tinner Sam', who back in the mists of time, had manufactured cooking pots and pans, for the steam trawlers. The valueless, yet priceless heirloom was the most coveted of prizes. Harold whispered into the Mayor's ear and the announcement was made.

"This year's winners, by one goal to nil are the fishermen."

Cheers erupted from the winners but these were drowned by the boos and cries of, "fixed, fiddle, rigged" and other words linked with strong expletives by the less controlled, red element. This was a strange result, as at least four goals had been scored in the short period following the interval, three of these scored by the firemen.

"I only count t' first 'alf goals," explained Harold, when questioned by a delegation from the losers. "It all gets too daft in t' second 'alf."

A large, valuable silver cup, complete with lid, dating from the turn of the century was awarded to the winners of the tug of war, though this was a poor consolation to the reds. This trophy was quickly retrieved by a sober charity official from the victorious captain to be taken away for safe keeping.

The winners of the races were in turn awarded a bottle of rum and a bottle of whisky, runners up receiving chocolates. Both bottles were swiftly decanted into the gold cup, which was then passed among the players, the Mayor wisely refusing the first drink.

His Worship coughed to clear his throat, then addressed the gathering, to say a few words relating to the worthy work of the Fishermen and Firemen's Charity Fund. He went on to say how everyone should be grateful to the fishermen, who spent much of their time at sea in all weathers, catching food for our tables. He continued to say that thanks to the firemen, we could all sleep soundly in our beds at night. Most of the crowd hooted and clapped, all the players booed. The Mayor thought the firemen were from the fire station.

The brief ceremony concluded, the players vacated the Lifeboat House, most of them crossing the road to the Lord Nelson carrying the gold cup between them. I tagged along together with my mates but was feeling a little queasy.

Once inside the busy establishment, the cup was passed to the landlord behind the bar to be topped up. He obliged with mild and bitter beer and various spirits from the optics. The cup was then passed around the hostelry for any of the customers prepared to take a sip. Most were pleased to join in the fun, though one or two declined the invitation. Virtually all the patrons were local people, the Boxing Day tradition was popular with everyone. It was probably the busiest day of the year for the harbourside pubs. Wives and mothers on this one day of the year, left husbands and children at home, touring in groups around the 'bottom-end' public houses.

The cup was carried by winners and losers from pub to pub on a grand tour, though some hosts were reluctant to fill it. The landlord in the Dolphin filled it with beer then asked the white leader for payment. Drinkers at the bar, standing observing, made adverse comments, "scrooge, greedy bugger and shame on ya, it's only once a year," which persuaded him, against his instincts to hand over the brimming trophy. Again it was passed around for general consumption though I wasn't interested in drinking any more. I sat down at a table to find I was sitting next to Soapy. He had two glasses in front of him, both partly consumed.

"Why are ya drinkin' two at once Ernie?" I asked. "Well," he slurred, "me Mam was in 'ere about an hour ago, askin' when I was goin' 'ome. I said I'd come 'ome when I'd finished that pint," he said, pointing to the glass on his left. The beer looked flat, warm and unappetising. "I've decided not t' finish that one jus' yet, I've 'ad three more since then," he said, a silly grin spreading over his face.

Now early-afternoon, the party atmosphere in all the hostelries was in full swing. Women, decorated in trimmings and globes from denuded Christmas trees were singing, dancing and requesting kisses from many of the men in the room. Some of these women were quite old, probably in their thirties. Feeling decidedly rough, I avoided their overtures, deciding instead to make my way home.

The street began to spin when the fresh air hit me and I can recall little else of the day, except that I was violently sick in the bathroom when I reached home and that Dad was less than pleased. Mum was out for the day with her sisters. I awoke the following morning feeling dreadful, much to Dad's delight. "You'll learn, you'll learn," was all he said.

Mum wasn't her usual self either, I guessed that she too had 'enjoyed' Boxing Day.

New Year came quietly; it wasn't an occasion as in Scotland, to be celebrated formally. The boats were back at sea on the second day of the year. I spent the next week in the *Osprey's* bait shed, listening to the stories of the men, as they casually baited two lines while I raced to complete one. The ladies skeining mussels recounted their Boxing Day exploits, giggling and laughing together at secret jokes.

Old Ben, a bachelor in his mid-seventies, woodbine cigarette permanently between his lips, cap over his eyes, was sitting quietly on a stool, skeining flithers. He would never sit on the stool without first putting a newspaper atop, for fear of a chill. Ben was very protective of his health, always wearing an overcoat and scarf even on warm days, yet he smoked eighty cigarettes a day.

Ben, who still operated a rowing boat from the beach each summer, taking children around the bay, lived at home with his mother who was in her nineties. She would go each week to the post office, for her own and 'the bairn's' pension.

Chapter VIII

The 'Vindi'

The day before I was due to leave home, I was instructed by Dad to get my hair cut. Reluctantly I visited the hairdresser, asking for a light trim, not wanting to lose my fashionable, collar length hairstyle. On arriving home following this trim, I was dispatched, not without argument, to get a proper haircut.

The following morning I woke early, packing a few final bits and pieces before leaving. Dad was at sea, my sisters still in bed. Mum heavily pregnant, gave me a huge hug, not quite managing to avoid a tear saying, "phone home when you arrive, be sure to write, look after yourself," and all the things that Mums say to their kids when they leave home. The walk to the station, toting my case was interrupted several times with "good luck" from neighbours and friends. Everyone seemed to be aware that I was going off to join the Merchant Navy.

It was a long journey to Sharpness. I changed trains at York and again at Birmingham. I took a bus from Gloucester to Berkeley and a final bus to my destination. There were many boys of my age on this final bus, speaking in a variety of dialects. The lad sitting next to me had long, black, straggly hair. In a thick scouse accent he asked if I was going to the 'Vindi'. I confirmed that I was. Most of these boys were from cities and seemed very loud, appearing to have lots of confidence, shouting to each other across the bus as if old friends. The boy adjacent spoke again, "I'm Docker, wher' ya from la?"

"I'm Fred, I'm from Scarborough in Yorkshire, it's on t' coast."

"They 'aven't gorra footbah' team, ya not a fuckin' Leeds fan are ya?" He spat after the name Leeds, with obvious disdain.

Warily I explained to 'Docker' that it was fifty miles to the nearest big city from where I lived. Middlesborough, Hull and Leeds were all about the same distance. York was the nearest league side, but they were in the Fourth Division.

"We fuckin' 'ate Leeds at the Pool," he said, in what I took to be a threatening voice.

I was a keen footballer, having played for my school and for an under sixteens side on Saturdays. I occasionally watched Scarborough play Midland League opposition, all of which I assured my compulsory companion, "but I don't support any big teams." I made a mental note to watch for the Leeds United results in future, in the hope that they'd beaten Liverpool, Everton and Manchester United.

The bus stopped outside what appeared to be an Army camp; there were numerous Nissen huts and a regulating office close to the entrance. Approximately thirty boys disembarked, walking the few yards into the camp. A group of a similar number were gathered close to the office. We were greeted by an officer in uniform who invited us to line up in two ranks to confirm our names. We were then issued with a number. Mine was eight-one-five-six-two-seven. This would be my identifying number for the duration of my stay. It was only necessary to use the last three digits as the through put of boys was such that I would leave before eight-one-six-six-two-seven arrived. There was considerable laughter and a little scepticism when we were informed that the previous 007 was called Bond.

This done we were now to get our hair cut. Clearly most of these lads were in need of more than a trim but I wasn't. I approached the 'two ringed' officer as he lead us to the barbers.

"I 'ad my 'air cut yesterday, sir."

"Everyone gets a regulation hair cut when they get here Yorkie," he replied not unsympathetically.

"'Ow did y' know I was from Yorkshire?" I said looking perplexed.

He just smiled at my naivete. Until that moment it hadn't occurred to me that it wasn't just the other boys that had strange accents.

If the officer seemed friendly, the barber was the opposite. He took great delight in shearing each head 'down to the wood' as he put it.

"Are you from the North or the South?" he would ask each unsuspecting victim as they sat in his chair. If the reply was North he began shearing from the front, if South, he began from the back, either way the result was the same. The floor was heaped with varying colours and lengths of dignity. It was a subdued column of convicts who paraded back across the square to the stores to collect their kit. Dad thought it highly amusing when I informed him in my first letter that I'd had three haircuts in two days.

We were issued with navy blue berets, battledress type uniforms, working fatigues, boots and toiletries. Curved cloth flashes to be stitched on each shoulder stated 'Merchant Navy'. A metal cap badge was initialled M.N.

We were divided into our relevant departments, seamen or stewards, then allotted accommodation accordingly. My group of ten were appointed to hut A7, then handed over to an instructor, who led us to what was to be our home for the next three months. The hut was sparse, containing five cast-iron bed frames, each with an upper and lower section. Two coarse blankets, two blue sheets and a pillowcase were placed on each mattress. Adjacent to the beds, an olive green locker, similar to those in the swimming pool back home, completed the furnishings. Close to the entrance, a small room was sectioned off from the main billet. Every hut housed permanent personnel, presumably to monitor and control excesses from the lads residing within. 'Mr P. Short', stencilled in red was on the door of ours.

"That's me," our reident instructor informed us, pointing to his name. "I'm a light sleeper and I don't like noise, so if you lot keep quiet after lights out and don't give me any trouble, we'll get along fine."

Pete Short was a short, stocky man with a round weathered face. His black curly hair, with extended, greying, lamb chop sideburns contrasted starkly with our crew cuts. Mr Short had been an Able Seaman, sailing from Southampton for most of his sea career. He had experience and a wide knowledge of most seagoing merchant ships, from liners to tramp steamers, which in later weeks he imparted readily, filling eager ears with his sea and shore going exploits.

Following instructions, we each located a bunk and locker; mine was close to the door. Ditching our kit we hurriedly reassembled outside, to be loosely marched through the camp in the direction of the ship, as yet hidden from view in a small valley beyond the camp. En route, several old lags shouted ominously in our direction, "you ain't never goin' 'ome, new boys."

We reached the top end of the camp from where, looking down the hill we caught our first sight of the hulk, 'Vindicatrix', moored in a siding, off the Sharpness to Gloucester canal. Our group were marched down the slope to the canal path, leading to the gangway. High above us on the top deck, almost the full length of the ship, boys were leaning on the rails, chanting the same words we'd heard previously, only this time to the tune 'tavern in the town'. "You ain't never goin' 'ome, goin' 'ome, you ain't never goin' 'ome. You ain't never, ever goin' 'ome, you ain't never goin' 'ome."

This was followed by jeering and calls of 'new boys'. I thought this was quite intimidating, but the city boys in my group thought it great fun, showing two fingers to the crowd and shouting "fuck off," in reply.

Once on board, we sat at bare wooden tables with matching benches for our first meal, which consisted of stew and potatoes, followed by steamed pudding and custard. The custard was made with water. The food was served by trainee stewards and wasn't very appetising; some of it was rejected by the lads. Two boys found dead cockroaches in their stew. "If you don't want your grub, we'll eat it," the stewards informed us. "Eat all you can, we don't get a lot." This proved to be the case. The principle seemed to be that if the inmates could cope with the food on 'Vindi', they could cope with anything any other ship could dish up when they went to sea.

We were free to roam the 'tween decks for'ard and the whole of the upper deck following our meal, mixing with the other lads. Few would brave the exposed upper deck at all during January and February, unless new recruits were arriving. We were subjected to a series of songs, which everyone but our group joined in, singing loudly. The lyrics mostly bemoaned the lot of the poor 'Vindi' boy and his lack of food and freedom. By the following week, we would be singing the same songs to the next batch of new boys.

'Tween decks midships, was the galley and messdeck, while aft was the officers' pantry and accommodation. The quarterdeck area aft was for officers only. A cadet watchkeeper was ever present to prevent anyone entering this area unless on business, though it was the last place on the ship most boys would wish to visit. The entire lower deck was fitted as classrooms.

There was an obvious hierarchy in the camp depending on time served. "Where are you from, new boy?" was a frequent question. The majority of the compliment seemed to be from the North West and Midlands. I only met two lads from Yorkshire, one from Bridlington, the other from Halifax. Though we slept in the huts, all lessons and meals were taken on board ship. The T.S. Vindecatrix had been a sailing ship, though her masts had long since been removed. Painted black, she was built of iron, with plating almost an inch thick. I discovered nothing of her history while in the camp, though I suspected it to be extensive. A tuck shop opened each lunchtime and again following the evening meal, selling sweets, crisps, chocolate, stationery and cigarettes. These were 'Players Weights', which were sold in packets of five.

Instruction had finished for the day prior to our arrival, so we were able to explore our new surroundings a little, before lights out. There was a communal hall housing a television, which proved to be popular. Top of the Pops was the favourite programme with a large audience. Each week a boxing contest was held in the hall between willing boys, refereed by the sports instructor Mr Buffrey. Slightly balding, he was a muscular man who during any day would wear tracksuit bottoms and athlete's vest, exposing his hairy shoulders. The ring was also a place for grudges to be settled, though this usually proved who was the best fighter, not who was right or wrong.

We had yet to learn the names of most of the officers and instructors in the camp, but discovered one more early the following morning when we were called rudely from our beds at six o'clock. "Come on you young beggars, hands off cocks and on socks." I was lying still for a moment, collecting my thoughts when I felt a jet of ice cold water on my face. "Come on, I mean now, get out of your pit." I tumbled from my bed to see a purple faced, thickset man in officer's uniform, grinning from ear to ear, directing water at me from a plastic detergent bottle. He quickly circled the hut, giving each lad still in bed a squirt. We had met 'Squeezy' Jackson.

I was one of several hundred boys, lined up in rows on the parade ground at six thirty, to be counted by our instructors, then given thirty minutes of physical training by Mr Buffrey. He was a very enthusiastic sportsman, insisting that everything was done 'at the double'. At the end of each row the instructors watched, some grinning, as we jumped and swung our arms. None joined in with the exercises.

The First Officer of the 'ship', three gold rings on his sleeves and flanked by a pair of two ringers, addressed the gathering, welcoming the new arrivals. He made various announcements relating to the day's programme, then left the instructors to carry out the detail. Cleaning the huts and the camp in general was the first job each day, to be completed before breakfast, which was served at eight o'clock. Standing on the parade ground looking around brought to mind a story I'd heard about Stan back home in Scarborough.

When Stanley left school at the age of fifteen, his first job was as van boy for the local shoe repairer. His task along with the driver, was to collect footwear in need of repair from customers in the more remote parts of the area. They would deliver shoes to the workshop back in town, later returning the repaired articles. The duo covered a large part of North Yorkshire, including Catterick Army Camp.

One day the pair arrived at the Army Camp, where Stanley was dispatched to collect boots in need of repairing. As he walked across the parade ground, whistling to himself, he was suddenly confronted by a screaming Sergeant Major yelling at him to, "get fell in."

"But I've only come for..."

The rest of his words were drowned by the bawling N.C.O. "I said get fell in, and I mean now!"

Stanley joined a bunch of new recruits in line on the square, then tried once more. "Excuse me Sergeant, I've onl... " but was interrupted again.

"Shut up you 'orrible little man, squaaad, leeeft turn, quiiick march!"

The van driver was getting impatient, he'd been waiting for what seemed ages for his assistant and eventually went to look for him. He found Stanley, still on the parade ground, marching up and down, still trying unsuccessfully to explain to the now grinning Sergeant Major, that he'd only come to collect some boots for repairing.

I wasn't long getting to know my fellow inmates. I had more in common with the northern lads and was christened 'Yorkie'. I began to lose my reticence, realising that as at school, I could use humour to make friends. I was popular for telling jokes and being a general hut clown. Though one of the smaller inmates, I wasn't bullied and seldom exchanged harsh words with anyone.

Each day following breakfast we were given instruction in the various aspects of ship work. I already knew the thirty two points of the compass from sailing with Uncle John, but learning to steer in quarter points was something new. We were taught the different types of cargo hatches, from modern 'McGregor' type, constructed from steel plate, opened and closed by the ship's winches, to old fashioned beams and boards, made water tight by three canvas covers. Mr Short explained the order in which the covers should be used, showing us how to batten them down correctly. Many ships have foundered when their hatches were breached by the sea in heavy weather.

I was top of the class at 'bends and hitches' as I'd learned all the knots, splices and whippings on the boats or at school, though I'd never learned how to rig a paint stage, a bosun's chair or to reeve a three-fold purchase. This was the ability to pass a rope through two sets of pulley blocks, each block containing three wheels. A three fold purchase was used to lower and raise ship's lifeboats from their davits.

No one was allowed out of camp during the week, but following hut inspection by the First Officer at midday on Saturday, we were free to do as we pleased for the remainder of Saturday and Sunday following the church service. There was little scope to do much in this down time, though a football match, organised and refereed by Mr B, was well supported. He was so enthusiastic, he tried to officiate and play for both sides. Berkeley, a four mile bus ride away was the extent of our freedom and most of the lads made for there. A small coffee bar with jukebox playing the latest pop music, was extremely popular.

The Manchester and Liverpool fans, Docker included, would wait avidly for the late regional newspaper carrying the football results. It was glorious one Saturday when Leeds United knocked Manchester United out of the FA Cup. I resisted the urge to stand up and shout, "yes!" I had difficulty hiding a smirk as all eyes looked in my direction.

The only other attraction in the little town was the cinema. It was the smallest picture house I'd ever seen, smaller even than the one in Fraserburgh. No one had heard of the films shown, but it was somewhere to go to relieve the tedium of weekend camp life. The camp gates were closed at nine each evening so the lads attending the cinema watched the matinee performance and were able to catch the eight o'clock bus back to camp.

One Saturday, about halfway through my course, I was with Dave, one of my hut mates, a tall good-looking lad from Blackburn. We were chatting to two of the only three girls in the village. This was a major coup considering the hundreds of boys in the area. Intent on our suit, we eventually realised that we'd missed the last bus by at least half an hour. This was a big problem. Anyone caught out after the gates closed could be liable for an extra week on their course. The gate was manned by cadets, but these lads were informed that if seen admitting anyone after nine o'clock, without first calling the duty officer, they would get a week on their course. This was quite a deterrent. Not many were prepared to take the chance.

Dave and I set off at a run down the road in the direction of Sharpness, knowing we hadn't a chance of arriving on time. With battledress and heavy boots we were both gasping and perspiring heavily, despite the late February chill. Our berets were stuck inside our jacket tops, another crime; they were supposed to be worn at all times. We'd covered about half the distance, running down the dark country road, our eyes accustomed to the lack of illumination, when a car approached from behind, headlights blazing. We stepped to the roadside, sticking out our thumb in the forlorn hope of a lift. 'Vindi' boys were not very popular with the locals. Even this desperate act was a risk. The Captain of the camp had a car and was merciless with any cadets found hitchhiking. He was a nasty, officious piece of work, best avoided if at all possible. Stories of his unpleasantness were widespread. He'd sent boys home or given them extra weeks for trivial offences.

Amazingly the car stopped, the driver lowered his window and said, "do you lads want a lift?" We couldn't believe our luck. We climbed in the back of the car to discover that the occupants were a young couple. The man spoke as he drove, "I'm not at all surprised to see you two running along here. I was a 'Vindi' boy myself, I remember it well. My wife and I are newly married and are touring the area, I wanted to show her the old camp." We'd been rescued by an ex 'Vindi' boy. We arrived at the camp at two minutes to nine. The watchkeepers had no choice but to let us in and close the gate behind us. We were heroes back in the hut. Not only had we chatted the girls up, even arranging to see them next week, we'd missed the last bus and still beat the deadline, what kudos.

At the end of each month, an amateur concert party arrived from Gloucester to perform a show for the camp in the recreation room. This was well supported by the inmates; the hall was packed to the doors. The acts were varied, a fumbling magician was not too well received, similarly a male classical singer. A teenage accordionist was very talented and was applauded but two young female singers, dressed in miniskirts and performing pop songs, brought the house down. These concert performances were very much appreciated by all hands and I'm sure none of us realised the strenuous efforts by the organisers on our behalf.

Attendance at the concerts was voluntary, not so the pox lectures. These were mandatory and explicit. The civilian lecturer pulled no punches. "You boys are going to sea. You will travel the world. Statistics show that at least forty per cent of you will catch some type of very unpleasant sexually transmitted disease." He showed many coloured slides of men and women with syphilis, gonorrhoea and other horrific sights. It was shock treatment, designed to discourage casual sex.

By now we were familiar with the names of all the officers and instructors. Some of them were cheerful and friendly, Mr Glendenning being one of the best, though he smoked like a chimney, coughed frequently, and it was rumoured had a terminal illness. One particular instructor, Mr A. was a pure bastard. No one ever left an encounter with him unscathed. He seemed to enjoy being unpleasant.

I wrote home several times to report my progress, often complaining about the food, so I was delighted one day to receive a large food parcel. Mum had been in Maggie Bean's bakery and when asked, informed Maggie I was fine, but the food was dreadful. Maggie insisted on giving Mum lots of cakes, including a Christmas cake, biscuits and buns to send to me. What a wonderful feast we had in the hut, adding to my popularity.

As the sentence progressed our group began taking evening and night watches throughout the camp. The gate watch was a miserable job. Even wearing the duffel-coat provided, it was no fun standing by the gate for an hour at a time in the early hours of a March morning. It took the remaining hour of duty to thaw out in the regulating hut. The night watches on board the ship were much better. The sole duty of the galley watch was to ensure the coal-fired stove was kept glowing, boiling huge vats of water, enabling the cooks to produce porridge for breakfast. This was invariably followed by a very small fried egg and two similar sized pieces of bacon. We'd heard previous watchkeepers talk of cockroaches on the ship, we'd discovered them frequently in our food, but now we were able to witness the evidence for ourselves. There were hundreds to be seen during the night in the galley, it was sport chasing them. The creatures dropped to the stove top as the rising heat stunned them, which explained their presence in the food.

One day while standing as watchman on the quarterdeck, with nothing to do except ring the bell to signify the time each half-hour, I was approached from the direction of the officers' pantry by the Senior Steward Officer universally referred to as 'Chop Chop', though not in his presence. He was thus named due to a peculiar voice inflection. Prior to speaking, he cleared his throat, rattling his teeth and sounding as if he was saying, "chop chop."

Tall and thin with wavy silver hair, he was probably nearing retirement age, having spent his entire seagoing career on the same passenger liner. He had sharp features, watery eyes and the worst set of ill-fitting false teeth I'd ever seen. He said, "chop chop, here boy, eat these," handing me a plate, which I thought contained sandwiches. This seemed odd, as Chop Chop wasn't keen on anything to do with the deck department.

I said, "thank you Sir," and he quickly turned away, heading back to the pantry. I looked at the plate in my hand. He'd given me the edges cut from the officers' evening sandwiches. I was holding a plate of crusts. Without thinking I picked one up and put it in my mouth, it was tasteless. "What are y' doing?" I suddenly asked myself. "You may be hungry, but you're not starving, do y' really need these?" I'd answered my own question. I left the plate untouched on the floor outside the pantry door. Chop Chop was most indignant when he saw I hadn't eaten them, but I'd have felt humiliated if I had.

Everyone counted the days they had left to serve. Ninety days seemed an eternity, but now I was down to my last three weeks and was an old lag. The days were growing longer; spring was coming. It was pleasant on the top deck of the 'Vindi' when the sun shone. I was given the job of 'Postboy'. This was a cushy number and was a much sought after position. Each morning after breakfast, I reported to the office in the main block, where two pleasant female civilian secretaries and the Purser worked. Here I sorted the cadets' post into numerical order, each envelope showing the name and three digit number of the recipient. The secretaries always gave me a cup of tea and biscuits. I made the work last until lunchtime each day, carrying the cadets' mail to the ship in an official looking mailbag. I was stopped frequently as lads said, "anything for me Postboy?" giving their name and number. I'd check, then give them their mail or commiserations and hope for the next day. Immediately following the midday meal, I stood on a bench in the messdeck and shouted out the names and numbers of the lucky recipients.

The worst honorary position in the camp was that of 'Captain's Tiger'. This sounded an interesting appointment but the catering lads dreaded it. For a month, the poor unfortunate given this job, was virtually a slave to the whim of the Captain and his wife. He kept their house clean and was frequently seen carrying shopping, flowers or walking the dog.

It was drawing closer to the leaving date. My hair had grown to a respectable length once more but sadly, no one was allowed to leave the camp without another haircut. Each of our group opted for a cut during the penultimate week, which at least gave some room for growth before departure. Passport sized photographs were taken of each boy holding a board with his six digit number on. We were informed that anyone smiling when the photo was taken was liable to another week on his course. Now we really did look like prisoners.

At last the big day arrived; we were leaving 'Vindicatrix' forever. We all exchanged addresses, promising to write. Each boy was issued with travel documents, but there was a shock still to come. We were not going home, our documents were for transportation to our nearest Shipping Federation Office. We were instructed to report to this regional office, to enquire if there was any immediate requirement for our services. Only if there were no berths could we go home. This wasn't a problem for the Liverpool and Manchester lads, their Shipping Office was in their home town. Mine was in Middlesborough. Finally we were instructed not to change from our uniforms. Anyone caught in civilian clothes would be returned to camp.

I reversed my outward journey. It seemed a lifetime ago that I'd travelled south. Not alighting at York, I remained on the main line train till Darlington then changed for Middlesborough, where I arrived late in the afternoon. Laden with suitcase and kitbag, I was hot and breathless when I arrived at the Federation Office, minutes before they were due to close. Explaining that I'd come from Sharpness, a fact fairly obvious as I was still in uniform, I asked if I was required to sail. The clerk was most sympathetic, "where are y' from lad?"

"Scarborough."

"Go home, we'll give you a warrant. Ring up in a few days and we'll see if we've anything for you. You should have rung up earlier, it would have saved you a journey." Travel document in hand and somewhat relieved I thanked him then turned to leave. As I approached the door he called out, "I'd get rid o' that silly uniform if I were you, most of the lads wear Wranglers or Levis and denim jackets."

I rang home from Middlesborough Station, telling Mum to expect me back later in the evening. The Scarborough to Whitby line had recently closed, so I had to take the circuitous route via Darlington and York, arriving home three trains later.

As I walked through the door at ten o'clock that night, I received a hug from Mum who immediately insisted on showing me my new baby sister, Alison, now three weeks old and fast asleep in her cot. Now I had four sisters. Dad welcomed me home then asked about my day of travel. He said it would have made sense for all the lads to have rung their respective shipping offices before departing from Sharpness. He was quite right.

Next morning I was keen to visit the harbour to see what had changed. Nothing much had, it was almost empty. The winter fishing had finished, Easter was approaching. There was much activity on the slipway as the pleasure boats were preparing once more for the coming season. I looked in vain for Tom, Mike, Herb and other contemporaries, but it was a fine day and they were all at sea. Sandgate Corner hadn't changed either. As I approached, one of the committee noticing me said, "you're 'ome then young Nommy, when are ya goin back? 'Ave ya brought any fags?" There was no, "pleased t' see ya" or "welcome back lad," just a request for duty free cigarettes. It was quite reassuring really, I was home, though not for long.

I met my pals that evening as each came in on their respective boats to land their catches. All spoke and asked how long I was home for, but things seemed different, I didn't feel part of the gang any more, time had moved on. Maybe it was me having travelled from home, met other people, got into other routines. I couldn't explain it, things just seemed different.

I rang the Shipping Office each day reminding them that I was at home awaiting a ship. Eventually on the Thursday of that week I was promised one on the following Monday. The remainder of Thursday and Friday morning passed slowly, I was out of sorts. Time was hanging heavy, though this changed the moment I had the opportunity of a trip to haul pots with Ernie and Dicky Elliott, his partner. Their coble, a traditionally built vessel, was called *Who Cares*. It summed up these two men's attitude to life. They were so easygoing and pleasant.

When we were younger, my pals and I would often visit their bait shed. Ernie and Dick only fished with a few lines, baiting their own to save expense. We would all assist them in their work; they in turn regaled us with scary or funny stories. Dick told tales of spooks, seen in and around the rickety old houses and of ghostly women, walking the alleys of the harbourside. I'm sure he gave us nightmares and I for one was very wary of walking these lanes alone after dark.

Ernie was a fund of funny stories, he always made us laugh. When he wasn't at sea he'd go to the Leeds Arms at lunchtime, for a few beers with other coblemen, then go to bed for the afternoon. He told us of the day his mother had arranged for his bedroom to be repainted and papered. When the tradesmen arrived, he was in bed. Ernie refused to get up, suggesting that they worked round him. The men did exactly that, moving his bed, with him in it, around the room to access the four walls.

He told a story of when he was a youngster during the war, when he and some friends were exploring Scarborough Castle. While in a prohibited area, they discovered a cache of ammunition, which they thought to be blanks. The boys took some, deciding to play soldiers. Splitting into two groups they were to attack or defend the remote eastern section of the castle, known locally as 'The Battery'. This part of the castle had a big, heavy oak door which was closed. One of the boys threw a dud hand grenade at the door but it exploded, blowing the door off its hinges. The lads were petrified. They abandoned the remainder of the ordinance, scattering in all directions. A police investigation followed but they were never caught.

I felt much more at home when we got back to the harbour on the *Who Cares*, we had a good haul of lobsters on board too. My pals were all in port and I spent a great Friday night with them at the new discotheque. The ultra violet lighting in the building was weird. It highlighted all the bits of dust on my suit shoulders, it seemed as if I had dandruff.

The lads were still ashore on the Saturday so we decided to visit the boating lake at Peasholm Park, which was newly opened for the season. The lake covers several acres, with a large island in the middle. There were six in our group so we hired three canoes for an hour of fun. I shared with Baz, Tom was with Mike, Herby paired with Ray.

All went well for the first twenty minutes, then, when all our craft were in the lee of the island, unseen by the boating attendant, Herby began splashing Tom's boat with his paddle. This was countered to a greater degree, Baz and me joining the fight. In no time this splashing had escalated into a full scale water fight. Eventually, when we were all drenched, a truce was called. Herby and Ray manoeuvred their canoe to the bank side, intending to empty the water from it. The two stepped ashore, hauling the craft stem first from the lake. Once on shore they inverted the little canoe, pouring gallons of water from it. Preparing to relaunch, Herby suggested to Ray that he should get in the boat prior to launching. Ray declined suggesting that Herb should get in and that he, Ray, would then launch it. After all it was Herb's idea.

Baz and I held onto the bank side. Tom's craft was held alongside ours as we watched events unfold. Herby sat in the boat towards the stern, his back to the water, paddle poised, waiting to control the canoe as it hit the water. Neither of them had taken Herby's weight into account. Ray, stooping, took a hold on the bow with both hands then shoved. The craft moved down the slope but the angle didn't change when the vessel hit the water. It immediately submerged leaving Herby spluttering in the chest-deep pond.

We were helpless with laughter as Ray attempted to haul his erstwhile shipmate from the lake. Herby holding Ray's hand, gave a mighty heave, pulling Ray into the lake to join him. At this point we dryer four abandoned our craft and scrambled ashore, before we too were tipped into the lake. Our three canoes were left floating or semi-floating in the lagoon. The attendant, hearing from disgruntled boaters of the mischief behind the island, arrived puffing just as we were leaving, "you're all banned, don't come back, I know your faces." It happened every year.

Dad was ashore on the Sunday and as it was my last day at home, he insisted on taking me to the pub for couple of pints. We went to the 'Leeds Arms', which was the nearest. I'd not been in this pub before, as the landlord was aware of my age. His son was in my class at school. "Is it alright if I bring t' lad in lan'lord? 'E's sailin' tomorra."

"As long as he's with you, that's no problem, and his first pint's on the house," came the reply.

We played dominoes in a foursome with Soapy and Bill Sheader. It was a most enjoyable couple of hours. Bill had us crying with laughter with his tales. He'd recently visited the doctor when an irritating rash had developed around his midriff. Following an examination the doctor said, "it's only a mild infection Mr Sheader."

Bill had replied, "it must be t' beer in t' Turk's Head, that's t' only place I drink mild."

Jitta was in full flow with his stories, saying Julie had been telling him for weeks to fix the carpet on the stairs in his home. The stairs were quite steep, and turned sharply to the left near the top. The carpet was lifting on the bend and was dangerous.

"If you don't do something about it soon, I'm going to get the carpet fitter to come and you'll have to pay."

Faced with this ultimatum Bill had no choice but to confront the problem. It seemed fairly straightforward; just a few tacks should do it. How wrong he was. No matter which way he tried, the carpet wouldn't fold down. There was either lots left over at one side or large lumps hanging over the steps. After an hour of frustration, he left the house and walked to his workshop at the harbour. He returned with pieces of wood, one of many available for constructing crab-pots. He nailed the wood over the offending lumps in the carpet then called Julie, informing her he'd fixed the carpet. The fitter arrived the next morning to fit a new one.

Dad and I left the pub together following an extremely pleasant lunchtime to a feast; an extra special Sunday dinner, made in my honour. Sunday dinners were always good, but this was more like a Christmas dinner.

CHAPTER IX

THE MERCHANT NAVY

At seven o'clock on Monday morning, dressed in Wrangler jeans and jacket, I took a final look at the harbour before collecting my kit from home and making my way to the station. My pals were all at sea, having sailed with the first of the flood tide.

My three-train journey was uneventful. I made my now familiar way to the Shipping Office, where I signed on as Deck Boy on the eleven thousand ton iron ore carrier *Ribblehead*. She was owned by the implausibly named Bolton Steamship Company and was bound for Sept Isles in the St Lawrence Seaway, Canada. My pay was to be fifteen pounds a month, though weekends at sea were classed as overtime. The clerk arranged a taxi to take me to Smith's dry-dock across the river at Southbank, where I made my first encounter with the huge, black-hulled ship. She was no longer in the dock but berthed at the adjacent quayside. It was the biggest ship I'd ever seen close up. I'd observed many colliers passing Scarborough on the Tyne-Thames run, but nothing to compare with this vessel.

The crew accommodation, galley and mess facilities were aft, the bridge with officers' quarters midships. She had four holds with Macgregor hatches, two aft of and two forward of the bridge. I walked up the gangplank, feeling the vibration of the generators as I stepped onto the afterdeck. I was met by the First Officer on his way ashore. On explaining that I was a Deck Boy, he directed me to take the first cabin on the main deck, port side, aft. He said the Seamen and Bosun were berthed on the port side, the Firemen and Storeman to starboard. "Firemen?" I asked myself, "it can't be a coal burner," but didn't pursue the subject.

The Mate said the ship had recently left dry-dock, and that the crew would arrive shortly but officially they wouldn't 'turn to' until the following day. I was to familiarise myself with the ship. There seemed to be no one else on board. I found the entrance to the accommodation on the port side. A small, plastic engraved label on the door said 'Deck Crew'. The label on the first cabin said '2 Ordinary Seamen'. I entered, wondering who I'd be sharing with. The cabin was quite spacious with two iron-framed bunk-beds, two wooden wardrobes, two chairs and a small four-drawer chest, the top doubling as a table. A single porthole faced forward, with a view of the main deck and two after hatches.

Leaving my gear I continued aft down the long alleyway. The first of three doors on my left said, 'Recreation Room'. I looked into a large, wide room that crossed the ship connecting to the Firemen's corridor on the starboard side. The main features were two long tables with cushioned benches, several chairs, a bookcase with mostly paperbacks and a dartboard. Ashtrays, a pack of cards and a cribbage board featured on the first table. Feeling like a trespasser, I backed out to explore further down the passage.

The second door on the left was a washroom with toilets and showers. Almost all the remainder on this side was blank wall, which appeared to have engine-room space behind. There were twelve cabins on my right, each door stating, '1 A.B'. They were identical with single bed, locker, chest of drawers, chair and porthole. The end door on the right was titled 'Crew Mess'. Inside were three rectangular tables with benches either side. More ashtrays, salt and pepper, ketchup and brown sauce bottles topped each table. Noticeably the bottles were lying on their sides.

Directly opposite, the only other door on the left was marked 'Pantry'; it too was communal to Seamen and Firemen. The pantry, which had a connecting serving hatch from the galley at the stern, contained sink, draining boards, refrigerator, several worktops with cupboard space below and a large, steaming hot water boiler. I crossed the pantry to discover the starboard side alleyway was a mirror image of the port.

Hearing activity beyond the serving hatch, I stepped out onto the afterdeck where I found the galley door. Peeking inside I saw a short, but immensely fat man with black tussled hair. He was having difficulty stowing cooking utensils under a preparation table. Standing erect and perspiring freely, he exhaled loudly looking in my direction. "Hello laddie who are you?" he asked in a mild, easily understandable Scottish voice.

Timidly I said, "I'm Fred, the new Deck Boy, it's my first trip."

Holding his belly with both hands, eyes sparkling, he said, "hiya Freddie, I'm Jock, the Second Cook an' I'm too fuckin' fat, I like my ane grub tae much."

I guessed him to be in his mid-thirties. He was very friendly and immediately put me at ease. He offered me a pot of tea, then insisted on frying bacon and eggs, which he put between two thick slices of newly baked ship's bread. As I munched my way through this mountainous snack, Jock explained there was only a skeleton crew on board. Most of the forty plus compliment were on leave, but would probably be back by evening. A few of the hands lived locally so would arrive for breakfast in the morning. We were due to sail 'light ship' (with no cargo) on the afternoon tide.

Forty seemed a huge crew but Jock explained that the ship was an oil burner so carried firemen to monitor the boilers. There were also twelve deck crew, supervised by a Bosun, Captain and four Deck Officers with two apprentices, Chief Engineer with three other Engineering Officers, Chief Steward plus Officers' Steward, two Cooks, Messman, 'Sparks' (Electrician), 'Chippy' (Joiner), Storeman and last and least Deck Boy.

After chatting comfortably with the cheerful cook, I left him preparing vegetables for the evening meal, returning to my cabin to unpack. It seemed I was the only Deck Boy and as there were no Ordinary Seamen either, I had a double cabin to myself.

I wandered around the deck, exploring the ship, avoiding the bridge area and engine-room for fear of meeting any officers. A paint store and joiner's workshop were midships at main deck level. In the afternoon as I sat in the recreation room, engrossed in a James Bond paperback, the first of the hands began to arrive. Some had clearly come from an extended visit to the pub. One man, elderly, quite small, with several days growth of grey stubble staggered to where I was sitting. He reeked of booze. "Whothefuckareyou?" he burbled. I found it difficult to understand what he'd said. His slurred words in a strong north east accent, came out as one.

"Pardon," I asked politely.

"Dinna fuckin' pardon me ya little c—, I saaaid who the fuck are ye?" his words this time distinct.

I grasped these words immediately and the threatening manner in which they were delivered by this nasty little man. Fortunately one of the other crewmen, taller and younger stepped up to the odious person. Putting an arm round the old man's shoulders and speaking in a similar dialect he said, "leave the lad alane Billy, he's dein' nay harm."

Without saying a word the old man turned away and staggered off to his cabin, where he was to remain until the next morning. "Tak nay notice o' him bonnie lad, he's had wan too many, he'll be alreet in the mornin'." He introduced himself as Andy, from Newcastle, an EDH.

I repeated my name and rank then asked what an EDH was. It was a term I wasn't familiar with.

He said it stood for Electric Deck Horse. I looked perplexed. "Naw, not really, it means Efficient Deck Hand. Its a similar rank to AB 'able seaman' but they gets ten bob a month mare fo' havin' a lifeboat ticket. Y'all find most o' the crew ar' EDHs."

About four thirty in the afternoon the Mate knocked on my open door, where I was lying on my bed, engrossed in James Bond's seduction of yet another beauty. He said I was to report to the pantry, to serve dinner to the two messes aft. The Messman was not due back until the following day, so I would have to be 'Peggy'. This was another term I wasn't familiar with but clearly it meant 'crewman/messman'.

Jock was peering through the serving hatch when I arrived. He asked me to count the number of crew on board, on both sides of the accommodation, then set places for three courses in each mess. I was to put mugs on the table, then brew two pots of tea from the steaming boiler. This wasn't too difficult. There were six firemen and five seamen. There would have been six seamen, but I made sure nasty Billy didn't wake up as I 'whispered' to him that dinner was ready. I don't suppose he'd have woken up if I'd bawled at him, but I didn't. I'd had enough of him for one day.

My new friend, the second cook passed the plated starter of curried, chopped frankfurter sausages with rice, through the hatch. I dispensed these plates to the two messes, alternating, to show no favour. Next I brewed and delivered the two large teapots, similar in size to those on the drifters, but much cleaner.

Jock suggested I filled the sink with soapy water so I could put the empty plates to soak as they were returned. He said there was unlimited scalding hot water, it came straight from the boilers. When all were eating I sat in the crew mess to eat mine. "I've never tasted curry before," I said to the two men sitting opposite, who were tucking in with relish. I stabbed a piece of sausage with my fork dipping it in the sauce. For a second it tasted really good but then the after-burn came. I gasped; they laughed. I shot off to the pantry for a drink of water. I wouldn't be eating curry again for some time to come.

The main course of chicken with potato and vegetables was very good. When all the plates were in soak, I delivered sherry trifles in individual glass dishes and was most surprised to find that only half of them were required. There were four spare in the sailors' mess, I ate them all. For some strange reason few of the deckies ate dessert. I loved sweet puddings, so it appeared I was to have an unlimited supply of desserts for the foreseeable future. As I washed the dishes, Jock looked through the hatch and said some of the boys were going ashore for a few beers and did I want to join them. I certainly did.

Six of us, Jock, Andy and three others, as yet unknown to me, walked to a pub called the Junction, not too far away. It was a good 'run ashore' Andy said, though to me it looked quite run down, as did the streets we passed through to get there. I was pleased to be in company, the area was quite daunting. The building may have looked shoddy, but it was lively inside and the jukebox was loud. Andy put a clean ashtray in the middle of the table, next to the one in use. "It's a quid in the kitty boys, if ye

havna got wan put in what yous 'ave got. It's a tarpaulin muster."
This was another new expression.

Jock explained that in port, when the crew hadn't much money,
they threw what they had into a central communal pot enabling
them all to go ashore. This was a tarpaulin muster. It felt good to
be part of the ship's crew, though I didn't have much to say. I was
amazed at the beer when it arrived at the table. The froth was
piled high like a Harbour Bar ice-cream. "It's Vaux's Exhibition,
it's good stuff," I was told.

It sure was, I'd had six pints by half past ten, and was feeling
slightly dizzy. Two really good looking girls had joined our
company, both wearing short skirts with low tops. One had jet-
black hair, the other was a vivid blonde. The illusion was broken
somewhat when they spoke, as they spoke roughly and were foul-
mouthed. I'd never heard girls swear before, I found it fascinating
if distasteful, even in my inebriated state. There was much rude
talk between the sexes, I was intrigued, they were very attractive.
Jock whispered in my ear, "dinna even think aboot it laddie, ye'll
get more that ye bargain for if ye go wi' either o' those twa, they'rre
on the game."

"What game?" I asked naively.

"They're prossies," he said. "They'll be full o' pox, steer clear."

'Prostitutes', I'd been warned about them in the lectures back
in camp. I thought they were all old bags, not good looking lasses
like these. It had certainly been a day for learning.

Ten minutes later I was staggering back to the ship with Jock,
Andy and Smithy, a tall skinny EDH in his twenties, whose name
I'd discovered during the course of the evening. The other two
hands were nowhere to be seen, neither were the girls. Jock was
singing an alternative version of the 'Banana Boat Song' with rude
words. One verse was about women on bended knees with two
ABs. We joined in the chorus of "Dao Daaao, daylight come an I
wanna go home."

I was awoken next morning from a deep slumber by a rapping
on my door.

It was opened by a big man with ginger hair, bushy eyebrows and sideburns. He wore an old faded blue boiler suit. "Aye aye young un, I'm the Bosun, it's time to turn to. Can you go to the galley and dish up the breakfast? The messman's not back yet," then he was gone. I heard him knocking on other doors in the alleyway as he went aft.

I felt rough, my mouth was furry and my voice croaky. I sat on the bed for a while then picked up my jeans from the floor where I'd dropped them. Stripped to the waist and bare footed I crossed to the washroom, where I brushed my teeth and swilled my face liberally with cold water. I felt slightly better until I turned up at the galley. Jock, bright as a button, was singing to himself as he put a tray of bacon into the oven. There was another cook in the galley, younger, probably in his mid-twenties.

"G'd morning ma friend, how are you today?" Jock said very loudly, grinning at my appearance. He introduced the other man. "This is ma boss, the Cook, Stuart. This is ma wee friend Freddie, from Scarborough."

The younger man nodded in my direction.

"I hope ya feel better than ya look son, 'cos ya look bloody awful," said the Cook.

Lying, I assured them both that I was OK then left to set the tables. At eight o'clock all hands arrived for breakfast, there were more new faces. I was pleased to note Mr Nasty was subdued. He probably wouldn't remember our encounter but I did, I'd keep him at arm's length in the future. I served a breakfast of porridge, followed by fried eggs, bacon, beans and tomatoes but didn't fancy any myself. Following the meal the Bosun detailed the crew to work, most of them soogee moogeeing, which I discovered was washing paint work with a water and detergent mixture. Two hands were dispatched to splice eyes in some new mooring ropes. I was instructed to sweep and wash the floors in the accommodation area, after I'd finished the washing up. Two pots of tea were to be ready for 'smoko', which was the mid-morning break at ten thirty. I was to be 'Peggy' until the Messman returned later in the day.

I was feeling better by the time the lads trooped into the mess for their tea and biscuits. It was literally a 'smoko'. Everyone was either smoking or in the act of rolling home-made cigarettes. The mess was like an opium den. I was offered several but declined, the men seemed genuinely surprised that I didn't smoke. Noon came and still no sign of the missing steward. I wasn't enjoying the housework but it wouldn't be for much longer. I was quite hungry now, so having served up fish and chips for all hands, I sat down for mine. It wasn't very good fish. The crew ate it heartily enough, but I thought it was a bit off. But then I'd never eaten fish more than a day old before.

Following the afternoon break the Bosun sent all hands for'ard and aft to single up the moorings. We were preparing to sail. The main engine was throbbing, vibrating the cutlery that I'd piled on the table. I kept looking at the gangplank through the messroom porthole, hoping for a late arrival. My heart lifted when I saw a man coming aboard but it sank again when I realised it was the river pilot. The gangplank was hauled inboard on his embarkation.

First the headrope was released by a docker on the wharfside, then the sternline. Soon there was only the stern spring attaching the ship to the shore. I felt the vibration increase as the engine engaged stern gear. The remaining rope tightened as it was used to spring the bows off the berth. The wooden pilings on the pierside creaked, as the stern bit into them. With the bows now angled from the quayside, the engine eased, then picked up again in head gear. Still no last minute, gasping, arrival. A gap appeared between the stern and the pier; it grew wider. Shit, shit, shit, shit, shit, no messman, I didn't need telling I was 'Peggy' for the coming voyage, it was obvious.

I stood out on the poop deck, watching the deckies stowing the thick ropes below, as the sides of the riverbank passed slowly by. A couple of kids sitting on a wall waved as the ship's stern grew level. Everyone waved back. I asked the Bosun when he came aft, if we would be going through the Pentland Firth or the Channel. Off handedly he replied, "I don't know, north about, south about, what difference does it make?"

It made a difference to me, I wanted to see Scarborough as we passed by. The ship reached Teesmouth Piers, continuing out through the buoyed channel of the fairway, then turned to starboard. We were going south about. I dished up the evening meal, occasionally stepping onto the deck to look at the land. I could see Whitby lighthouse, the short, stubby, white tower nestling on the cliff edge. Later, when everything was washed and stowed away I stepped out again. The sun was setting over Robin Hoods Bay on our quarter and there on the starboard bow, was what looked like a big rock. It was Scarborough Castle headland. The little square pimple on the top was the castle keep. I felt quite melancholy, wondering when I'd see it again.

The evening was spent in the recreation room. I played darts with a couple of the younger crew. Two old hands played cribbage, a complicated game, which I tried to follow but couldn't comprehend. A serious game of poker was the main entertainment, some competing, others watching. The constant fug of smoke filled the room. Beer and lager were available by the case at duty free prices from the Chief Steward, Mr McGregor. Anything required was deducted from pay, due at the end of the voyage. Most of the crew kept a case in their cabins, bringing out their requirements each evening.

During the following day we passed white cliffs to starboard, we were entering the English Channel. Resigned to my unwanted job, I soon got into a routine. The crew, a mixed crowd from all parts of the country, were good fun. I particularly liked Magnus from the Isle of Barra, Western Scotland. His voice, a slow, soft drawl, every word considered, his general demeanour, placid and affable. Billy, Mr Nasty, was not popular, though was tolerated by most. He spent his spare time reading cowboy books or watching the poker games. Not speaking much at all, it seemed he was only nasty when drunk.

Before turning in that night, I set the tables, putting mugs, cereals and dishes, cruet and relish on the tables. At some point during the night we entered the Atlantic hitting a gale force wind. I felt the ship rolling but was not concerned. Next morning as I approached the seamen's mess, swaying down the alleyway to compensate for the rolling of the ship, I heard rattling and the tinkling of crockery. On entering I immediately thought, "what an appropriate name; mess."

Choking back tears, I looked at the broken dishes and mugs, mixed with brown sauce, ketchup, cornflakes, dissolved sugar, salt and pepper; all sliding from one side of the cabin to the other as the ship rolled. An almost identical scene greeted me in the firemen's mess, though someone earlier in the evening had laid the sauce bottles on their sides. These had stayed on the tables, held by the raised edges, though both were chipped from colliding with each other as they slid too and fro.

I was devastated. I didn't expect a ship of eleven thousand tons to roll about like a keelboat. The cleaning up didn't really take too long; everything went into the dustpan and was thrown over the side. The mop and bucket soon cleaned the floor. My major concern was that I had no replacements for any of the broken items. These would have to come from the Chief Steward, a tight, stingy man who had whinged the previous day when I asked for tea, tins of evaporated milk and sugar.

McGregor went absolutely haywire when I informed him of my problems. He was apoplectic when I requested twenty four mugs, a similar amount of dishes plus all the replacement ancillaries. His face went from red to purple and I'm sure there was smoke coming from his ears. He screamed at me, calling me a stupid little bastard, asking if I had any sense at all. Didn't I know the Atlantic Ocean got rough, didn't I know ships, especially ships with no cargo, rolled.

I wanted to scream back at him that I didn't ask for the fucking job, I was a deck-hand not a fucking steward, that I was doing it under sufferance. I didn't, I just kept swallowing hoping not to shed a tear. He finally gave me the required items in a cardboard box, which I took to the pantry, placing it temporarily on the deck at a suggestion from one of the deckies. "That's gravity stowage son," he said grinning, "they can't fall off the floor."

The crew were fairly sympathetic once they'd stopped laughing. "Wet the tablecloths liberally with cold water before you set the table, it prevents stuff from sliding about." This was a useful hint, which I found worked really well. I'd realised already that sauce bottles and cereal boxes couldn't fall over if they were on their sides. The bad weather moderated and the days passed routinely.

Only the wind and the clocks changed. Following each fifteen degrees of longitude to the west, the Second Mate would advise all hands that the clocks were to be moved back one hour. On the first Sunday at sea, following dinner, 'tots up' was announced by the Bosun. The crew grabbed a mug each and made their way to the Mate's cabin below the bridge. "Haway young un, 'tots up', grab a mug," Andy encouraged me.

I followed the crowd to the Mate's cabin where all hands were given a liberal helping of 'Four Bells' duty free rum, probably the equivalent of four or five optic measures. As he dispensed my dram, he asked if I wanted to do my Helmsman's Certificate, which required ten hours of steering the ship. I was keen to do this, so he said I was to report to the bridge the following evening after dinner. The rum was quite smooth but the quantity made me giddy. Subsequent Sunday tots were shared with the lads in the rec' room.

For the next five nights, when my duties were completed, I reported to the bridge. The ship was normally controlled by automatic pilot in open water, but this was switched off for me to take the helm. It was good fun to begin with. The dimly lit compass card, calibrated in degrees, was only a repeater. The main gyro compass was in the chart room. I was expected to keep to within two degrees either way of the ship's heading. To begin with I was up to five degrees out but soon got the feel of her. It was much easier than steering the *Floreat*. The weather was fine; I was able to divert my gaze occasionally, attempting to take in my surroundings, but there was nothing to see except the silhouette of the lookout on the wing of the bridge. All was in darkness, save a red light in the chartroom, from where the Mate occasionally emerged to check my course. The red light enabled him to plot the ship's position frequently, but didn't impair his vision when returning to the darkened bridge.

He never spoke. It was as if a caste system existed. With the exception of the occasional "watch your head," if I was straying off course, there was no dialogue between us. I quickly realised that socially, there was no interaction at all between officers and crew, it was an 'us and them' situation.

My next three tricks at the wheel were mundane, but it was different on the fifth night. The weather deteriorated, the wind changed to an easterly direction increasing to gale force. Steering the ship became much more difficult. Being 'light ship' we were pushed along by huge rollers, bouncing on each as it surged under our vessel. Vibration ran through the ship each time the propeller emerged from the water, dying as she slipped back into a trough. It was impossible to hold my course as the ship sheared to port or starboard each time she was pushed along by a big sea.

The Captain came onto the bridge ordering his First Officer to alter course. He said we'd be better dodging head to wind until the storm eased. "Hard a port," the Mate said in my ear.

"Hard a port," I repeated, remembering the instruction learned at the 'Vindi', spinning the wheel quickly to my left. When it reached the stops at thirty five degrees of port rudder, I eased it back a couple of spokes, then said, "wheels hard a port, Sir."

"Thank you," was his reply.

He watched the compass card spinning rapidly as the numbers reduced, though he was forced to grab a stanchion, one of two iron pillars connecting the deck to the deckhead, as the ship lurched violently, while broadside to the swell. The Captain, holding the other stanchion, observed in silence. Grasping the wheel with white knuckles, legs braced wide apart, I was able to keep my balance. Two more big lurches then her head began to come up into the wind. The Mate was back at my side. "Ease the wheel," he said.

"Ease the wheel," I repeated.

"Midships."

"Midships," I echoed.

"Steer oh nine oh."

"Oh nine oh," I called, putting ten degrees of starboard wheel on to counter the still slowly swinging card. On achieving the required heading I said, "steady on oh nine oh."

"Well done, thank you," he said formally. These were the most words he'd spoken in the five days since I first attended the bridge. Steering was different now. The ship was easier to control. I could see the shadow of the bows as they climbed through the white wall of each oncoming wave. This watch passed much quicker, it was ten o'clock before I knew it. The Mate didn't revert to autopilot; he ordered the lookout to take the wheel. I was instructed to send up another watchman to relieve the lookout, when I went below.

We were still dodging head to wind the next morning, though the swell seemed to have fallen away a little. Following breakfast I took the 'gash bucket', containing the remnants of the recent meal, out onto the stern, in the lee of the accommodation to dump it over the side, as I did three times each day. In port it was dispensed into a fifty-gallon drum hanging over the stern. This was tipped into the sea once the vessel was under way.

Looking out to starboard into the gloom and spindrift, I was amazed to see a trawler, heading on a parallel course to ours. With all lights blazing, her crew were on deck, gutting fish. Their yellow oilskins and sou'westers were shining, reflecting the glare. This brave little ship was plying her trade, dragging her heavy gear along the bottom, towing an easterly course into the big seas. She cut a swath through each, spray flying mast high.

Here we were, in an eleven thousand ton ship, dodging in the opposite direction to where we wanted to go and alongside was a vessel, one hundredth of our size, engaged in fishing as if the weather didn't exist. I felt a great elation. I could feel my heart pounding with pride for these unknown men. That's what I should have been doing, and at that point I just knew that eventually I was going to be a fisherman.

The weather eased and within two days the Ribblehead was feeling her way through a series of islands as we approached our destination. I'd known land wasn't too far off after viewing the fishing vessel. The Atlantic Ocean is too deep for trawlers, so I'd deduced we were on the shoals of the famous 'Grand Banks' fishing grounds. It was fascinating watching the strange land with the brightly coloured houses, as we approached the port's ore terminal. I hoped to explore a little following the midday meal, though I'd have to be back for 'smoko'. It was mid-morning when we finally tied up alongside and the gangway was lowered. The crew began opening the iron hatches, each section clanging as it was hauled back, swivelling from horizontal to vertical on its retaining wheels, the sections concertinaed tightly together.

I hurriedly washed the crockery, gave the floors a lick and a promise with the mop, then hurried below to change into clean, going-ashore gear. I was gutted on reaching the gangway, to find a sign saying, 'No Shore Leave'. I walked for'ard dismayed. Conveyors were shooting ore into all four holds simultaneously, filling the air with an orange, choking dust. I quickly returned below and changed back into my working gear. The fine dust was permeating everywhere.

We were in port for little more than twelve hours, in which time about fifteen thousand tons of iron ore was loaded. By mid-evening the crew were re-covering the holds prior to sailing. I'd expected the holds, which were boarded out with heavy timber, to be full but this was not the case. A pyramid of ore, filling not much more than half of the available space, was contained in each. The stuff was so heavy that the ship would probably have sunk had the holds been filled. As it was, we were loaded to the WNA mark on the plimsoll line, on the ship's side. This was the maximum cargo allowable for 'Winter, North Atlantic'.

It was rather disheartening. I'd crossed the Atlantic Ocean, seen Canada, but never set foot there. So much for joining the navy to see the world. We were back at sea before midnight, bound for Glasgow. The ship had a different feel to her now. The deck was much closer to the water. She didn't roll as much, tending to plough through waves, not lifting over them, though the weather was reasonable.

The routine was much the same on the return trip, though I never visited the bridge again during the homeward voyage. We encountered a north easterly gale during the night, a few days into the passage. I was wakened by the sound of water, washing about on the deck outside. As the weather worsened, rollers were swilling down the deck, thumping on my cabin side, which faced forward. It was quite disturbing, I went out into the alleyway to check the storm door was securely fastened. No other crew members seemed to have been disturbed by the conditions, so I went back to bed, though I didn't sleep too soundly.

The wind shifted to a more northerly direction during the night. It was fascinating to watch the water as it washed across the deck, viewing from my forward facing porthole. That evening, with the weather still poor, I served dinner from the pantry as normal. Jock was his usual good-humoured self, exchanging banter, as I dispensed the food. When he'd shut the serving hatch I put washing up liquid in the sink, then turned on the hot water tap, intending to return shortly to turn it off. I was delayed in the seamen's mess, completely forgetting about the running tap. The first indication of my mistake was when a small wave of scalding soapy water lapped over the door sill, as the ship rolled heavily to port. Dismayed I dashed to the door, entering the pantry as she rolled back to starboard. Steaming water was overflowing freely from the sink. I could feel it burning through my plimsolls. As I dashed towards the sink the ship began rolling back to port again and a wave of scalding water was heading towards me. My feet were already hot. Visualising severe burns, I leapt to the worktop until the wave receded. I tried twice more to reach the overflowing sink, but with near boiling water flowing back and forth with each roll of the vessel, it was impossible to get near it.

The crew, with their feet safely on the benches thought it hilarious. None of them were prepared to help me. Water was now flowing down the alleyways towards the cabins. "It'll stop when the boiler in the engine-room runs dry," one wag suggested. It probably held thousands of gallons.

I had a brainwave. Dashing down the alleyway, I went hot foot through the recreation room to the firemen's corridor. I could see water flowing from the pantry at the other end. Opening the storm door to the deck on the lee side of the ship, I made my way aft to the stern, where I was able to enter the galley. The two cooks were oblivious to my plight. "Can I open t' servin' 'atch?" I begged, breathlessly, then proceeded to do so without waiting for an answer.

The cooks looked baffled until steam billowed through the open hatch. I climbed onto the bench, kneeling on the work surface to reach into the pantry. With the assistance of a kitchen towel for insulation, I was able to shut off the offending tap. I felt relieved, but physically sick. "You'rre up to yorr neck in hot water agin, ma wee friend," Jock observed. After a few minutes I was able to enter the pantry to begin mopping up operations. The floors were probably the cleanest they'd ever been since the ship was new. I never left the tap unattended again.

One afternoon, a couple of days before we were due to arrive in the Clyde, I heard a cheer from the firemen's passage. Curious, I went to investigate. In one of the cabins, a radio was blaring loudly. Half a dozen men, beers in hand, were listening intently to a football match broadcast on the world service. "Da 'Pool 'ave jus' scored," one of the Scouse firemen informed me. Of course, it was the cup final, Liverpool were playing Leeds United. I sat on the floor, keen to follow the game. Someone gave me a can of Tenants lager and a stainless steel piercing tool. I followed the commentary avidly. Leeds equalised and I cheered, then realised that everyone was staring at me in silence. The cheer died in my throat. Sadly, well into the second half, Liverpool scored the winner. It pleased the others in the cabin, but I was a little miffed. At least Docker, my former 'Vindi' acquaintance wasn't there to gloat.

We sailed up the Clyde, taking on a pilot at Greenock before finally arriving in Glasgow, a city with a reputation for being tough. I was really apprehensive about visiting this place. I'd heard stories of the Gorbals district and of razor gangs. As the ship drew alongside, a young, thin-faced man with sharp features, holdall in hand, stood waiting to come on board. "Hiya Archie, boy have we missed you? Wait till you hear the stories," one of the men standing aft shouted.

This had to be the Messman. Oh was I pleased to see him. Now I could be a Deck Hand. He came aboard, dumped his bag in his cabin in the midships section, then came aft to commence his duties. When I greeted him warmly, saying he was welcome to the job and to Mr Bloody McGregor, he laughed pleasantly. After chatting a while, discovering he'd had problems at home which explained his absence, I left him to his thankless employment, reporting to the Bosun that I was available for deck work. He said I'd be on day work, nine till five. He had sufficient watchkeepers for the three sets of four-hour rotations required to operate the ship day and night.

The ship was in Glasgow for three days and two nights. It took much longer to discharge than load. The ore was grabbed mechanically, then dumped into a hopper on shore. This fed a fleet of lorries taking it to some unknown destination. I went ashore both nights with Magnus, Jock and Archie and was pleasantly surprised to discover that the people of Glasgow were amazingly friendly. Nowhere did I find the slightest unpleasantness or trouble; the city's pubs closed at ten o'clock and the law was very strict applied, though strangely I was never asked my age.

With most of the cargo discharged, the Bosun ordered me to hose the decks, washing off the ore dust, which was everywhere. There were several water valves along the deck for connecting the pipe, so oilskin clad, I began the task. I was liberally hosing the hatch combings, when I heard a harsh yelling from the hold below. Looking down over the edge, I saw a dozen angry Glasgow dockers looking up in my direction. Their combined threats indicated they were going to put me in hospital. I'd accidentally allowed the jet of water to shoot over the combing into the deep hold below, not knowing that the men were shovelling the remaining cargo into grabs. I was quite scared, believing they intended to carry out their threats. My first impressions of Glasgow flooded back. I kept well clear of this part of ship until they'd gone ashore and the ropes were let go.

After a pleasant evening cruise down the river, bound for Sweden, an amazing spectacle was to be seen at the 'Tail of the Bank'. Anchored in the Firth of Clyde, where the river widened, seemed to be the entire British Navy. There were dozens of warships, from the biggest carriers to the smallest sweepers. Grey painted naval ships, anchored as far as the eye could see. It was a breathtaking sight. I wondered if we were going to war, but the Second Engineer, who was standing on the after deck close by, said the Queen was coming to Greenock to inspect her fleet. It was certainly impressive.

This was only a short voyage, north about through the Pentland Firth, crossing the North Sea, then into the Skaggerak and Kattegat. We steamed southward, down the narrow channel between Denmark and Sweden, passing Copenhagen on our starboard side, where Nelson won his famous victory. Soon after, our ship rounded into the Baltic, heading north, though I saw little of this. For three days, along with the men from the eight to twelve, then the four to eight watches, I was sweeping and shovelling, down below in the holds. The Bosun said all four holds were to be swept clean, as the ore which we were to ship, was a special grade and was not to be contaminated.

We accessed each hold via an inspection cover. There were two between each pair of hatches. The vertical iron ladders, lit only by a single wandering lead seemed to go down forever. It was impossible to see the base of the hold until my foot touched it. The lead light on its extensive cable, was lowered down to me and I pulled it to the middle of the hold, clipping it onto a splinter of damaged bottom board. I was joined by the men from the watch. Our eyes gradually became accustomed to the gloom and starting at the far end, the four of us began sweeping the heavy ore towards the ladder. It was choking work, the clouds of dust filled the air as we swept. Few words were exchanged other than those necessary. Our mouths were kept shut.

We shovelled the ore dust into drums, formally five-gallon paint tins with handles, intending to heave them by rope through the inspection hatch, then tip them overboard. When full the buckets were so heavy, it was almost impossible to lift them. The most we could manage was a quarter of a drum. It was back-breaking work, 'smoko' was very welcome, though the daylight was intense when we emerged, covered in red dust. I felt more like a miner than a sailor. At midday we broke off to eat. The three watchmen in our party were now stood down. They would be on watch at the corresponding time in the evening, though no work, other than lookout or possibly steering would be required. As a day worker I continued again in the afternoon with the next watch.

After two days of tubbing out, the holds were deemed to be satisfactory. The following day we arrived at Oxelosund, a small town on the East Coast of Sweden. This ore was certainly different. It wasn't dust at all, but small rocks, not red but black, with speckles and veins of silver embodied throughout.

There were only two conveyors to load the cargo, so we were in port overnight. I went ashore to a small bar with most of the crew. For the last three days, each evening in the rec' room, there'd been talk of Sweden, the land of free love, where the girls were all beautiful and all liberal with their favours. Maybe it was sailors' talk, maybe all the beauties stayed at home that day, but whatever the reason, the only two girls in the bar were rather large and quite old, though I think they appealed to certain members of our group. It was a very funny evening despite the lack of girls, the lads were telling tall stories, hilarious jokes and being daft in general.

During a brief, quiet period, late in the evening, Jock asked me if I'd seen the golden rivet on the ship yet. A general chuckle went round the table. Totally unaware, I replied I hadn't. He went on at some length, explaining that the last rivet hammered home on every ship was made of solid gold. I was a little sceptical, but couldn't see why not, or where the tale was leading. "Ask the Steward tomorrow laddie, he kens wherre it is, he'll show ye."

The crew all laughed knowingly. I realised I was the victim of a wind up but still couldn't see the joke. "I wouldn't ask t' Steward for anything," I said.

Magnus rose unsteadily to his feet, put one hand on his hip, patting the air theatrically with the other. In his lovely, soft lilting voice, with a very feminine slant, he said, "rheport to my cabin in da mornin' wit your trousers folded neatly ofer your left arm. I'll show you wherre the golden rifet is." Everyone howled at this. I realised there was a homosexual connection in the joke, but still didn't see it. The more I looked perplexed the more they laughed.

"It's the rivet about a foot below his porthole," someone chipped in. I visualised the scenario of being very vulnerable with my head stuck out of a porthole, and it dawned on me and I joined in the laughter.

Two more of the crew stood up, in what was clearly an often used routine. "Oh what's that?" the first said in a painful voice, holding his bottom.

"Just the roll of the ship," the second said reassuringly. "It feels more like a roll of wallpaper," replied the first, squeaking.

This sketch reduced everyone to tears. Andy then told a tall story of when he joined his first ship. The Bosun showed him a large barrel, tied to the mast. The barrel had a bunghole in the centre. He said "I know young lads of your age get frisky with sexual urges, so you can relieve yourself, using the barrel. You can use it any day except Wednesday."

When Andy asked why he couldn't use it on Wednesdays, the Bosun replied, "Cos on Wednesday it's your turn in the barrel." This brought another howl of laughter from the crowd. Similar jokes and bawdy stories flowed until it was time to return to the ship.

There wasn't much humour to be found early the next morning. Everyone was subdued, few required more than coffee for breakfast. Andy and Smithy arrived back on board during the breakfast period, both looking decidedly rough, but both grinning broadly. The stories they told then, and at 'smoko' broadened my limited sexual knowledge considerably.

Our next port of call on leaving Oxelosund was Middlesborough, from where I was able to spend a night at home, though arriving at ten at night and leaving again at six the next morning, made it a fleeting visit. It was lovely to see all the family, to spend a night, albeit a short one, in my own bed and to see the almost empty harbour again, before dashing off once more. I saw few familiar faces, other than the early critics on the corner, but as I scanned the familiar peaceful haven, an inner voice was saying, "stay here, don't go back." I knew I had to go, that it wasn't the right time. I turned my back on the passive scene and headed for the bus station. The bus would take me to Whitby; a train went from there to Middlesborough.

Our next voyage was to West Africa, which sounded really good. This was the foreign travel that I'd signed on for. We were bound for Port Etienne, in Mauritania, West Africa, a country I'd never heard of. It was a fine weather cruise, passing in sight of the Canary Islands. The islands, shrouded in cloud, were pointed out to me by Magnus while we were soogeeing one day. Most of my mornings were spent washing paintwork, afternoons chipping and painting, just as Mr Tribe, my headmaster had predicted. This was brought home more starkly when I was washing the wing of the bridge one day. I observed the Mate showing an apprentice how to 'shoot the sun'. He was using a sextant to take a reading of the sun's elevation. When taken at midday with various corrections; height of the observer above sea level, sun's semi diameter, refraction and index error (the error in the instrument), the ship's latitude could be calculated. I'd learned this at school. I was now washing paint when, had I listened to advice, I could have been using the sextant. I hadn't even got to sea any sooner. I was due to leave school about the time I sailed on my first voyage.

Port Etienne wasn't a port in the conventional sense of the word. It was a jetty off from a desert, at least the ore terminal was. There were no physical signs of habitation. The ore was brought to the ship by conveyor belts, from somewhere over the horizon. The shore workers, directing the cargo into the hold, arrived on the back of a truck. There was nothing to see, only sand and a pier on one side and sea on the other. At least I saw some of Canada, even if I didn't step ashore. Here I didn't want to step ashore.

When I mentioned this to the lads at 'smoko', the general opinion was that I should be in a general cargo vessel if I wanted to see the world. These tramps visited many ports, with varying lengths of stay. The company that owned the Ribblehead also had two general cargo vessels, the Ruysdael and the Rembrandt, named after Dutch painters. The suggestion was I should sign on one of these when we arrived back in the UK. I decided I would.

The highlight of the visit to Port Etienne was the fish. When Archie tipped the gash bucket over the side, thousands of silver, bream-like fish could be seen in the clear water, fighting for the food. During the lunch hour I rigged up a fishing line with galley waste for bait. Every time I dropped the line in the water I caught a fish instantly. The fish, about ten to twelve inches long with big scales and sharp pointed spines, similar to those on a gurnard, gleamed in the bright sunshine. Soon all the crew were engaged in this fishing frenzy. The Steward, totally out of character I thought, provided some line and hooks for those who had none. Soon heaps of fish were scattered around the deck, it was great fun. The Steward returned with an assistant, carrying a large laundry basket, which he almost filled with fish. We ate the bloody stuff every other day on the way home. It must have saved him a fortune in provisions and it tasted like mud.

I was almost tearful saying goodbye to my shipmates when paying off at Newport, South Wales. I'd met some really good men, who accepted me as a part of the crew, despite only being ranked as a Deck Boy. I shook all their hands as I made for the gangplank and they in turn stood around to wave me off as my taxi left for the station.

I spent three weeks at home, which passed at the speed of light. It was great to see everyone again. It was summer and the town was very busy, nothing much had changed; the passenger boats still plied their trade. My pals were mostly at sea, though I met up with them at weekends. On my last night ashore, before joining the Ruysdael in Liverpool, I was standing at the bar in the Dolphin with Tom and Mike, when Soapy came in to join us. Concealed in the palm of his left hand were coins to buy his drink. As he ordered a pint of beer, he picked up the lifeboat collection box on the bar with his other hand, inverting it, covering the coins previously palmed. He shook the tin then revealed the coins which appeared to have come from the collection box. We laughed, though we'd seen him do this before.

A little old lady with her husband were being served with drinks adjacent to Ernie. The woman witnessing this apparent crime was incensed. "You horrible wretch, how dare you take money from the lifeboat? Those men risk their lives, going out to sea in all weathers and you come in here, stealing their money to buy beer." As she yelled, she began beating him over the head with her umbrella. Such was the ferocity of the onslaught that Ernie, arms around his head to protect himself, retreated for the door his beer untouched, leaving us helpless with laughter.

CHAPTER X

GENERAL CARGO

I boarded the five thousand ton general cargo ship Ruysdael in Birkenhead, Merseyside to discover I'd been promoted to the dizzy heights of JOS (Junior Ordinary Seaman). I was still the lowest form of life on board, but it meant another four pounds a month wages. The crew were mostly Liverpudlians and Glaswegians and my first impressions were favourable. With the exception of one man with ginger hair, staring eyes and an abrupt manner, the others were young and friendly. It was exciting being in Liverpool, even if it was only for a few days. I went ashore with the local lads and found the place buzzing. Football and The Beatles were constant topics. The major disappointment was seeing the Steward, Macgregor come on board. I thought I'd left him behind on the Ribblehead.

The Ruysdael was laid out differently to my previous ship. All the accommodation was midships, crew on the main deck, officers above on the boat deck. There were two holds forward and two aft of the accommodation. It was interesting watching the cargo, as it was stowed in the holds. Each article was stamped with its destination and everything was stacked in reverse order. The final items to be stacked marked, 'Port Sudan', would be the first to be discharged, so Port Sudan was to be out first port of call. While at home I'd bought a world map, which I pinned to my cabin wall. Surveying it, I realised Sudan was in the Red Sea, which meant a voyage through the Mediterranean, and a passage through the Suez Canal.

We left Liverpool fully-laden with a very mixed cargo. There was soap, tinned foods, sewing machines, vehicles and many other articles, too varied to relate. It was an uneventful voyage, except that for the first time I was a watchkeeper, assigned to the eight to twelve watch. This meant an early breakfast, then deck work during the morning. The evening was spent on lookout, or steering if a helmsman was called for, but mostly the ship was on autopilot.

The days passed quickly. We passed through the Straits of Gibraltar, then continued east. The weather was warm and sunny, though the true temperature was masked by the speed of the ship. The crew were becoming tanned from working on deck each day. I learned to avoid Jake, the man with the staring eyes. He took a perverse delight in being unpleasant to me at every opportunity. Perhaps it was because I was young, or maybe he wanted to continue the 'War of the Roses', as he wasn't aggressive with any of the other lads. Either way I gave him a wide berth. Fortunately he wasn't in my watch, so I didn't see much of him.

Early one evening, while on the bridge during lookout duty, several days after passing Gibraltar, I noticed a peculiar smell in the air. I mentioned it to Charlie, my watch relief, when he came up to the bridge. "Dats Egypt la,' it's da Sewerage Canal ya can smell," he informed me, with typical Liverpool wit. He was correct though. Within the hour we were dropping anchor to await daylight and a pilot into Port Said.

The Captain mustered all hands in the recreation room that night. He said he was prepared to let the bum boat traders on board when the ship tied up to the buoys, but no one was to buy any booze or substances. Elaborating he said, "a whisky bottle doesn't always contain whisky, even if the label says it does. It could be anything from cold tea to coloured spirit, which could lead to loss of control and sanity and even have permanently damaging effects. Don't buy 'Spanish fly' or any other drugs. If you are caught with any illegal substances I cannot help you, and in some cases you could be liable to a long spell in a filthy jail or even a death sentence."

This was a sobering talk, which left more questions than answers as far as I was concerned. The booze aspect was self-explanatory. What were 'bum boats'? What was 'Spanish fly'? What drugs was he talking about? My queries were answered as a general discussion took place following the 'Old Man's' departure. The bum boats were small wooden trading vessels, mostly with two crew, powered by oars or sail, laden with all manner of goods, which came alongside to trade. If not allowed on board, these traders would use light lines to send garments, sandals or souvenirs up the ship's side in baskets, for assessing, before bartering a price.

The crew spoke of various horrifying incidents they'd seen when illicit booze had been consumed. I learned that 'Spanish fly' was supposed to make girls mad with desire for sex, though no one seemed to have any anecdotal evidence, having bought it. I guessed maybe they had, but if it didn't work they wouldn't admit it. Joey, one of the scouse EDH's, who'd been through the Suez before, instructed us not to leave our cabin doors or portholes open. "Deez theivin' Gypos 'd swipe da gol' teet' from ya mout' if ya left it open."

During the eight to twelve watch the following morning, a pilot came on board. One of our watch was sent to the bridge to take the wheel. Joey, Charlie and me were sent for'ard with the Mate, to prepare for mooring. Joey said we'd probably tie up to buoys in Port Said, until there were sufficient ships for a convoy. The canal is only wide enough for single traffic and there are few passing places along its hundred and eight mile length. He seemed very knowledgeable when it was possible to understand him. The heat was intense now that we were near land and the ship had slowed down. I wore only shorts and flip-flop sandals. We were instructed to haul two of the heavy plaited ropes from the foc'sle, where they'd been stowed during the voyage. These were to secure the ship to a buoy for'ard. Two more ropes would be used at the stern. We passed one hawser end through the fairlead, lowering it until it almost touched the water, in readiness for the boatmen. The remainder of the rope was secured to prevent it running out.

My eyes were on swivels as we cruised slowly into the busy port and canal entrance. There were huge, white, imposing buildings on both sides of the waterway, gleaming in the sun. A myriad of craft, of many types, were travelling in all directions, but the dhows with their triangular sails, moving gracefully in the light breeze were the most striking, so clearly Eastern. The pervading smell was now overpowering.

As we approached our designated mooring buoys, a small boat powered with an outboard motor came close under our bows, keeping pace with our dead slow speed. One man steered while the other reached for the dangling eye of the rope. Looking up he shouted, "more slack Johnny, more slack." The Mate instructed us to take the turns off the bits, allowing the rope to run out into the boat below. Joey put his foot on the rope preventing its flow. "We'll gerra laugh 'er la's. Don' gif em any till I say, den fire it at 'em 'ard as ya can."

We could see the impatient tugging on the heavy rope and could here the voice from down near the water line. "More slack Johnny, fuck you, more slack." the voice was becoming a high-pitched scream.

"Now la's, gif em some slack." We propelled many fathoms of the heavy cable through the hole as fast as we could. More shouts and curses came from over the side. We raced to look at the results of our mischief. The two boatmen appeared to be buried beneath a huge coil of rope, arms and legs akimbo. The pair screamed and jabbered in a foreign tongue as they climbed from beneath the mass of rope. One of them produced a gleaming machete from the side of the boat. We looked at each other in dread, were we to be chopped up for our prank? Was there to be an international incident? We needn't to have worried. The man didn't look in our direction again. He hacked at the rope, still dangling from the ship, cutting it clean with three or four swift strokes. His partner gunned the engine and the pair shot off for the shore, leaving us with half a rope.

When the little craft was clear of our bows it slowed down and two boatmen turned in our direction, gesticulating rudely. The one with the knife, standing among the rope turned again. Raising his gown he bent over, exposing a large brown bottom. The engine was revved once more and the boat and rope set off for the shore.

"I tol' ya da bastards 'd nick anyt'ing, but dat takes da biscuit," chirped Joey grinning.

The Mate, exceedingly angry, asked all in earshot how he was to explain to the Captain, that half a headrope had been stolen from under his nose. Deciding to say nothing, he quickly ordered us to get another up from below. The real mooring boat was approaching.

The instant the Ruysdael was tied to the buoys, before the pilot had left the ship, there were half a dozen bum boats alongside. The occupants were throwing heaving lines on board to attract attention. Joey crept to the lines unseen, making them fast to any secure point, preventing their owners from recovering them. This brought howls of protest and more cursing from over the side. Soon the after deck was like a market place, where the traders had set out their wares. It was impossible to move anywhere near without being accosted to purchase fruit, stuffed miniature camels, sandals, carved pyramids and sphinxes. I was discreetly offered whisky, Spanish fly, flick knives and dirty photographs. These men would try to catch our attention by many ruses, the most common by asking, "hey Johnny, where you from?"

No matter what place given in answer, whether a well-known city, small town or village, the next words would be, "oh fucking hard case eh?" I'm sure they hadn't a clue where Scarborough was. Another approach if the reply was Manchester or Liverpool was, "ah Bobbee Charlton" or "Biill Shankley."

I quickly learned it was better to ignore them completely, though they were most persistent. I did buy some Egyptian stamps, at what was probably an extortionate price, to add to the collection I'd started at junior school. When some of the Arabs were discovered wandering around the crew's accommodation, they were all instructed by the Captain to get off the ship, but it was virtually impossible to make them go; they were extremely crafty.

More ships began to arrive, lining up behind us, also awaiting passage so the bum boat men finally cleared off to try their luck on these vessels. Just before dark, the north bound convoy passed by, leaving clear passage through the canal. A pilot came on board, our ropes were released intact by the boatmen, and we began the journey through the canal. Our ship was the first in line of about twenty vessels, Shell and BP tankers and general cargo vessels of many nations.

At eight that night I made my way to the bridge for my turn at the wheel. I was quite excited at the thought of steering the ship in this famous waterway. The Egyptian pilot looked in my direction then turned to the Captain shaking his head and waving a single finger. "No, no, too young." I felt humiliated. I'd steered the ship many times and was confident I could do it, but was not allowed to. The Captain could have overruled the pilot, but would have been foolish to do so. He sent me below to ask for another helmsman. I consoled myself, quietly standing at the ship's side, watching the Arab families in the glow of their camp-fires, as we passed villages close to the canal.

During the next morning our convoy stopped, tying up in a bypass for a couple of hours allowing the ships travelling in the opposite direction a free passage. It looked very strange seeing a convoy of ships passing close by, as if floating on the desert. I foolishly joined half a dozen of the crew, swimming over the side during this enforced stop, not thinking of any possible contamination and was rewarded with a dose of galloping gyppy tummy.

The following evening, twenty four hours after leaving Port Said, we entered the Gulf of Suez, heading down towards the Red Sea. I was reinstated to steering duties, though we were soon back on autopilot. It was extremely hot now as we approached the tropics, the accommodation was unbearable. Along with most of the deck-hands, each night when not on watch, I slept on the cargo hatches. The stars were unbelievably bright, giving a magnificent show. Shooting stars could be seen almost by the minute. It's no wonder the heavens were studied so intensely by Biblical characters.

Port Sudan was our first stop, but only a small amount of cargo was designated for this port; the stay would only be a few hours. There was none of the hurly-burly of Suez. The natives were quite lethargic and docile, nothing seemed to be done in a hurry. The intense heat may have had some bearing on this.

There was no opportunity to go ashore, but two days later we were in Assab in Ethiopia. Most of the crew were working or trying to sleep, but as Joey and I were on the eight to twelve watch, we were free for the afternoon. Joey asked permission for us to go ashore and we were given a couple of hours leave, but were told the ship was sailing at four, and not to go far. It was very hot as we wandered past the large, corrugated-iron cargo sheds, serviced by ancient steam railway engines. Joey seemed to know where to go, and a short walk found us in a rickety, dimly-lit bar, also constructed of corrugated-iron and wood. These appeared to be the only building materials available in this run down dock area.

There were eight or nine other occupants in the building, part of the crew of a Russian ship berthed adjacent to ours. They were drinking and singing, one of their number playing a squeeze box. Their men were clearly having a good time, with the exception of a thin faced, serious looking character sitting quietly, observing the proceedings. "Dat'l be da party man. Dey ain't allowed nowhere widout a minder." Joey whispered.

He was right as usual, I subsequently noticed wherever we went, the Russian crews always went ashore in large numbers, and there was always a Communist Party man in attendance, who didn't mix with the group. Joey bought drinks with a US five dollar note then we joined the friendly foreign sailors, some of whom had a smattering of English. The party man scowled but said nothing. The time went quickly. During the afternoon a tall, black, African girl appeared on the scene and it was clear she was 'on the game'.

Having had a few beers by now, in company with our new Russian friends, Joey was keen to go with the 'bit o' black', as he put it. I thought it was a good idea too. She took him off to the back of the building and I began to get quite excited at the thought of this slinky, ebony Ethiopian. My shipmate seemed to be gone ages and I was almost beside myself with anticipation, when he finally returned. I was immediately deflated when he said, "eh come on la' look at da time we're gonna miss da bloody ship."

I felt instant annoyance, but sobering a little, was relieved I didn't have to follow him with the African woman, and it was nearly four o'clock. We waved goodbye to our Soviet friends, who in turn bawled and yelled a friendly farewell, apart from the loner, still scowling near the door. I wondered what he did for fun. The ship was ready for sailing as we arrived back, and now I didn't have to go with the woman, I expressed my annoyance with Joey for spending so long with her.

Our ship was now almost at the extreme southern end of the Red Sea, so it wasn't long before we passed through the narrow straits of the Gulf of Aden to dock in Djibouti, in Somalia. This was quite a civilised place, of French influence on the western side of the gulf. We were still in Africa. On the quayside, an Arab trader was selling souvenirs, displayed on a carpet. Some of the crew must have broached the cargo, for most of his goods were bartered for with bars of Lux toilet soap. His handcart was piled high with hundreds of bars of the product when he left the pier, much to the annoyance of the officers, watching from the bridge.

It was only a short, overnight passage across the water to Aden, but we were going to another continent. This was the only port of call on our voyage not in Africa. Part of the cargo was for the British Army, stationed in the Protectorate. Our ship was moored to buoys offshore from the quays, the cargo discharged onto lighters with our ship's derricks. This was one of the few places we used our own equipment, mostly we were discharged by the ports' dockside cranes.

Each hold on the ship had two steel derricks with independent winches. One derrick was raised over the hold, the other at right angles to the ship, plumbed over the barge. Tension was taken on the derrick over the hold, raising a piece of cargo. Strain was taken up on the derrick plumbed over the lighter as the first one was slackened. The load was gradually transferred from the first to the second derrick, thus the cargo was suspended over the lighter to be lowered for transporting ashore. It was such a simple arrangement. I spent some time watching the Arab dockers as they ably discharged tons of freight.

Following the midday meal, a group of the crew requested shore leave to have a look round this corner of Arabia. The Captain gave permission, but warned there was civil unrest; the Yemenis were protesting at the British presence and were seeking independence. Knowing little about politics, only wanting to see the local colour, I went along with the group. We were ferried ashore in the agent's launch.

There was a sense of hostility even as we walked from the landing stage towards the town. I was pleased to be in a group of what seemed to me to be tough men. The tension was almost tangible. A few trinket sellers were initially friendly but they too became abusive when realising we didn't want to trade. We retreated to an upstairs bar which had an outside balcony overlooking the main street. Bottles of cold beer were ordered as we sat in the sun, relaxing a little and debating the situation. Someone mentioned it was a shame there was chicken wire surrounding the veranda, as it kept the birds out.

The proprietor, who was serving the drinks from a tray, pointed out that it kept hand grenades out also. At this point the beers were quickly paid for, supped, and we made our way back to the landing stage with unseemly haste. Once back on board we felt safer, but it wasn't until the Ruysdael was back at sea that everyone was entirely happy. With the exception of Joey, who at this point had occasion to visit the Steward, requesting treatment for a nasty, embarrassing, venereal infection. I got the last laugh, realising how close I'd come to sharing his fate.

The ship was on an easterly course in the Gulf of Aden, heading towards the Horn of Africa, where she would turn south, then almost south west into the Indian Ocean. As she turned on the new course, without warning, literally thousands of dolphins of varying sizes, including many babies approached from all directions, swimming along with the ship. We'd seen these lovely creatures every day, but this massive gathering, stretching as far as the eye could see, was unbelievable. Everyone on the ship not sleeping, gathered on deck to watch the phenomena.

South and westwards the ship sailed, heading on the five day, twelve hundred mile voyage towards Mombassa in Kenya, which was our main destination. A large part of the cargo was due ashore here. During the afternoon of the fourth day, while sitting on the hatch combing nursing a pot of coffee, one of the engineers produced a large tub. He secured this between the accommodation and the fore side of the hold, close to where I was sitting. I hardly noticed when he half-filled the barrel with water from the deck hose, but when he tipped in several buckets of thick black oil and 'chippy' deposited buckets of sawdust and shavings, my curiosity was aroused. Next, the cook, grinning in my direction, threw in the galley slops, making an evil smelling, witches' brew. I quickly realised there was mischief afoot.

Immediately following dinner, along with two other deck-hands, an engineer and both apprentices, I was seized, and taken to the foul container. Someone, I knew not who, was dressed in a poorly-made 'King Neptune' costume. I finally realised we were about to cross the line. How could I have been so thick not to realise it was a ceremonial ducking for those on board who hadn't previously crossed the equator. The entire crew, including the Captain and Officers, were gathered round the area, though out of splashing distance.

There was little ceremony to the event. King Neptune with his wooden trident in one hand, can of lager in the other, charged us jointly with trespassing into his domain. He sentenced the entire group to be dunked, head first if resisting or feet first if voluntary. Everyone volunteered, at least that way we got to hold our noses and it was only a quick duck. I was third in line, following the apprentices. The mixture was disgusting. Even holding my nose and with my other hand over my mouth, I could taste the oil. The Junior Engineer, a large rotund lad thought he'd escaped the worst when the gunge only reached his chest due to his inability to crouch in the bin. Someone however, had thoughtfully foreseen this eventuality and promptly decanted a bucketful of best reserve over his head, as he stood in the barrel grinning.

If the ceremony was short on words it was long on celebration, though only following a painful scrubdown. The deck hose removed most of the offending material, then a long wash with detergent took the remainder, along with some skin. The Captain and Officers remained long enough to consume a couple of G & T sundowners before retreating to their quarters, but the 'Old Man' was kind enough to relax watch duties to a minimum for the remainder of the evening. It was a clear night, with little or no shipping about. Each of the eight to twelve watchkeepers spent only an hour of the evening on lookout duty before returning to the party. From eleven to midnight the Mate stood watch alone, fortunately for Charlie, who was so drunk he couldn't have climbed the bridge ladder without assistance.

Entering Mombassa was a terrific experience. The natural harbour of Kilindini was overlooked by a fabulously sited hotel with views of the bay and the Indian Ocean. Ships of all nationalities were anchored in the bay or tied to the quays, including the large aircraft carrier HMS Eagle, which I'd seen previously in the Clyde.

Once the ship was tied alongside, I went ashore again with most of the deck crew to see the sights. Joey said they were going to the Seamen's Mission. I thought he was joking, that it was perhaps the name of a bar he knew but I would wait to see.

The bustle of Mombassa was amazing. Outside the dock gates were dozens of touts handing out introductory cards to the countless bars and clubs of the city. Beyond these, in the centre of the main road and stretching for hundreds of yards, were traders, selling every possible carving imaginable, though mostly of animals. Some were really good, especially the elephants, rhinos and antelopes. There were wooden masks and spears, drums and shields, covered with zebra skins. The sellers were all shouting and offering to barter for their wares, keenly, though not aggressively. We spent ages viewing the goods before moving up the road. I made a mental note that I must take some home as presents.

Further along, much to my surprise, we arrived at the 'Mission to Seamen'. The sign of the 'Flying Angel' is known worldwide. There are 'Missions' in all the major ports in the UK but this one was a revelation. There was a swimming pool, restaurant, bar, TV lounge, games room and even a full sized football pitch. No wonder Joey directed our party here; it was home from home. I spent most of my spare time when not working on board at the Mission, surprisingly not visiting any of the bars or clubs that were freely advertised. The Superintendent of the establishment arranged a friendly football match for our crew against the crew of a Polish ship berthed nearby. He even provided the kit, though I had my own boots. They hammered us four goals to one. The heat was too intense for walking, so playing football in it was madness, though good fun. I quickly realised how unfit I'd become since being shipbound.

Leaving the ship on my own one afternoon, I'd almost reached the dock gates, when a group of sailors from the carrier Eagle stood in a line barring my path. I got the impression they'd been drinking and were going to be unpleasant. There was no point in running; maybe I was wrong, perhaps they were being mischievous. I took a deep breath and kept walking towards them. As I drew close I called out cheerfully, "now then lads, are you off that Carrier out there?"

They didn't move for a few seconds then one of their number shouted, "'ang on lads it's Fred." I was gobsmacked, it was George, he'd been in my class at Graham Sea Training School until he left to join the Royal Navy. Here he was thousands of miles across the world, and probably saving me from a hiding. The atmosphere changed immediately. His pals carried on back to their ship, while George and I stood talking for ages, about what we'd been up to since leaving school. Sadly he was unable to take up my invitation to come back to the Ruysdael or go to the Mission, as he was due back on duty. It would be several years before I'd meet him again back in Scarborough.

One morning, while sitting on the foc'sle splicing new cargo slings with my watchmates, a small, twelve-seater coach with the word 'Safaris' pulled up on the quayside, adjacent to the ship. A tall, lean, tanned man wearing bush-gear shouted to us, asking if our crew were interested in a full day Safari. He would take twelve people for ten pounds each to the game reserve. It sounded a great idea and a deputation of hands visited the Captain to request permission. It was denied. He wasn't prepared to allow twelve of his crew to be absent at one time. Everyone was disappointed. It costs hundreds of pounds to travel to Kenya on safari. We were there, offered a trip for a tenner and couldn't go.

The day before leaving, the Captain said we'd been challenged to a football match against a team of African stevedores and he'd accepted on our behalf. Much to our surprise when we turned up, they were changed, ready for the game but were playing in bare feet. I thought we'd whoop them but they were very skilful, making us look silly. The soles of their feet were like leather and all could kick the ball further unshod than we could with boots on.

When we'd conceded about eight goals Joey realised that the soles of the opposition's feet may be rock hard, but the tops were quite sensitive to football boot studs. He 'accidentally' stood on several black feet while tackling. There were shrieks of pain as the opposition fell to the ground holding their battered feet. Each time Joey sportingly grabbed a hand, helping the fallen player up. The recipient always smiled broadly, jabbering at Joey in Swahili. I don't know what they said, but judging by how their team mates laughed, I don't think the smile and words meant the same. We were thrashed by so many goals that we lost count and were pleased to fall into the swimming pool at the final whistle, before making for the bar to get wet inside too.

After five days in Mombassa, with the holds now containing less than a quarter of their capacity, we sailed for Tanga, a small port in a remote bay further south, where we anchored for a few hours, discharging part of the remainder of our freight onto barges. Upping anchor, we sailed south once more to our southernmost destination, Dar es Salaam, in Tanzania. On our port side, not too distant was the exotic sounding island of Zanzibar, but sadly we had no cargo for there.

Dar es Salaam was an imposing city with many fine Arabian-style white buildings, though it lacked the vibrancy of Mombassa. Our holds were finally empty, but loading began immediately with cargo for the UK consisting of raw materials, sacks of coffee beans, husks and bundles of stinking cow hides. We didn't stay in port long here but there was more cargo to be collected at Tanga and Mombassa on the passage north. There was time to seek out the 'Flying Angel', which was equal to its sister establishment further north.

It was in the Mission that I observed Jake taking money from the cash box in the restaurant. He realised I'd seen him and approached me, prodding me in the chest with his fore finger, his eyes blazing malevolently. "Keep yor fuckin' mout' shut la', it's a long way back to England. Anyt'ing could 'appen." Having left me with that thought, he slinked off back to the ship with his ill-gotten gains.

Shortly after he'd left, there was cry from the restaurant when the Tanzanian waiter realised the money was missing. The Mission Superintendent asked everyone if they'd seen anything. To my shame, I said I hadn't. I didn't have the guts to name the culprit, even when it was announced that the waiter would have to make up the shortfall himself. I felt sickened by this episode and began to wish I was home. For the first time in weeks, I wondered what was happening in Scarborough, even though I did get occasional letters from Dad. What activities would be taking place at the harbour? What would Baz and the other lads be doing now? It was October, Dad would be preparing for the winter line fishing. Mum would be skeining mussels again soon. Baby sister Alison would be seven months old now.

Time began to hang heavy. Days that were once filled with new events now dragged. Cargo was loaded in Tanga and Mombassa, where I went ashore only to buy wood carvings for family presents. I was pleased when the holds were finally full and we could batten down the hatches for the passage home. Once at sea, I began to get excited at the prospect of getting home, though it would be several weeks sailing yet before the ship docked in Avonmouth. Talking to Joey in the mess one day during the passage north, I mentioned that I was having difficulty sleeping, I was constantly dreaming of going home. He said, "you've gorra bad attack of da 'channels' la'. It's early days t' be gerrin' dem."

He was right. It's a condition I'd heard mentioned before, though not experienced. It was the feeling of restlessness sailors got when approaching the English Channel, knowing they would soon be home. The passage through the Red Sea was more bearable northbound. Charlie showed me how to convert an empty cardboard box into a wind scoop. Stuck through an opened porthole, tied in place, it funnelled a constant draught into the cabin, cooling it wonderfully.

There were no more stops until the Ruysdael reached the southern end of the Suez Canal just before dark. We arrived in time to be the tail end vessel of a north bound convoy, so didn't tie to buoys. Following dinner, I stepped onto the deck to look at the sights on the banks, as we cruised slowly through the cut. I was aware of a strange sensation which for a few seconds I couldn't explain. Then I realised, I was cold. For the last three months I'd worn sandals, shorts and occasionally a tee shirt while on board ship. Now I had to don jeans, a long sleeved shirt and jumper to feel comfortable. I felt very overdressed.

The voyage through the Mediterranean was slow and uneventful. I mostly managed to avoid evil Jake, though when I did see him, his eyes said the words that his voice didn't speak. It was late November when the ship finally crawled into Avonmouth.

The low temperature was a vast contrast from the heat of the Indian Ocean; a keen frost lay on the ground as we berthed alongside the quay. I wore several extra layers of clothes to keep out the cold. We were paid off almost immediately the ship was tied to the bollards. Almost all hands were leaving the ship. I said hurried goodbyes to most of them and would miss some, though I was glad to be rid of evil Jake. I shared a taxi to the railway station with Joey and Charlie. They'd been good shipmates and I was sorry to wave them off, as their Liverpool bound train pulled out.

My train departed only fifteen minutes later. I arrived back in Scarborough in the late afternoon, deciding to walk home through the main street. My bags, one in each hand didn't seem unduly heavy. The street was quite busy as I made my way down through the town. Out of the crowd I noticed a familiar figure heading towards me, it was my Mum, out shopping. Though my folks knew I was coming home, they didn't know the exact date, I decided to surprise her. Averting my gaze until almost in front of her, I dropped my bags, held out my arms and called, "hello Mum!"

Her first look was of consternation, she didn't recognise me, though only for a second. "It's me bairn, it's our Freddy. Just look at the colour of you, you're nearly black. Look at that hair, it's blond, and it needs cutting." Then she grabbed me in a rib crushing hug, as if I been away for years rather than months.

It was great to be home again. Baby Alison was growing. Janet was now attending High School with Sue and Chris. I greeted them all as they arrived home from school. They all seemed to have grown in the months I'd been away. As soon as possible I went down to the harbour. The *Rosemary* was in port, her catch was landed. I found Dad in the baiting shed with his fellow fishermen and Micky, each completing a line. Dad was clearly delighted to see me and the men's conversation stopped as they asked the expected questions; where had I been? What was the ship like? How long was I home for?

I asked why they were still here at five o'clock; they were usually home by this time. It transpired that they'd been at sea since three o'clock that morning but Ernie was ill and hadn't been able to bait his usual quota of lines, so they opted to make up the shortfall, rather than have insufficient to take to sea the following morning.

The men all looked tired, but were cheerful. They'd had a good catch and were keen to sail with a full compliment of gear.

I offered to help but was told there was no point in getting covered in mussel juice and they'd soon be finished, so I sat on the stool by the fire, listening to their talk and enthusiasm for their job, watching as they worked as a team. As the first of the four lines was completed, that man immediately helped someone else to finish. No one ordered, no one asked, it was expected. This was a different world from the one I'd just left. It was a world that I dearly wanted to be a part of. I walked from the pier with them to hear Tom say, "same time in t' mornin' lads, if we get away early we'll get a good berth."

There were so many boats operating, those sailing earliest were able to select the choice grounds. These men would be home for six o'clock, in bed before nine, then up at two thirty the following morning to do it all over again. Hopefully Ernie would be back at work, then at least they could go home when their catch was landed.

I wasn't intending to return to the Bolton Steamship Company, so was a free agent. When ready to return to sea, I'd contact the Shipping Office in Middlesborough, to enquire what ships, if any, were available. Though it was only late November, I had no intention of missing Christmas at home. I'd wait until the New Year before looking for a ship. Meanwhile I could bait lines, go flithering, help the boats to land, all the things I enjoyed. Dad couldn't complain too much, after all, I was on leave, though already dreading returning to the Merchant Navy.

I'd been home for two weeks and was working with three other men, all quite elderly, baiting lines for the *Osprey*, starting at five o'clock each morning. Robin, the youngest of the men was one of seven brothers and was father of nine children, including seven sons. An ex steam trawlerman, a maker and mender of trawls, he was probably the fastest baiter of lines in the port. He was slightly built with piercing, twinkling eyes, mostly hidden behind streaked glasses, supported at the hinges by Elastoplast. Straggling ends of silver hair protruded from beneath his cloth cap. He would occasionally remove the cap, exposing a fine tussled mane as he subconsciously scratched his head when making a point in the varied conversations.

I sometimes wondered when Robin shaved, as he always seemed to have a two-day growth of grey stubble. Without him knowing, I would attempt to race him as we baited our lines. I went as fast as I could, while he didn't seem to rush at all. Occasionally he'd stop and sit down to roll, then enjoy a cigarette. He said he couldn't work and smoke with wet hands. I'd keep going, making the most of the advantage. No matter how I tried, Robin still would bait more than two lines to my one.

Jim, another of the men was known to all as 'Ruffan'. In his youth he'd been a hero and was given an award for rescuing two young girls from a burning house. He'd probably been a 'rough un' too, hence the name. Even now he was quite fiery, despite having poor eyesight. Ruffan constantly wiped his red rimmed, watery eyes with a dirty handkerchief, drawn each time from his jacket pocket.

He was a habitual user of snuff, the evidence easily visible; a brown mark between his nose and upper lip. Ruffan had sailed in cobles when younger but was now a box mender, fish weigher and jobber for a fishing agent, baiting lines in his free time. He was suspected of leaving occasional 'sleepy hooks' in the centre of the coils of line. The crew of the boat would frequently come ashore complaining of dangerous incidents relating to unbaited hooks in the middle of a line. He denied the accusations of course, so I surreptitiously began observing him at his work.

Jim's vision was very poor, he seemed to work mostly by feeling. The knot of a snood was encountered on every third coil of line; this was run through thumb and forefinger to the hook. The different baits were contained in separate dishes and were grabbed in loose handfuls, any surplus to requirements returned to the container.

I noticed on one occasion, when his mussel bait dish was empty, he dropped the hook into the middle of the baited line then refilled the dish from the bucket on the floor. When he returned to the bench he began turning new coils of line, burying the bare hook. "You've left a sleepy 'ook there Jim," I said, too quickly and too loudly.

He turned in my direction. " Y' clever little shit, 'ere's you, straight fro' school tellin' grown men 'ow t' carry on. You're still wet be'ind t' ears. Jus' keep y' fuckin' place as a boy."

He then continued baiting his line as if nothing had happened. I was stunned into silence. The others were quiet too, not commenting on the incident. No one spoke for what seemed ages, then gradually non-controversial conversation began again. Robin lightened the atmosphere, saying to Jim, "d' ya remember that bromide stuff they used put in our tea durin' t' war, to stop us feelin' randy and sexy."

"Aye I remember," came the reluctant reply.

"I think it's started t' work."

This restored the harmony in the room, much to my relief. When Ruffan's line was completed, he fastened it tightly to the skep with the securing bands before taking it outside. Robin took the opportunity to turn in my direction, "we all know it's 'im young 'un, jus' go easy on 'im, it's not 'is fault, 'is eyes are knackered. E's havin' t' put chalk lines on 'is weighin' scales nowadays 'cos 'e can't see t' numbers. We'll mark that line an' cut t' 'ook off before we go." It was impossible to bait these rogue hooks once discarded, as their position in the sequence of rows was lost.

The third man working in the shed was old George, tall, stooped, with thinning grey hair, he was the eldest of the group. Though from a fishing family he'd never been to sea. His only job since leaving school was at the gas company, from where he'd been retired for many years. He'd been taught to bait and skein as a boy by his father. George lived on a new estate on the outskirts of the town, about three miles from the pier. He would walk this distance each morning, hours before the first bus was available. When he'd completed his four lines, he'd walk home again. When I asked why he didn't take the bus home, he replied, "it weren't there this mornin' when I wanted it, so why should I use it now?" This seemed rather perverse but if he was prepared to walk home, who was I to argue?

Unless the weather was too bad, the boats fished for six consecutive days. Saturday was usually a non-fishing day. The fishermen turned out after breakfast on this day to 'cave' their lines, removing any remaining bait from the previous day, untangling fouled parts, replacing damaged or missing hooks, eliminating worn or chafed parts and re-splicing the lines. It was a time for general maintenance and good husbandry of the gear.

Before noon the skipper would go to the agent's office to settle his boat's account. He'd return with cash, the net proceeds of the week's fishing after deductions for bait and other expenses. The skeiners and baiters pay was subtracted, the balance then shared between the crew, the owners of the boat and the fishing gear. There was often a little extra for the shore staff if the week had been particularly successful. Loose change and oddments were left with the shoreman for incidental purchases.

For a couple of hours early on Saturday afternoons, the fishermen and their shoremen could be found in the many harbourside pubs, before making their way home for their much-too-brief free time. Some would take their wives or girlfriends out during the evening, but if the weather was reasonable the men would be sailing again early the following morning.

One foggy Saturday in mid December, I was sitting in the bar of the Newcastle Packet with Bill Sheader, Soapy and several others, enjoying the general good humour. Soapy bought a beer for little Joe Dwyer, the eighty year old window cleaner, after accompanying Joe in his favourite song, 'Throw out the lifeline'. Everyone was now listening to the little man reciting the many verses of Tennyson's, 'The Charge of Light Brigade'.

Joe demonstrably yelled out, 'into the valley of death rode the six hundred.' As he reached the line, 'cannons to the left of them' the first of the maroons was fired announcing that the lifeboat was required. By the time the second maroon was fired, Joe's solo performance was just that, the pub was empty.

When our group arrived at the boathouse a crowd of onlookers was gathering around the opened doors. Bill pushed his way through, making a path for others. The powerful tractor, engine growling, was being shackled to the lifeboat carriage by willing hands. The crew of six, mostly fishermen, were counted into the boat by the coxswain, as they climbed the wooden stepladder. Bill

Sheader, now serious, was a very different man to the humorous, relaxed character I'd been sitting with five minutes earlier. He was a consummate seaman.

The last of the team paused at the foot of the ladder. Alan, Bill's brother-in-law wasn't a fisherman, he was the retained engineer of the lifeboat, paid by the R.N.L.I. His role was to maintain the vessel in a constant state of readiness. Alan was a massive, immensely powerful man, round of face with greying hair combed straight back. His stance was erect, that of the former guardsman, which he was. It was Alan who'd fired the maroons to summon the crew, in response to the Coastguard's telephoned request. He spoke earnestly to Bill, relating the situation, before climbing the ladder to take his place in the boat. When at sea he'd be under the cockpit, manning the radio. As Bill made to mount the stairs, I made eye contact with him and said hopefully, "'ow are y' fixed?"

He paused for a moment then replied, "we should be alright but get in anyway."

My heart leapt. I hadn't been hopeful. I'd been on a few practices, but never before on a service. The willing crew were helping me fasten the complicated buckles on my lifejacket, as the carriage was trundled through the fog. It was only a short distance to the water's edge, an indication that it was almost high water. The deck beneath my feet began to vibrate as the twin diesels below burst into life.

The boat was secured to the carriage by four heavy chain strops, each attached by a quick release clip. I was instructed to stand by the port one for'ard. As the boat was pushed deeper into the water, Bill leaned far outboard, checking the level against the caterpillar tracks, until he was sure there was sufficient depth to float the boat. Standing upright again, he turned to the tractor driver and held up his hand to say, "halt." The carriage stopped. He turned forward and in a very crisp, clear, commanding voice, shouted, "right lads, knock out."

I removed the locking pin, then hit the release bar with a hammer, purposely stowed to hand. Three others did the same. The four chains fell into the sea simultaneously. The nose of the boat tilted forward and she was catapulted from the carriage by pulleys, as the tractor and trailer were driven hard in reverse. Coxswain Bill pushed the throttles to the stops and the boat surged forward into the swirling fog. Looking aft I could see him consulting with the Second in command, Tom, Dad's skipper. These two were a good team. "Keep a good lookout, we'll be about twenty minutes," Bill yelled to the four of us standing in the for'ard welldeck.

Turning to Ces, the crewman standing nearest, I asked what we were going for. He replied, "t' coastguards reported some anglers, ashore in a small boat, in t' corner o' Cayton Bay, beyond t' 'igh scar. Daft buggers should 'ave more sense than t' go out when it's like this." His arm pointed to the grey void ahead of us. He continued a tirade, aimed at all amateurs who sailed the seas, ill-prepared.

I looked aft again at Bill, his hands on the helm, his face expressing total concentration, his eyes fixed on the compass. Occasionally he glanced at the clock, then quickly scanned his command. This was a totally different character to the man who was joking, laughing and drinking pints of beer, half an hour earlier. Though he could see nothing, he knew exactly where he was in relation to the land. When we'd been steering south east for about twenty minutes, Bill eased back the throttles, until the engines were ticking over dead slow.

"We should be almost at 'igh scar, now he shouted, it's about top o' tide, so we'll go o'er it alright, keep yer eyes an' ears open." Although not academically bright, his knowledge of the sea was unsurpassable. Every man in the boat had total faith in this Coxswain. He calculated distance, course, weather and tide in his head. He knew how much water was over the scar and was confident there was sufficient for safe passage. This reef was exposed at low water.

If proof was required of his skill, not more than a minute later he yelled again, "I'm jus' marking shalla water on t' echo sounder now, were over t' top of t' 'igh scar."

One of the men on the other bow suddenly called out, "there's somebody shoutin', I just heard 'em."

Bill pulled the controls to neutral, stopping the boat. Everyone listened intently. Faintly, we all heard the shouting again, "ahoy, over here!" It wasn't easy to say exactly where the call came from, due to the distortion of the fog, but consensus was it came from the starboard bow.

The engines were engaged in slow speed and the wheel put over, until we were roughly heading towards the direction of the shout. It came again, more clearly, then out of the mist appeared a small, varnished, open motor boat. Three oilskin-clad figures were looking in our direction and waving. The boat was not ashore, as Bill was aware, monitoring his depth gauge. He manoeuvred his lifeboat close to the drifting boat, enabling two of his crew to catch hold of the small craft with their boat-hooks. They drew the little vessel close alongside.

It transpired they'd sailed earlier, before the fog had enveloped the coast. They had no compass aboard to steer back to port by, but to compound this omission, they had no anchor and cable either. This at least would have allowed them to maintain their position until the fog lifted. With the option of drifting, they had instead, attempted to guess their way back to the harbour, only to run ashore on the rocks to the west of their original position. Luckily the weather wasn't bad or the little craft would have quickly been smashed beyond repair by the jagged boulders. They'd been seen by passing ramblers on the shore, who had reported the incident to the coastguard. Meanwhile the three men had managed to refloat their craft, preventing damage to the hull, but were now drifting helplessly in the tide, close to the rocky shore.

There was no criticism of their actions from Bill at this point, but Ces could be heard muttering, "amateurs, bloody accident waitin' to 'appen," and other descriptive, derogatory terms, all aimed at the hapless mariners. Following an instruction from Bill, we pulled a strong nylon rope from a locker in the bows of the lifeboat. An end was passed to the casualty, where it was secured to a strong point in the stem. The remainder of the coil was paid out over the stern, as the lifeboat began to head east, away from the land and the casualty.

When he was satisfied there was sufficient cable for a comfortable tow, Bill said, "that'll do lads, catch a turn." Several turns were passed around the steel post on the starboard quarter and quickly made fast. The rope between the two vessels rose from the sea with a snap, dripping water. The casualty's bows were hauled round to follow the tug, almost jerking the angling party from their feet. It was difficult to hide a grin as they staggered to keep their equilibrium.

Once clear of the shore, Bill put his command on a reciprocal course, gradually increasing the throttle, to prevent the tow from snatching. Fifteen minutes later, our straining ears picked up the dull boom of the foghorn, sounding out from the lighthouse at the pier end. This was reported to the Coxswain, who slowed down the boat, allowing most of the towrope to be recovered. He requested only sufficient rope to allow him to manoeuvre both craft into the harbour.

The shamefaced anglers were escorted to the Golden Ball slipway, where they were left to make their way back to their moorings. As we departed, Bill quietly said to the presumed boat owner, "get yerself an anchor an' cable, an' a little compass. It won't cost much, an' it'll save yer a lot o' trouble in t' future." The message was delivered without fuss, or malice but it carried authority, and would be acted upon.

It took a further half-hour of teamwork to rehouse the boat, hauling it from the water across wooden skids with the tractor, assisted by shore helpers. The tilted carriage was steered to the stern of the boat and the sturdy craft was soon hauled back into position ready for another launch. Boat and cradle were towed back to the boathouse, to be hosed and cleaned free of sand by Alan. The crew, having lost their brief, weekly leisure period, would go home.

One of the shoremen assisting in the recovery of the boat was Sam (Toddy) Cammish. Sam was at the Somme during the 'Great War'. He saw so much carnage and was so distressed that he decided he'd had enough and returned home. He was never caught, court martialled or discharged.

Another of the helpers was the Curate of the old, Parish Church of St Mary, which commanded a wonderful view of the town. Mr Bubbins, or Charlie as he was universally known, was an ever-present figure at the harbour and had, on occasions, sailed on the lifeboat. In excess of six feet tall, broad, he could have been mistaken for a rugby player, yet this appearance disguised the real man. A more gentle soul, it would have been impossible to meet. He had slightly greying tousled hair and a large roman nose dividing a pair of piercing, challenging eyes. The fact that few fishermen attended church, mattered not to the Curate. He sought his flock at their place of work, or wherever he could find them. This was sometimes the pub, where he enjoyed a pint or two and a game of dominoes with Bill and the lifeboat crew. It wasn't unknown for him to over indulge in this company. Following a couple of minor falls, the vicar suggested that perhaps Charlie shouldn't travel on the top deck of the bus, when making his way back to the vicarage.

On completing the remaining line before the Christmas break, we discovered there was a quantity of bait left, though not enough for a full line. "Rather than dump it, why don't y' shoot a 'trot' '(a short length of line) on t' sands?" Robin suggested. "There's a piece of old line on t' shelf." This was a good idea, the tides were right, high water was about three o'clock in the morning. I took the line, and skep, from the shelf. There seemed to be three or four score of hooks on it, ideal for the purpose.

When the others had gone, I baited the line with mussels, flithers and a few worms. It didn't take too long, it was only a third of the size of a normal line. I left the prepared trot in the shed, returning about nine o'clock that evening. I brought with me a couple of old building bricks, recovered from a demolition site en route. Wearing a thick donkey jacket and short seaboots, I carried the line and bricks down to the beach, stopping close under the pier wall, only a few yards from the water's edge. My eyes soon became accustomed to the dark. It was low water, waves were constantly breaking on the shore close by.

I fastened the end of the line to one of the bricks, then dug a hole in the soft sand with my hands, burying the brick. Walking very slowly, parallel to the breaking waves, I carried the skep in one hand, dropping each baited hook as required, in sequence, until the tray was empty. I retrieved the other brick then tied it to this outer end. Stretching the line tight, I made another hole, then buried the second brick. The line was now in place, though it would require a few fathoms of twine attaching, from the inner end to the pier-wall, to enable me to haul the line while it was still immersed in the sea the following morning.

The flowing tide would cover the line at some point soon. It would remain covered until about seven o'clock the following morning. I would haul it in at six, before the line became exposed. Any fish caught could be washed off the hooks in the swell or taken by scavenging gulls if left longer.

It was gone ten o'clock when I got home. Mum was about to retire for the night; Dad had been in bed for a while. Sleeping was difficult that night; I dreamt of big catches on the line and was out of bed quickly when the alarm went off at five thirty. I found the kettle still warm on the stove; Dad couldn't have been gone long. I downed a quick cup of tea, then was on the way to haul 'my gear'. There was a sharp frost on the ground and my enthusiasm waned as I trudged along the pier, hands in pockets, hunched against the chilling breeze.

Locating the down line I gave it a heave, hauling the buried brick from its place. The wet line felt icy in my hands. As I hauled the brick up the pierside, several hooks became exposed in mid air. On the fourth or fifth was a big flatfish. All thoughts of cold evaporated, I'd caught a fish. With the brick in my hands, I gave the line a big heave, dragging the other brick from its hole. As the line tightened it exposed more hooks and another fish, a codling. Hand over hand I began to haul the line, coiling it and the snoods in my right hand, the hooks hanging in the middle of the coil. Each small handful was placed on the skep. The flatfish was a flounder, locally known as a 'mudbut', similar in shape to a small halibut, but of little value.

I took the flounder, then the codling from the hooks, dropping them to the floor. Both were dead and had been for some time, they were stiff with rigor mortis. Excitedly pulling the line, I was now sweating profusely. Another flounder appeared, then another, each caught on flithers, the remains of which were evident on the

*The hulk T.S. Vinicatrix in her berth near the Sharpness
to Gloucester Canal. Photo unknown*

THE CREW OF SCARBOROUGH LIFE-BOAT — THE "J. G. GRAVES OF SHEFFIELD"

*The author with the Scarborough Lifeboat crew, circa 1967.
Left to right: Jack Rowley, Fred Normandale, Bill Sheader,
Ces Bean, Bob Swalwell, Alan Rennard, Tom Rowley.
Tractor driver Jim Firman assistant Ross Tyson. Photo RNLI*

The bulk carrier Macauley loading phosphate in Dakar, Senegal, circa 1966. Photo FG Normandale

Jann Denise on trials leaving Fraserburgh harbour, circa 1971. Photo Jan Borowski courtesy of Bob and Ann Walker

hooks. Another codling came up, caught on mussel, then more flounders. It was a disappointment when the angle of the line became depressed, almost to vertical, but there was one more 'mudbut' before the brick appeared. I was delighted with my haul. Two codlings, weighing about three pounds each and seven flounders with a total weight of about half a stone.

I gave them all to Robin, who'd arrived early to help cave the previous days lines. He said mudbuts were good eating fish, that he couldn't understand why no one would buy them. He said it was the same with monkfish. This I could understand, monkfish were so ugly, no one would want to buy them.

Christmas and Boxing Day rapidly came and went and were the usual riot of hilarity, but the New Year came in with a bang. The wind went to the east, sticking in that direction. The older hands called these easterly winds, 'sheep's head' winds. They said that's all they could afford from the butchers, when they couldn't get to sea. The boats didn't sail for a week and still the wind didn't shift. It was cold, miserable and money was scarce. Everyone had spent up over the festive season. I'd nothing left of the pay I'd accumulated 'big boating' and there was nothing to be earned locally. Though not really wanting to, I decided to ring the Shipping Office, to ask for a ship.

I was offered an Ordinary Seamen's berth in a ship called *Macauley*, shipping phosphate in the form of fine, light coloured sand, from Dakar in Senegal, West Africa, to Billingham, a small wharf further up the Tees from Middlesborough. There were no other ships available so I took the job, leaving home early the following morning. This would get me through the difficult spell, then I'd reappraise my situation in the spring. The easterly wind still hadn't shifted; it felt raw on my face as I made my way to the station. The wind was blowing directly from Siberia, as high pressure persisted in dominating the weather.

The *Macauley* was grey hulled, about six thousand tons, with all accommodation aft. She had four 'Macgregor' hatches in line for'ard. I was pleased to see a familiar face on board. Andy, the EDH from the *Ribblehead* was joining the ship at the same time. I felt like an old hand as we chatted, waiting to sign on. We sailed, light ship, that same morning, leaving no opportunity for a night ashore, which was fortunate as I had little money to spare, though a tarpaulin muster would have ensured I wasn't left on board on my own.

It was to be a three-week, return voyage to Dakar. It would be good to feel the African sun in January, after the recent frosts of home, though I felt unsettled now having left again. I was in limbo, not knowing quite what I wanted to do. This feeling was temporarily dispelled while sailing through the Channel in thick fog, on the second day, outward bound.

I'd been assigned to the twelve to four watch with Andy. We were dispatched to the foc'sle head, to keep a lookout in the freezing fog. Crouching below the bulwarks, with only our heads showing, we were able to peer into the thick pea souper while avoiding most of the icy blast, created by the ship's own momentum. The intercom, connecting the bridge to the foc'sle buzzed. Andy pressed the button, acknowledging the caller. "Keep a sharp lookout, there's a ship dead ahead, let me know the instant you see it," came the instruction from the 'Officer of the Watch'.

We stared into the gloom, imagining weird ghostly ships coming out of the fog, when suddenly there was ship, a real one, looming out from the void. It was passing only a few yards away, on the starboard bow, close enough to throw a stone on board. It was upon us, out of the fog in seconds. The converging speeds of the two vessels made it impossible for us to call the bridge in time to give any warning. Andy and I stared at each other in disbelief. It had missed us by a hair's breadth. We watched as it drew level, then the buzz of the intercom pulled us from the surreal world. This time I answered it. "Hello?"

"Hello! Is that all you bastards have got to say? You were sent up there to keep a look out. We missed that bloody ship by a whisker, no thanks to you two. You're worse than useless, the pair of you."

"It was on us before we 'ad a chance to do anything," I replied defensively. "We couldn't 'ave let you know before it 'it us, it was impossible." He was slightly mollified by my comments, but was not about to accept any blame for the near miss, which according to Andy later, would have been his fault, for not reducing speed in restricted visibility.

"You should have called me, that's why you were sent there," The officer said sternly.

At that I just said, "sorry, there jus' wasn't time." If the two ships had collided head on, the intercom, situated on the bulwark in the ship's stem, would not have survived the impact, but there was no point in pursuing the dialogue. He wasn't going to take the matter further, without implicating himself.

The run to Dakar was without further event though we passed close to our sister ship, the *Thackeray*, going in the opposite direction. Strangely she had only three hatches. Apparently our ship had at some point been cut in half with an extra section inserted. I found this a little unnerving, though I was never given any cause for worry and wouldn't have known, had we not seen the other ship.

Going ashore in Dakar held little interest. Maybe I didn't want to sub my wages; maybe foreign places had lost their appeal. Either way, arriving in the early hours of the morning, then sailing again before midnight fully loaded, gave little opportunity to explore. I stayed on board and strangely was not too bothered. Not long ago I was desperate to see foreign ports.

After two trips to Dakar, I managed a weekend at home and was surprised to see a few of the keelboats rigging to go trawling. It was very early in the season, but some trawlers at Bridlington had been getting phenomenal results catching cod with trawls, rather than lines. This was a new departure from tradition. I stood on the pier looking at a new arrival I'd not seen before, the *Whitby Rose*. Tom Pashby had given up the *Osprey* to take this newer command. As I studied the vessel, Tom climbed the ladder to where I was standing. "Now then me ol' kid, what are you doin' 'ome? I thought you were away in t' Merchant Navy." Tom referred to almost everyone as 'me ol' kid', I wondered if he remembered anyone's name.

I said I was, but was home for the weekend and was sailing again on Monday.

"Well if ya get fed up ya can 'ave a berth wi' me," he said.

This was the opportunity I'd been waiting for. "I've got t' go back on Monday, I'm still signed on, but I'll on'y be away three weeks, can I come wi' ya then?"

"Aye OK me ol' kid, we'll be trawling then, come an see me when ya get back." He walked off in the direction of the Pier Hotel. I was elated, it was the right time, I knew it was, but first I had to tell Dad. Would he approve?

I met Dad in the Leeds Arms half an hour later and told him of my offer.

"If that's what y' want t' do, I can't stop ya, but 'e's a strange one. 'E can't keep a crew, that's why e's askin' you." This was an approval from Dad. I knew Tom was very superstitious, I'd learned the hard way from saying the wrong things in his presence, but this was my chance to go fishing.

Feeling that some mitigation was required, I explained I'd seen some of the world, as he had, though my service hadn't been in war time, but now I wanted to go fishing. Kit, an old fisherman standing next to us in the bar, partly listening to our conversation, interrupted saying to Dad, "I've been all over t' world as well Fred. I've been t' Shields, 'artlepool, Grimsby, Lowestoft, loads o' places."

I laughed, but Dad nodded sagely, saying "aye you've been around as well Kit," to the man whose perception of the world, extended to fishing ports along the East Coast of England.

My final trip on the *Macauley* was interminable. The ship seemed to crawl through the water. There were two days of delays in Dakar due to mechanical problems with shore equipment. This was previously unheard of. Eventually the ship berthed in Billingham and I was paid off. It was Friday, on Sunday morning I would be sailing on the *Whitby Rose* as crew.

CHAPTER XI

FISHING AT LAST

On Saturday, I arrived early at the boat to seek Tom, knowing there'd be work to do preparing for sea the next day. He was already aboard with his two crew men, mending a split in the trawl, damaged the previous day. The tear had been laced together quickly enabling fishing to resume, but now it required repairing correctly. The *Whitby Rose* was fishing on rocky ground. A string of twelve inch diameter iron and rubber wheels, 'bobbins', on the bottom of the net assisted it over rough ground, but snagging and tearing was an occupational hazard.

John was a Scotsman who'd first arrived in Scarborough on a herring drifter but had decided to stay. Not surprisingly, he was known as Scotch John. Bruce, the other hand, had recently sold his coble and was sailing with Tom for experience, before seeking a keelboat of his own, a fact that Tom was well aware of. He was reluctant to divulge much, if any, of his fishing knowledge to someone intent on being a rival.

My arrival was greeted with mixed feelings by those present. John was quite amiable but Bruce was less so. I suppose he felt his job was threatened now there were four on board. Tom was pleased to see me and immediately gave me several jobs to do. "Get three boxes of ice from t' ice factory an' cover it wi' a canvas sheet under t' fish market fo' when we ger in tomorra night." This ice would be sprinkled on the fish to chill it until the auction the following morning. "Go t' chandlers fo' some mendin' twine, bring some distilled water from t' electrician." I was a gofer, go for this, go for that. Meanwhile they would continue to repair the net.

On my return with the twine and water, Tom took me below into the engine-room demonstrating how to top up the bank of batteries with distilled water, using a small filler bottle. Touching the batteries made my wet hands tingle. I wiped them subconsciously on my Wranglers. In the days to follow I would have inexplicable holes in my jeans, and would eventually realise that they were burned by the battery acid.

The batteries filled, I returned to the deck, where the trawl was now repaired as new. Tom had gone to the agent's office for the week's settlings. Bruce was below in the cabin, compiling a list of food required for the coming week. While we were waiting on deck, John made me laugh with a story of a man back in his village at home. The man was involved in an acrimonious divorce from his wife, who was claiming a large amount of maintenance money for herself and their twins. The man swore that only one of the children was his.

Our sailing orders were for three o'clock the following morning. I didn't go out that evening, opting for an early night and was down on the pier at five minutes before three, with my oilskins and seaboots under my arm. These would now remain on board. There was wood smoke coming from the cabin chimney and a light showed down in the engine-room. Tom would be starting the engine.

I surveyed the craft on which I was to spend my first days as a real fisherman. She was light blue in colour, similar in length to the *Floreat* but newer, with sleeker lines. The winch was fore side of the wheelhouse and the trawl was worked from the starboard side. For'ard and aft on this side were two metal 'gallows', standing about six feet high, which the trawl wires were guided through. The two wooden trawl boards sat comfortably between the gallows and the boat's side, held in position by securing chains. The doors would be heaved outboard with the winch, to hang by the chains, prior to shooting the trawl. The boat's bulwarks were only raised about nine inches from the deck. I would need a good balance to avoid falling overboard.

John emerged from the cabin pushing back black, straggling hair from his eyes. He greeted me with a grin. Bruce could be seen walking along the pier, sea bag in hand, so I unfastened the mooring ropes. John caught a turn to the pier ladders with a light line, keeping the vessel alongside. As I climbed down to the deck, the engine burst into life with a clatter and a cloud of smoke. A minute later Tom clambered from the engine-room coughing profusely, a thick, hand-rolled cigarette still held firmly between his lips as he coughed. His face was redder than usual. Reluctantly he took the cig from his mouth, shouting to John, "ar' we all 'ere me ol' kid?"

John nodded. "Righto, chuck 'er off then." The line hitched to the ladders was released as Bruce stepped aboard, though we didn't set off immediately. The boat drifted slowly from the quayside while Tom spent a few minutes setting up the 'Decca Navigator'. This electronic equipment in a small, grey, metal cabinet, consisted of a display of four circular flashing dials. Three of these, the slaves, indicated position lines. The fourth, the master clock, was a reference to set the other dials correctly. Responding to radio signals from transmitters throughout Europe, the position lines enabled the user to fix his location by cross bearings on any designated chart within the system.

Skippers were able to plot the positions of known wrecks and obstacles on home-made charts, hopefully avoiding them in future. 'Fasteners' were reported by fishermen to their colleagues so obstructions could be avoided. The equipment was quite accurate when conditions were good, but could be erratic in the dark. In thunderstorms or heavy rain the system went completely haywire, the clocks spinning uncontrollably.

We steamed from the harbour, heading north east for about ten miles, to an extensive area of flat rocky ground, where fishing had been favourable during the previous week. I was informed by Bruce that Tom never left the wheelhouse from leaving port to returning, except to haul or shoot the trawl. He did all the steering to and from grounds and also took all the trawling watches. This was a tremendous feat of concentration and stamina daily, the boat had no autopilot or hydraulic steering.

Bruce and John occupied two of the four bunks during this brief passage. I felt a little queasy, so after making Tom a mug of tea, I spent the remaining period dozing on the seat locker in the cabin. I quickly learned that the skipper required frequent fill-ups, amounting to a dozen or more each day.

An hour and a half after leaving the harbour, we arrived at the grounds. Tom brought the *Whitby Rose* across the slight breeze, taking the way off with a gentle kick astern, then joined us on the deck. The doors were lifted outboard with a wire from the winch, then the net and bobbins were heaved over the side. Most of the work was done by Tom himself. In his enthusiasm he would never use the winch if his own strength would do the job. When the work wasn't progressing fast enough for his liking, he'd say, "ger out o' way me ol' kid, I'll do it."

As the skipper passed me, en route to the wheelhouse, he glanced at my hands and noticed for the first time I was wearing protective, plastic-coated gloves. He tutted, rolled his eyes, then reached for my hands, pulling the loosely fitting sheaths from them. In the same movement he threw them over the side. "Ya won't be needin' them me ol' kid, you'll get soft wearin' them." I'd been used to wearing gloves for heavy-duty work on the ships and though a recent introduction, they were being used more often on the fishing boats, but not it seemed on this one.

John released the brakes, allowing the net to slip astern. The bridles snaked across the deck, running outboard through the gallows as the boat moved through the water. Bruce manned the for'ard door; I was instructed to attend the after one where Tom could keep an eye on me. The boat was now picking up speed. Soon the bridle ends attached to the wire warps, were checked in the gallows as John applied the brakes. Bruce and I shackled our respective bridles to the back of each door, then clipped the warp to the front bracket, finally releasing the securing chains. The warps zinged, snapping taut as they absorbed the weight of the gear overboard.

The *Whitby Rose* was now turning in a large circle, in a similar way to how I'd seen Dad and Uncle John shoot their gear. Bruce joined John at the winch brakes; I was positioned at the boat's side to ensure that the two wires didn't meet or cross. Occasionally, when they became close, I would yell "check." They immediately parted as tension was put on the brakes; water resistance acting across the surface of the boards. Soon the gear was on the seabed, with a hundred fathoms of wire out. John and Bruce screwed down the brake handles. The cables were secured at the stern by Tom and me. We were trawling.

While Bruce cleaned the deck of debris previously hidden under the net, without using a brush, (which was unlucky according to Tom), I assisted John to prepare breakfast. This was a large fry-up of bacon, sausage, eggs, tinned tomatoes and beans, with fried bread. A plate was deemed too small for Tom's needs, so his meals were delivered in a large pie dish, referred to as his 'trough', though only beyond earshot. The skipper had a voracious appetite, but refused to go below to dine, choosing to eat his meals standing up, in the cramped confines of his wheelhouse.

I was despatched to deliver Tom's breakfast, which John passed to me from below. "Careful mon, he'll snatch it frae yor han's," cautioned the Scotsman, as I carried the meal aft, along with cutlery, sauce and seasoning. Sure enough, the skipper, observing me crossing the gently rolling deck, dropped the sliding window in anticipation. As I drew near, he reached out wordlessly and grabbed the dish from my outstretched hand. I returned for his pot of tea. "Did 'e grab it frae ye?" asked John on my return. I nodded.

John told me about Kevin, a crewman on board previously, who disliked this habit so much he was determined to cure it. Kevin put the trough into the coal-fired oven until it was glowing hot. Taking it out carefully, with towels for insulation, he filled the container with the days dinner. Tom saw him coming across the deck with his meal and dropped the window, preparing to grab it. "Careful Tom, it's hot," warned Kevin. The warning went unheeded, as two huge, knarled hands reached out, snatched the dish, then promptly released it again. The meal dropped to the deck through singed fingers. "I told y' it was hot," said Kevin smiling. He was asked to leave at the weekend.

Following breakfast and the washing up, I kicked off my boots and rolled into my bunk. It seemed only minutes before Tom was yelling down the hatchway.

"Haway me ol' kids, it's time t' net was up." I slid from my snug berth and sat on the seat locker; my two shipmates did the same. The kettle was steaming on the stove top. I expected a quick cup of coffee before hauling, but was disappointed. Bruce and John began donning their seaboots and oilskins immediately.

John saw the look on my face, "he disna like hangin' aboot waitin' f' us, he wants t' haul at wance. If we dinna get there quick 'e starts wi' out us." With that he disappeared up the ladder. This was a different routine to what I'd been used to. The Merchant Navy was much less frantic. I followed Bruce to the deck, where John had already engaged the winch clutches. The skipper was releasing the chain, which harnessed the warps at the stern. He dashed back to the wheelhouse easing the throttle. John engaged the winch and the barrels began to rotate. Bruce and I stood by the gallows, waiting to re-secure the boards, as they emerged dripping from the water.

It was so much easier handling the doors at waist height, into these purpose-made steel frames. I passed the short length of chain through the towing bracket, then made figure of eight turns on the iron cleat, securing the board in place. On the *Floreat*, which had no gallows, the doors were fastened to the boat's inner bulwarks, inches from the deck. This could only be done on hands and knees. It took seconds to unclip the bridles from the door and almost immediately John was heaving them onto the winch. The boat was lying comfortably across the wind. Soon the net would appear.

I glanced at the wheelhouse. Tom, looking extremely agitated, was puffing furiously on another huge cigarette. As the two wing-ends of the trawl appeared in the gallows, John stopped the winch, unclutched the revolving barrels, then re-engaged the machine leaving only the 'whipping drums' rotating on each end. At each wing-end was a 'quarter rope', leading to the heavy, ground gear on the bottom of the net. These ropes are usually taken to the whipping drums so the heaviest part of the trawl is hauled on board mechanically. Tom couldn't wait to use the winch. He hauled the after quarter rope, hand over hand, his cigarette puffing like the funnel of a steam trawler. John and Bruce heaved the fore end up using the winch, but Tom had beaten them by several seconds. The string of polished bobbins, shining from the constant ground contact, dropped to the deck with a thud, the sock of the trawl streamed down into the sea.

The skipper's agitation continued, as he cajoled us to pull the net in with words I was to hear hundreds of times during my stay on this boat. "Come me ol' lads, we're not on pay while it's on t' deck. Let's ger it down again as sharp as we can." Tom believed we were only earning money when the trawl was on the bottom. I felt constantly on edge, trying to save seconds, rushing every job I did. John on the other hand, took everything in his stride, ignoring the skipper's urgency.

The mixed bag of fish in the codend was soon heaved aboard, spilling into the pound in the centre of the boat, as the slipknot was released. The catch, wriggling and cavorting, was all clean fish, with only a few sea urchins and starfish sprinkled among it. There was no sand or mud to rake through, as I'd been used to when sailing with Uncle John. The bobbins prevented the net from scraping the bottom. It didn't look a bad haul, there were some medium sized cod, haddock, whiting, plaice, lemon sole and several other species easily identifiable. As John and Bruce prepared the net for shooting again, I began to pick up some of the fish, throwing them, struggling, into the boxes on the port side. There would be five or six full boxes, each box approximately six stone in weight. "It's not a bad first 'aul," I said to Tom conversationally, as he re-tied the complicated codend knot.

He snapped back, "Never mind t' fish when it's on t' deck me ol' kid, that's ours, jus' concentrate on gettin' t' net down again."

I was quite deflated. This wasn't the Tom I was familiar with, he always seemed really nice ashore. Dad was right, he was certainly a Jeckyll and Hyde character. "Dinna tak ony notice o' him, he'll ha' yer as mad as himsel'," John whispered to me later, as we stood side by side gutting the catch. He had a lovely temperament, nothing seemed to faze him, or make him angry.

My hands were beginning to feel sore with handling the gear and the sharp edges of the fish's gills, which dug into my fingers when gutting. Small painful cracks appeared at the edge of each finger nail.

We shot and hauled the trawl four times during the day without it snagging the bottom, which would have meant early hauling and some damage. Tom said I was a lucky bird, and it was the first day for ages that this had happened. We arrived back in harbour at seven that evening, with a catch of a hundred and twenty stones of prime mixed fish. It was discharged onto the pier, weighed, iced and covered over with a canvas to deter predators, feathered or shod. By eight thirty we were walking from the pier, having restocked with empty boxes and secured the boat for the night. Tom, John and I crossed the road to the Lord Nelson for a couple of beers, Bruce went home.

I was dead tired on arriving home, so after giving Dad a brief résumé of my day, confirming his observations about the skipper, inviting the expected, "I told y' what 'e was like," I had a quick bath, then crawled off to bed setting my alarm for three forty five the following morning. I'd forgo a cup of tea in exchange for an extra fifteen minutes in bed.

I staggered from my bed when the alarm sounded, only to catch one of the small cuts on my fingers, making it bleed. I found it difficult to fasten the buttons on my jeans; my hands were so stiff and painful, though they eased quickly when soaked in a bowl of warm water. I would continue this practice each morning until they toughened up.

Monday wasn't so easy, the trawl came fast on the bottom three times, losing several hours of fishing time, which caused Tom to curse and berate himself. Our catch reflected the trying day and there was an hour of net mending in the harbour, before we could go home.

By Friday morning I was dead on my feet and my hands were a mess. It had been the hardest week of my life. I'd often been to sea fishing for pleasure, but to work six consecutive days on a boat had been totally different. We arrived in port at five that afternoon, an early finish. Though still weary I'd perked up, having completed my first week as a fisherman. I celebrated with a night on the town with the lads, though I was home before eleven. I now knew why my mates seldom wanted to socialise during the week, making the Olympia the exception.

That night I slept as if dead and it was eight fifteen when Dad woke me for breakfast. I'd have slept all day had he not called me. By nine I was on board for the usual maintenance and to collect my wages. I joined Bruce and John who were already busily overhauling the trawl, looking for small holes to mend. Tom was nowhere to be seen. Tied alongside our craft was the *Marion* a potting vessel, whose crew were also working among gear. Kevin, one of the crew called out, "'Ows that skipper o' yours? Is 'e still as dingy as when I was wi' 'im?" Then he laughed.

Everyone in the port knew of Tom's mannerisms and superstitions. John smiled, saying nothing. I defended him saying, "'e's alright," but Bruce began a tirade of tales about Tom and his antics, which although accurate, would have been better left unsaid. Fifteen minutes later Tom emerged from the engine-room with a face like thunder. He climbed the ladders to the pier top without speaking, but his glare spoke volumes, as he made for the office.

Neither of my shipmates had been aware that the skipper was below. "Do y' think 'e 'eard me?" Bruce asked, when Tom was out of sight. We both shrugged but his question was answered soon after, when Tom reappeared from the agent's office. He was calmer now as he dispensed a wage packet to each of us. I glanced at the front of mine which said, Freddy, £37. This was wonderful, it was more than I'd earned in a month on the 'big boats'. It had been worth the hardship.

Looking up, I heard Tom say to Bruce, "that's it me ol' kid."

Bruce was holding his wage packet and his National Insurance stamp card. He spluttered, "is it full Tom? Does it need changin'?"

"No me ol' kid, that's it, it's ya cards." He turned to John and me, both standing in silence. "Do you two wanna go wi' 'im?"

We shook our heads and said "no," in unison.

He just said, "righto, four o'clock in t' mornin' then," and turned to climb the ladders, leaving us all speechless.

Bruce muttered something about never having been sacked before, then went below for his sea gear. John and I went to the Newcastle Packet to meet up with the crowd.

If possible, the work was harder during the following week, as we were short handed, though it was noticeable that Tom was more considerate towards us. I thought it might be the absence of Bruce, who the skipper clearly disliked, but John said he was always of a better temperament when short handed, he didn't want to lose any more crew. It would be extremely difficult to handle the heavy, bobbin trawl gear with only two men.

I slowly settled into working on the *Whitby Rose* and my body clock adapted to the long working days. Time spent in harbour for mechanical breakdowns or bad weather was gratefully received, allowing some free time and often an afternoon nap. Some mornings, when the weather was unsettled, we'd arrive at the boat to find Tom waiting on the pier. Other crews would be in attendance. The collective skippers' decision would be to wait for the shipping forecast, broadcast at zero six hundred hours. We'd then all board the *Caroline* or *Onward Star*, to sit round the cabin table and listen to the old hands talking of their war experiences, or of fishing exploits from years past. These were memorable occasions.

Though the food on board was good, it was basic and I had a good appetite, so I began taking extra supplies of biscuits, cakes and puddings from home, to supplement my diet. One day, soon after I'd put a tin of sponge pudding on the stove in a pan of boiling water, the sound of the engine easing down, caused us to rush on deck. This was a sure sign that the trawl had caught on an obstruction and required hauling immediately. We were trawling on rough ground, so this was common occurrence.

John dashed to the winch to commence hauling the trawl. I ran aft to release the towing harness. Tom manoeuvred the boat as the winch heaved the fishing gear to the surface, then the three of us hauled the net on board. The lower part was badly damaged and took more than an hour to repair before it was back fishing again. While Tom and I were repairing the damage, John dashed below into the cabin to re-stoke the stove. He came back grinning. "Ken this, yor puddin's boiled dry, so I've hoyed it in tae the oven."

Shortly after shooting the gear, the net became fastened again twice, so it was several hours before we were able to get below for a break. I opened the oven carefully, the sides were glowing hot.

My little tinned pudding was now bulging with the pressure within, and was shaped more like a football than a can.

"Ya ken this, it'll surely be cooked the noo," my companion needlessly understated, handing me a can opener. I was about to stab the swollen container, when he suggested I might want to put a cloth over it first. This proved a useful tip, for when I stabbed it there was a hiss of steam, and I was enveloped in a hot fog. I could see my shipmate rolling about on the cabin floor, laughing. When the mist cleared, I finished opening the tin and was dismayed to see there was nothing but a thin layer of toffee in the bottom. I threw it in the gash bucket in disgust. John, now crying with laughter, managed to say, "dinna dump it, ye ken it'll be awful handy wor we tae spring a leak."

The months passed by, summer was at its height; the days at sea, though long, were mostly fine and sunny. It was a drastic contrast to the cold miserable days when I first started. Occasionally we'd catch a heavy bale of soaked cardboard in the trawl, which squashed much of the fish. Three feet square by four feet long and held together with three metal bands, these were remnants of cargo from the merchant vessel, 'Fred Everard'. During the previous November, the ship had encountered blizzard conditions, while sailing from Norway to the UK with a deck cargo of baled paper. This cargo became saturated and shifted in the heavy seas, giving the vessel a thirty degree list to starboard. The crew began to jettison the bales, in an attempt to save the ship. Unable to do so, she had gone ashore under the towering cliffs at Ravenscar, at the south end of Robin Hoods Bay. The crew were efficiently rescued by the Whitby Lifeboat.

This paper legacy lasted for more than a year. Colin Jenkinson, who was now skipper of the *Margaret and William*, caught four of the bales in his trawl one day. The immense weight caused his boat to list to starboard. Her winch would barely heave the colossal weight up the little vessel's side. Gradually, an inch at a time, the winchman was able to gain a little, but the bales didn't seem to be coming out of the water. Suddenly, with a bang, the mast and its housing dropped through the deck, into the cabin. The winchman had been hauling the mast down, not the paper up. The net and bales were cut away, allowing the vessel to return to port for major repairs.

It was very pleasant working with John and Tom, though John had been quieter during the latter days. One Saturday, as we were given our pay, John said to the skipper, "that's me, I'm done wi' ye, I'll nae be comin' wi' ye next week." This was a blow, not only to Tom, but to me. John was my shipmate, sharing most thoughts; I was disappointed he'd said nothing.

Tom wasn't perturbed however, he'd seen this many times before. He instructed me to turn out at seven the next morning. Together we'd dismantle the bobbin gear, then replace it with a chain sand net. With only two men on board, this would be easier to handle. We would work nights, commencing on Sunday, fishing mostly for soles and plaice. The season for soles was just starting.

I met up with John later in the day and asked why he'd finished. He said he just felt it was time to move on, to look for another boat. He said he'd been getting vibes that he wasn't required; that he had outstayed his welcome. "The ol' beggar was nae lang choosin' tae change tae sole fishin' when I was awa'. Ah've kenned f' a while, I jus' wasna wanted." He was sure Tom wanted rid of him, so had gone before he was sacked. Sadly John was to drown a few years later, when the boat he was on ran ashore south of Whitby in a heavy easterly swell.

For all his faults, Tom was a master fisherman. In his youth he'd fished with his father and grandfather in these same waters. He had total knowledge of the seabed for many miles north and south of the harbour. The sandy grounds where we fished each night, consisted of an extensive narrow band, reaching from beyond the rock strewn shore with its various bays and promontories, to roughly a mile out to sea, though this varied. In places the sand stretched further out to sea; in other areas the rocky shoreline extended seawards. All this information was stored in Tom's head. The Decca Navigator was now switched off. He used landmarks and transits to ascertain his position. Even in the dark he had no problems trawling this area, using certain shore lights as markers. Had the net caught on any of the rock edges, it would certainly have been damaged, but it never did. No one in the area had more knowledge, and now there was only the two of us on board, his personality changed again. He began to point out the landmarks he was using. He would chat to me from the wheelhouse window as I delivered his pots of tea. We ate only sandwiches and tinned soups at sea, as sailing at six each evening, we'd both eaten at home. We'd eat a large breakfast each morning when the catch had been landed.

One evening midweek, when we'd shot the trawl, he tuned the radio to listen to a football match. This was unheard of. Apart from shipping forecasts, the radio was always tuned to intership frequencies. On this day England were playing Portugal in the World Cup. I'd never seen him so animated. He wasn't usually interested in anything other than fishing, but it was as though he was at Wembley. I stood at the side of the wheelhouse listening to the game through the open window, equally excited. When the final whistle blew and England had won, he was ecstatic, jumping up and down, shouting and flashing the boat's deck lights on and off. He couldn't have been more excited if he'd scored the winning goal himself.

A few days later, we were towing south east from Robin Hoods Bay, at a location known as the 'Off Hole' where the band of sand was very narrow, when a thick fog dropped suddenly. Though unable to see land, Tom was able to navigate our vessel and its fishing gear safely through this narrow passage, using only the depth sounder.

He ordered me to stand aft holding the warps and to yell out if they began to bounce or change configuration. Rather than steer his normal course hoping to get through the gap, he steered half a compass point to the east. The instant he marked a rough contour on the sounder, he altered to starboard, away from the danger, offsetting the course half a point to the south, until he again marked rock. By zigzagging several times, he was able to successfully guide us into the wider expanse of clear ground.

He later explained that had he guessed at the correct course, then marked rocks on the sounder, he wouldn't have known which direction he'd drifted off, and may have compensated the wrong way. By allowing a known error, he was aware of his position. Tom said he'd learned this technique during the war. He related it to navigating through a fjord in fog, without radar. If the water begins to shallow, and you're not aware which bank you're close to, it's easy to run aground. By gradually closing in a known direction, it's obvious which way to alter. This was a valuable lesson, one of many that Tom taught me during that summer.

Social activities always took place at weekends. One Friday night a 'men only' excursion was organised by the landlord of the Leeds Arms, to the 'White Horse Theatre', in a village about thirty miles away. There were several cabaret acts, including an extremely funny comedian. Following much barracking from one of our group, the comic retorted to Herby, "the last time I saw a mouth like that, it had a hook in it," which we all appreciated, including the victim.

A considerable amount of beer was consumed during the trip and everyone had an excellent evening. On the way back, Tony, feeling warm, took off his jumper. Someone began whistling the tune, 'The Stripper'. Encouraged, Tony continued to disrobe, walking up and down the central aisle while everyone on the bus clapped and whistled. He divested every stitch of clothing as he played to the audience. What he failed to realise, was as each garment was discarded, it was passed to the back of the coach, where it was ejected from the window.

Following his act, he pleaded for the return of his clothes, which he presumed had been hidden, before finally sitting in the nude for the remainder of the journey home. It was only when everyone had disembarked from the coach in the early hours that he realised his clothes were not on the bus. Fortunately for him, the driver took pity and delivered him almost to his door, though how he explained his lack of clothes to his wife, no one ever found out.

In the autumn following the sole fishing, when the weather began to get more unsettled, the bobbin nets were prepared again. We were joined by my pal Tom, who'd left the *Margaret Jane*. We got on very well, but I suspected that the skipper wasn't too happy having two young lads together. They may encourage each other to mischief.

A violent north to north easterly storm heralded the onset of winter in November, with winds in excess of force ten, gusting to hurricane strength. The fishing fleet was in port, but late one evening the lifeboat maroons were sounded, summoning the crew.

This was going to be a horrendous night for anyone at sea. I arrived at the boathouse along with many others to ascertain the nature of the emergency, which was to take the lifeboat out in such a storm. An oil rig, exploring for gas deposits five miles north of the harbour, two miles offshore, had suffered damage and was in danger of breaking up. The weather was too severe to launch rescue helicopters.

I looked up to the boat on the carriage, where Bill the coxswain, already kitted out in oilskins and lifejacket was waiting for one or two more of his crew.

"Are you OK?" I called up to him through cupped hands, enquiring if he had sufficient numbers.

He shook his head and waved the palm of his hand in my direction. "I'm not tekin' you on this one," he shouted back.

I wasn't sure whether I'd been refused because I was inexperienced or because he wasn't sure he'd be coming back. Bill wasn't kept waiting long for his regulars. Soon the tractor was pushing the boat and carriage down the beach into the teeth of the gale and to whatever fate had in store for these volunteers.

Along with a few others I went to the crew room to listen to the radio communications between the coastguard and the lifeboat. It was suggested that if the oil rig collapsed into the sea, Scarborough lifeboat wouldn't be able to cope with the disaster alone, further assistance would be required. The storm was so fierce it was impossible to launch the Whitby lifeboat. Whitby's piers pointed due north; the sea between them would be a maelstrom.

Teesmouth lifeboat was launched to assist in the service and was soon on her way south, making a fast passage before the huge following seas. Not long after, we were shocked to hear over the airwaves that her coxswain had been lost overboard. It was many long minutes before the next message came through to report that he'd been picked up again and the vessel was continuing on her way to the potential casualty.

The two little craft bobbed like corks downwind of the huge structure for the remainder of the long night, fortunately without needing to effect a rescue.

The storm was savage but short lived. As the darkness moved away so did the wind. At eight o'clock the following morning, the Scarborough boat entered her home port in a heavy swell but with hardly a zephyr of wind. Her weary crew's faces were caked in salt from the continuous flying spray. They were tired and one or two had been seasick, but otherwise they were none the worse for their ordeal. Their services had not been required, but they had been on hand and their standby was greatly appreciated by the oil rig personnel, who later sent a grateful thank you letter and a case of brandy to the station.

We fished up to Christmas with three hands, encountering no problems. Fishing was good, everything seemed to be harmonious on board, but a few weeks into the new year we were joined by one of the skipper's friends, also called Tom. This became very confusing, I was sailing with three shipmates with the same name. The recent addition, who volunteered to cook and was very good, answered to Tommy.

Gradually as the weeks went by, I began to get the feeling I wasn't needed. Tom the skipper hardly spoke, only when it related to the job. I couldn't understand why. One day, while we were gutting the most recent catch, he opened his wheelhouse window, enquiring of Tommy what was for dinner. Knowing that he'd obtained pork, a meat I wouldn't have dared order, and being aware of the superstitious nature of the skipper, I yelled back, "we're 'aving pork."

He scowled in my direction, slammed the window shut, then kicked the door closed. This was a serious temper, though I thought it none of my making. I didn't order the food. The meat smelt wonderful as it cooked in the oven. The crisp, golden crackling looked superb when the joint was taken out. Tommy loaded the trough with a large portion, delivering it to the wheelhouse, where, despite his superstitions, it was grabbed by Tom with the usual enthusiasm. On his return to the cabin, Tommy dispensed three more mouth-watering meals. No sooner had we begun to tuck in, than we heard the engine ease down, the net had caught an obstruction.

Dropping our meals, we quickly ran up the ladder to retrieve the trawl. I arrived on deck in time to see the trough, with contents plus cutlery, fly from the wheelhouse window, in an arc over the side. "Don't ever, ever, bring that fuckin' meat on 'ere again," he yelled at the top of his voice to no one in particular. No words were spoken as we heaved on the wires to the doors. Only the engine and winch could be heard as we recovered the heavy footrope from the sea. The net was badly lacerated. I kept my head down as I saw the skipper coming from the wheelhouse. He took one look at the paralysed trawl then yelled out, "pigs, rats, rabbits, say what the fuckin' 'ell y' like now."

Disgusted by this outburst, I looked at him saying, "what's wrong wi ya, you eat bacon every day?"

"An' I don't need any fuckin' cheek from you either," he screamed in my direction. I got my cards at the weekend, but wasn't too surprised, I knew it was my time to go.

It was early spring. Dad had recently left the *Rosemary*, having bought a small coble of his own, which he re-named, *Alison*. He suggested that I should go with him as crew. Sailing at five each morning, we fished with pots, along the shores to the north of the harbour, in the small bays of Cloughton and Hayburn Wyke. Each morning as we motored to the location of the first buoy, I'd cut the gurnard, dab or small fish from the trawlers, into sizes which would fit the 'bait band'. Once at the gear, I hauled the pots with the capstan. Dad would lift each inboard, empty, re-bait, then stack them ready for shooting again. We'd then swap places. He'd take the tiller, steering the boat into the required position, while I dropped the pots back over in sequence. The rope, which connected the pots, was laid in a heap in the bottom of the boat. It ran out swiftly, so it was important to keep feet away from it, or I'd go over the side with the pots.

Occasionally, when not paying attention, I'd grab a pot at the wrong end of a row, causing the correct pot to fly though the air, then over the side as the rope came taught, much to Dad's dismay. This was dangerous for us both, and it damaged the pots too.

We worked well together for a while, with occasional disagreements. When I was younger, I believed without doubt, everything Dad said. Now I suppose I had opinions of my own, but mostly we got on. The warm early mornings with the sun newly over the horizon and the sea barely having strength to break on the shore, were wonderful. One day we saw a fox scavenging on the rocks; on another occasion a deer, close to the cliff edge. Working close to land, it was possible to imagine prehistoric animals roaming the coastline. There was no sign of human habitation, no houses or roads. The cultivated fields on the cliff top were out of view. There can be few places remaining in our country that time has left untouched.

It was late morning each day when we arrived back to port. After landing our catch we'd work for a couple of hours, repairing or making new pots, then my afternoons were free. We'd take it in turns to visit the fish market each evening, to await the incoming trawlers for fresh bait. There was much rivalry among the potting fraternity for the scarce commodity. Some coblemen had regular suppliers; others took what they could get. The going rate was now five pounds for a seven stone box.

We would meet with Soapy, Bill Sheader and other 'potters' most lunchtimes in the pub, where good humour abounded. One busy day, a sixteen stone cobleman, universally known as 'Baby', for no other reason than he was the youngest of a family of six, was leaning on the bar, yarning with an associate, when a tall, well-built young stranger came in. He was having difficulty getting to the bar due to Baby's out-spread arms. Rather than ask if he could get through, the young man began elbowing his way in, saying, "get out of the way ya silly old sod."

It looked as if there was going to be a fight. 'Baby', without speaking, turned to face the obnoxious young chap. Grabbing the stranger's left biceps in his vice-like fingers, he squeezed. The man dropped to his knees squirming, still in the grip. "Say excuse me an' I'm sorry f' bein' rude," Baby requested. The young man murmured the apology. "Louder, I didn't 'ear you." The youth blurted out the words again, then leapt for the door the instant he was released. "Young uns o' t'day, they've no manners," Baby said, picking up his pint once more, concealing the glass in a hand the size of a shovel, as he continued his conversation.

Now I was in a coble, I'd more time to go on the lifeboat. I sailed on a number of exercises and these were very instructive; I learned to rig breeches buoys, handle the heavy anchor with a davit, stream the drogue and retrieve a simulated 'man overboard'. It was amazing how swiftly Bill could spin the boat around, allowing for wind and swell, then to place her alongside the floating object, within easy reach of the boat-hook. It came as second nature to him. He did manoeuvres like this every day of his life, when hauling his fishing gear.

One day while lying off the beach, idly waiting for the tractor and trailer to re-house the lifeboat, Bill opened the brandy bottle usually kept for cold weather services, giving each of the crew a tot. As we were gathered round he laughed to himself, then asked if we'd heard of Soapy's latest mischief.

He said that Gwen, who lived not far from the Leeds Arms, had recently bought some chickens, in the hope that any eggs would augment the family's food supply. It was expected to take several weeks for the birds to settle and begin to lay. Ernie, on hearing of Gwen's acquisition, late one night after visiting the pub, left half a dozen boiled eggs in the birds' nesting boxes. Gwen was delighted, telling everyone of her birds' early success, until she attempted to break one for breakfast. The probable culprit was immediately identified, forcing him to lay low for a while. Gwen was a formidable woman, had she found Soapy she would have given him a severe ear bashing.

I met up with the lads to go 'on the town' as usual each weekend. There were night-clubs and discotheques now, licensed to stay open until two o'clock in the morning. We'd visit most of these during the course of the evening. Some had a dress code, which denied admittance to wearers of jeans or leather jackets. Others were less particular. One dive, the 'Holiday', would probably have let us in wearing oilskins and seaboots. We inevitably ended the night in this dubious establishment. One particular night at the Holiday, we encountered two young ladies unfamiliar to us. Most of the local girls were known. Some who frequented this club were quite frightening, but these two were both friendly and attractive. What were they doing in a place like the Holiday? Baz and I asked them to dance, then we began chatting.

I danced with Olga, Baz with Dorothy. The two girls were from Hull, fifty miles to the south. In answer to an advertisement in their local newspaper for seasonal staff, they'd come to work in a small privately run hotel, 'La Baia'. It was their first week in town. This explained their presence in this sleazy dive. When the club closed, we walked the two visitors back to the hotel, saying goodnight, with a kiss. Olga had a boyfriend back in Hull but Baz arranged to meet Dorothy again, on Wednesday evening at a pub disco. I decided to turn up too, I quite liked Dorothy. I felt a bit of a gooseberry sitting with them so didn't stay long but I remembered this girl from Hull.

Several weeks later, for some peculiar reason, when the pubs closed at ten thirty on Friday night, I was the only one in the mood for 'clubbing'. Even Baz, who was usually game for anything, decided to go home early. Undaunted, I headed 'up town' on my own. I was sure to meet someone I knew. At the 'Candlelight', a 'strongman' cabaret act was performing on the dance floor. Unable to see the show for the crowd, I stood on a nearby table. Whether I was disorientated in the dark, or the worse for wear I don't know, but I fell from the table into the lap of two girls, spilling their drinks.

"I've fallen f' you," I muttered in the dark, hoping I hadn't hurt them. They said they were OK. Apologising, I was about to offer replacement drinks when the lights came on. I immediately recognised Olga and the lovely Dorothy. After a visit to the bar for fresh drinks I sat with them for the remainder of the evening, chatting as old friends. They were such comfortable company. Dorothy hadn't seen Baz since their midweek date, so at the end of the evening I asked her out. This was an encounter that was to change my life. We met most nights throughout the summer following this chance meeting. Dor, as she was known to her friends, was fun to be with, and had a great sense of humour. She must have had, she laughed at all my jokes.

Working split shifts as she did, Dor was never usually finished before nine each evening. It was only a ten minute walk for me up the hill, through the churchyard, to where I would wait on a bench across the road from 'La Baia'. Once, Dor came out of the building saying that Mrs Arecco, the owner of the hotel, had shown her a lobster, and asked if she knew what it was. Dor replied, "it's a lobster, we have them in sandwiches at my boyfriends." It was true, we did often. Dad would keep the undersized ones, which were illegal to land, to feed his family. Mrs Arecco refused to believe that anyone ate lobster sandwiches and was disgusted at this apparent sacrilege.

It would sometimes be one or two o'clock in the morning before I took Dor back to La Baia, leaving her at the door. It seemed as if I'd just got into my bed at home when Dad would call me for sea. We had some terrible arguments during the summer due to my, 'burning the candle at both ends'. I wasn't doing my job properly. At least once a day I'd get a crab-pot stuck on the capstan, causing it to revolve violently, threatening injury. Dad would have to disengage the hauler before it could be untangled. I would still occasionally grab the wrong pot to throw over the side when shooting the gear. There was a terrible atmosphere at home. Mum was torn between the two of us. Working together and living together became very difficult. We would take our differences back to the house. Eventually, much to Dad's relief I think, I decided to leave the coble to get a job on another trawler.

CHAPTER XII

'SUCCESS'

I secured a berth with Bob, on the *Success*. The other crewman and lifelong friend of Bobs, was Gordon. Both were in their late twenties. The atmosphere on board this boat was really good. I was treated more as an equal by these two than as a deck-hand and there was an element of fun to be had. The *Success*, one of the larger boats, though ageing, was Bob's first command. We were mostly working daily, so I still met Dor a few times each week and at weekends. My new skipper had, prior to securing this vessel, spent his time as a crewman on the *Progressive*, a Filey boat, so continued the tradition of not sailing on a Sunday. This was a bonus for me and my girlfriend.

For the first time in ages, I began to think that I too could be a skipper. This thought hadn't occurred to me since I left the Merchant Navy. For most of the time spent in the *Whitby Rose*, I had felt inadequate compared with the skipper, but Bob was younger, still learning his new trade and was making a go of the boat. This gave me hope and though I had a long way to go, I could see a light, a ray of hope.

The humour on board the *Success* was zany. One warm, sunny day, while fishing close to several other boats, we hauled our trawl to discover that the net was torn. It wasn't a bad tear; ten minutes stitching would repair it. With our boat stopped in the water, we stripped to the waist, setting to work with mending needles. Within a few minutes it became obvious that another boat was going to pass very close to our position. Judging by the gulls surrounding the vessel, her crew were on deck gutting fish. Gordon suggested we should remove the remainder of our clothes, leaving only our full-length seaboots to protect our feet and legs.

Agreement was reached without another word. We kicked off our trousers and drawers before re-donning our seaboots. It was very difficult to keep a straight face as the *Brilliant Star* passed within a boat's length of ours. We looked up from our task, waving in unison to the gawping men on the adjacent craft. They stood nonplussed, while we continued our mending job as though there was nothing unusual onboard.

The VHF radio, audible through the opened window crackled into life. Much to our amusement every boat within thirty miles heard 'Jocksey', skipper of the *Brilliant Star* say, "we've jus' towed past t' *Success* laid mendin', an' not one o' the buggers 'as got a stitch o' clothes on, they must all be bloody crackers aboard o' there."

On another occasion when a boat was passing close by, we hid behind the wheelhouse until the last moment, then bombarded the unsuspecting passers-by with eggs.

Several weeks later, with a south westerly gale blowing and the *Success* in harbour, I was standing on the pier among a group of pals when the lifeboat maroons were detonated. This caused a dash to the boathouse, where I was fortunate to get a place in the boat. We were going out to a small sailing catamaran, owned by an eminent QC, Gilbert Gray, a local man who'd been involved in many famous legal cases. His reputation said he was very good at his job, but he wasn't much of a sailor. In fact he was the lifeboat's best customer. In fairness, he preferred to sail in strong 'off land' winds, when the seas were comparatively flat compared with the wind's strength. His catamaran would gain exhilarating speeds of twenty knots or more in these favourable conditions.

Only a mile and a half from the harbour, we arrived alongside the dismasted, upturned hull, to be greeted by the legal eagle shouting, "what took you so bloody long? I've been waiting ages. The water's bloody freezing."

Gilbert knew Bill the coxswain very well, as they'd both grown up together in the 'old town', where Gilbert's father was the local butcher and a keen Salvation Army member. We helped him on board before taking his stricken craft in tow. He soon warmed up and began chatting, telling us of his days as a boy, out fishing during the war.

In 1943 at the age of fourteen, when other boys of his year were assigned to fire watching: looking for incendiary devices dropped from enemy aircraft, Gilbert had been given permission to do his 'war work' by assisting an old fisherman, Tom Birch, in his coble the *Florence*. They were fishing close to the shore near Robin Hoods Bay. The fishing was good, they were catching lots of lobsters. Not all the lobsters were of legal landing size, but undismayed, the old man was keeping the smaller ones, known locally as 'porks' for a special customer, much to Gilbert's disapproval.

They'd almost completed the fishing operations when an aeroplane came swooping low over the cliffs. "It's a German," gasped Gilbert, "a Heinkel III."

"Nay lad, it's one of ours," said the old man. The plane banked sharply, heading in their direction and a burst of machine gun fire hit the water a hundred yards from the little coble. Gilbert dived below the boat's side for cover, though the half-inch planking would have given little protection had the bullets been on target. "I told you it was a German," he bawled at the old man.

The old man took off his cap, throwing to the deck. "That Fisheries Inspector'll go to any lengths to stop us keepin' porks, 'e's even got t' Jerries on 'is side now."

Dor and Olga often used the hotel kitchen to cook food of their own, so one day I decided to take them a treat. While steaming back to the harbour, I selected a two foot long wolf-fish, locally known as woof. Though ugly and grey in colour with black spots, woof is a very tasty fish, with milky white flesh and a meaty texture. Woof feed on a diet of shellfish, such as crabs, whelks and sea urchins, so by necessity this fish has a formidable array of teeth, filling most of its mouth. As I picked this choice fish from the catch, it occurred to me that the poor creatures must have a terrible existence, spending a lifetime passing broken shells through their systems.

I chopped off the head and removed the skin before rolling up the remaining edible part in a newspaper. On completing our work at the harbour and running late, I dashed home for a bath and a change of clothes before going up the hill to meet Dor. She was sitting on the bench outside the hotel waiting, as I strolled down the road with the fish, held by the tail within the paper. "I've brought you a present," I said, as I approached. She smiled sweetly. "It's a fish, a woof." The smile disappeared.

"For one misguided moment, I thought you'd brought me some flowers," she said through clenched teeth. "I should have known better."

At the end of the summer season Dor and Olga returned to Hull, much to my disappointment. Dor found work in one of the many factories in the city, working on a production line. We wrote to each other often, and I rang her two or three times each week, though not from home. I preferred the privacy of a call box. Dor's family had no phone, so I rang her at the next door neighbours who were pleased to play 'Cupid'. Some weekends she'd come to Scarborough, travelling on the late afternoon train on Friday after work, and staying with us until six o'clock on Sunday evening. Unfortunately there were no trains to Hull on Sundays during the winter, so my poor girl friend was forced to endure a three hour bus ride home.

Towards the end of the year Gordon acquired his own boat, *Ocean Gift*, making way for Terry to join us on the *Success*. Our new man was a good cook, though his sense of humour wasn't on the same wavelength as ours. The ship lost some of its atmosphere.

While trawling one fresh breezy day, in the company of several other vessels on 'Filey Tow', we hauled our trawl to discover a very heavy object caught in the net. Unable to pull the net in by hand as usual, we used the winch and wire hawser from the lifting pole to raise this unwanted catch to the surface. Just how unwanted the catch was became more apparent as the lump emerged from the water at the boat's side. Surrounded by fish, seaweed and shells was a large, circular, sea mine with deadly horns protruding uniformly from the net. It was clearly very old, its casing decayed in places, enabling us to see the workings inside. "What are we gonna do with it?" was the question on all our lips.

"Lets tek it aboard an' 'ave a proper look at it," I very foolishly suggested. Surprisingly, the skipper agreed. Terry heaved some more on the wire and the giant conker swung inboard, to be lowered gingerly into the fish pound in the centre of the deck. Bob radioed the other boats in the area, informing them of our predicament, only to see them disappear over the horizon at a rate of knots. We were on our own.

We examined the ancient piece of ordinance, peering inside at the corroded wiring and sandstone coloured explosive, touching the horns, some of which were now bent with the rough treatment received. We presumed it to be German, of 'World War I' origin. History records that when the German fleet bombarded Scarborough in December 1914, the mine layer Kolberg sewed a hundred of these devices in a minefield between Cayton and Filey Bay, many of which served their evil purpose, hence the profusion of wrecks in the area.

Having deliberated on our catch, we were faced with the dilemma of getting rid of it. It's fairly easy, even in poor weather, to lift heavy objects onto the deck of a trawler. The design and layout of the craft is perfect for heaving anything inboard, but getting the same object outboard again is a totally different scenario. Nevertheless, somehow this unwanted object had to be returned to the sea, in a position where it wouldn't be caught again.

Bob decided to drop the mine close inshore on the very rocky ground near 'Filey Brigg', where it was impossible to trawl. He set the course and as we steamed slowly to the west, asked Terry to go below to rustle up some bacon sandwiches and a pot of tea. The heavy trawl boards were still hanging in the gallows overboard. As the boat was rolling quite heavily, the boards were frequently banging loudly on the boat's side. After steaming for about fifteen minutes, Bob, curious to see why his sandwich hadn't arrived, looked down into the cabin through the hatch. He saw Terry, frying pan in hand, holding it over the stove. Each time the trawl boards clanged on the boat's side, our cook jumped, so did the bacon in the pan. Hardly surprising with a thousand pounds of high explosives above his head.

Eventually we arrived at the designated dumping ground, where Bob stopped the boat. The *Success* was soon wallowing broadside to the swell. We began to debate the best way of jettisoning this unwanted cargo. It was decided to fasten a rope around the mine, then lift the thing from the deck with the same lifting pole and wire we'd used to lift it on board. It would still be in the centre of the vessel, so we would try to manoeuvre it overboard.

Terry was appointed winchman again and passed three turns of wire round the winch capstan, then heaved. The unstable explosive was raised from the pitching deck but immediately began to swing to and fro, pendulum like, with the rolling of the boat. It was impossible for two men to prevent a 1000 lb object from obeying the law of gravity, and we began to get a little worried. I shouted that rather than stop it swinging, if we were to encourage it, by pushing, eventually it would swing out over the boat's side. My knees were knocking and bowels rumbling as Bob shouted to Terry, "next time it swings t' starboard, chuck off t' wire and its momentum should tek' it clear of t' boat's side." Terry nodded.

Something must have been lost in the communication of this message, for instead of totally releasing the wire at the end of its swing, the winchman lowered it down about six feet. Here was our unexploded bomb, having reached the peak of its projection, now hurtling back at our boat's side.

It's true, your life does flash before your eyes. CRUMP! the explosive devise hit the boat's side with a crack. It didn't explode; it crumpled into several pieces then fell into the sea. No bang, no agony, everything intact. It was a dud. Could we have been this lucky? There was plenty of time to doubt the parentage of our cook as we headed back to the fishing grounds to get the trawl down again.

A new bar, 'The Bier Keller' had opened in town and quickly became 'the' place to visit on Friday nights. It had wooden tables and benches supposedly resembling those in Munich. The beer was lager type, sold in quarter, half or full litre glasses. It tasted sweet, but was quite strong. A terrific rock band played, while scores of dancers strutted their stuff on the tables or postage stamp sized, dance floor.

After a really good night out with the lads, we were making our way to the exit shortly before closing time, when we encountered Soapy, standing with difficulty and looking perplexed. Thinking he'd lost someone in the crowd, Baz asked if he was alright. "Can you lads tek' me t' door please, I know it's over there, I can see it but I've 'ad three goes at 'eading for it now, an' I never seem t' reach it."

Winter turned to spring and the weather began to improve. The finger-freezing days were left behind. Regular visitors to the town, familiar faces from the factory regions of West Yorkshire and the pit villages to the south of the county began to appear, heralding the new tourist season. After the dust and grime of the coalmines, the sea air was most welcome to these people. One such visitor was Carl. He'd spent many holidays in Scarborough, always staying with the same landlady, in a cottage in the heart of the 'old town'. He enjoyed the company of the fishermen around the harbour and was frequently to be found on the fish market or in the local pubs.

One evening as usual, Bob, Terry and I called into the Leeds Arms for a couple of pints, before going home. Carl was in the bar and the conversation centred on the contrast of occupations, that very few fishermen would wish to go down a coalmine, but then not many miners would like going to sea. Carl couldn't see any problem with going thousands of feet below ground, but said he didn't see any difficulty in going to sea either, in fact he'd quite like a trip on a trawler, for the experience. We warned him he'd be terribly seasick but this didn't seem to bother him. We were sailing again at four o'clock the following morning so Bob invited him along.

Our keen passenger was waiting on the pier ready to sail when we arrived at the harbour next day. The ropes were quickly thrown off by the hovering pierman, to be stowed by Terry and me as the *Success* rounded the pier-end, heading into a fresh easterly wind. Ahead of us was a two hour trip to the fishing grounds. Bob took the first watch so Terry and I decided to snatch a couple of hour's sleep on the outward passage. I suggested to Carl that he did the same.

The cabin on the *Success* was for'ard, as on most vessels. The hatchway was in the stem, the foremost part of the boat. It wasn't easy for Carl to get across the deck to the hatchway, as the boat was constantly lifting and dropping her head in the swell, throwing up a light spray, but he eventually managed. I pointed to the spare bunk at the bottom of the ladders then kicked off my boots to turn in. Terry was already horizontal. I watched until Carl was in the bed, then switched off the cabin light, in easy reach of my berth.

Lying in the dark, semi-dozing for a while, I heard the sound of urgent movement in the cabin. Looking out from my bunk I saw a pair of legs negotiating the ladder to the deck, it was Carl. I guessed he was feeling unwell. As it wasn't fully daylight and the weather poor, I felt compelled to check he was safe. I rolled from my bunk, pulled my seaboots on, then mounted the ladder, following him to the deck.

Carl was slumped against the side of the boat, wet with spray, his head and shoulders covered in vomit. My own stomach heaved as I looked at him. Bob, having seen the events for'ard in the growing light was now spewing from the wheelhouse window in sympathy. Carl had apparently, on feeling seasick, leapt from the bunk, shot up the ladder and unable to hold on any longer, heaved over the side the instant he reached the deck, unfortunately for him, into the wind.

It's a well-known nautical saying that you should never 'spit into the wind'. This also applies to peeing and spewing and if Carl ever goes to go to sea again, which is doubtful, I think he'll know why now.

Arnie was also a frequent visitor and a familiar face during the summer season. Familiar, but not popular. An undertaker by trade from Leeds, he was a real jinx, a 'Jonah'. Fishermen, superstitious in the extreme, avoided him like the plague. Many people tried to disprove the bad luck aura surrounding Arnie, but always to their sorrow. He could empty a pub of its customers in seconds. Some landlords refused to serve him, for if Arnie was in the bar, few others would enter.

He stopped to stroke a dog one day at the side of the harbour but the creature ran away, directly into the path of a bus. When on an angling boat, the boat's engine broke down. Bill Sheader, though superstitious, was a kind man and felt sorry for Arnie, misguidedly taking him to sea when he went to haul his lobster pots. Bill was a competent seaman, one who never got into difficulties. Nevertheless, on this day he fouled the *Constance's* propeller with his own pot rope, causing the engine to stop and sustaining damage to the gear-box. Arnie was never invited again.

A group of fishermen were sitting in the Lord Nelson one day, selecting horses from a newspaper for the day's racing. Sam, who was renown for backing losers, had written the names of four horses on a piece of paper, when Arnie entered the pub and joined the group. Cursing Arnie for his presence, Sam tore the betting slip into shreds. All his selections won.

Dor came back to Scarborough alone at the start of the summer season, having acquired work at the Valley Bridge Hotel. Olga had decided to stay with her boyfriend in Hull. During that spring Dor and I decided we'd get engaged. I can't recall asking her to marry me, it was just a natural progression; we jointly decided we should wed. We set a date in October, the end of the season. It would be four weeks past my twentieth birthday. Inevitably, almost everyone began to call Dor, Dot. My Dad was Fred, so I was young Fred, my mum was Dot, so Dor became young Dot. It was very confusing for her, in Hull she was Dor, in Scarborough she was Dot.

Gordon was doing very well in the *Ocean Gift*, proving himself to be a successful skipper, so with a government grant/loan scheme and a shrewd business partner, he commissioned the building of a new vessel. She was to be state of the art, with the latest electronic fish finding and navigating equipment, a two hundred and thirty horsepower engine and a comfortable cabin aft. Fifty five feet in length, she was to be built by James Noble of Fraserburgh, in the very yard I'd walked round with Dennis when we'd visited that port as schoolboys. Though she wouldn't be finished for many months, Gordon had asked me to be one of his crew when she was ready. I was thrilled with this, it was both a compliment and an opportunity to improve. Meanwhile I would stay with Bob until this new craft was ready.

Fishing continued to be good and I met Dot whenever I could, though still had occasional nights out with the lads. On one such night we met Arthur, 'Artie' an ex Merchant Navy AB, who after a period of fishing, was now working as boiler-man at the maternity hospital. Artie always had a fund of stories to tell. Most of the time it was impossible to assess whether he was telling the truth or tall stories. He related how he had recently attended the General Hospital for a series of tests, following a bout of chest pains.

"It were one o' them foreign doctors that examined me," Artie said, eyes twinkling, "he asked for a sample o' me water. 'E said that was OK, then 'e asked what colour me stools were. I told 'im they were brown, wi' cream tops, I was gonna tell 'im we'd just 'ad 'em re-covered, but 'e ran out o' t' room 'olding 'is mouth, chokin'. There's some funny people workin' up at that 'ospital."

Artie continued with a tale from when he was younger, during his service in the Merchant Navy. While in a Spanish port, along with two or three other members of crew, he went ashore to look around the town, then to find a bar. After sitting in a cafe-bar for a while drinking, they began to feel hungry. This was accentuated by the lovely smell of roasting chicken, emanating from the kitchen. None of the other members of the group could speak Spanish, but Artie assured them he was quite fluent in the language. He summoned the waitress over to their table with a wave.

As she arrived, Artie putting both hands on his hips, waved his elbows back and forth calling, 'Quanta Quanta Quack Quack.'

There were grave fears within the fishing industry that Britain was about to join the Common Market with no 'Fisheries Policy' agreement in place. Our grounds and fish stocks would be swallowed up by vessels from other European nations which bordered the North Sea and English Channel.

With this in mind and with the assistance of our Member of Parliament, four of the leading skippers on the coast, Will Pashby and Denk Mainprize from Scarborough, Jim Leadley from Whitby and Jack Sanderson from Bridlington, attended a highly publicised meeting with Prime Minister, Heath's negotiators.

This discussion was quite prolonged, but the skippers were elated on their return, thinking they'd won a vital victory. The men representing the leader of our country had assured them, "we'll give due consideration to the importance of your industry." In the years to come this statement was to reveal its true meaning.

During the summer, catches became scarce throughout the daylight hours. The water was very clear, perhaps the fish could see the net coming. We began to work thirty-six hour trips, landing every second evening. Late one wet, windy night just after dark, with the weather marginal for fishing, an emergency message came over the radio from a crewman on the *Ocean Gift*. Gordon had been lost overboard. The trawl had caught on an obstruction; one of the wires at the stern had suddenly tightened, catapulting him over the stern of the boat. Every fishing vessel in receiving range of this message hauled its gear, making for the scene, to join in the search. It was a forlorn hope. The night was pitch black with driving rain and a heavy swell. Gordon couldn't swim.

All the fleet, plus Scarborough and Whitby lifeboats, criss-crossed the area throughout the night. Crewmen shone torches and searchlights into the dark, surging waves. Oilskin clad figures stood at their boats' sides, listening in vain for a cry from the missing man. As daylight came, an extensive sweep of the area was organised by Will Pashby, a natural leader. Will ably arranged twenty boats, in line abreast, approximately a tenth of a mile apart, heading north. At the end of the sweep, on his word, each boat turned to starboard, moving east for two miles, before heading south again. It was a search of naval precision. The only objects found were a few fish boxes, which had been thrown overboard to mark the place where Gordon was lost. These had drifted with the tide. Had Gordon been on the surface, he too would have been found. He never was.

There was much gloom in the port during the following weeks. The missing man was a popular person, several of his brothers were fishermen. There was a feeling of great loss in the community. Eventually a memorial service was held in the Parish Church of St Mary. The old building was packed to the doors for the service, which was emotional, even for the hardest of men.

A trust fund was set up for the benefit of the lost man's wife and family. Among many other fund-raising events organised, Scarborough boats' crews arranged a football match against their contemporaries in Whitby, some of whom had been involved in the fruitless search. This game, played on Scarborough Town's ground, before a large all-paying crowd was a light-hearted affair, with a very drunken party to follow. The reason for the game was close to everyone's thoughts. Though Scarborough fishermen were victors on the day, the fund was the real winner.

It was fitting that Bob was asked to take over Gordon's new boat when it was ready, as they'd been friends from their school days. I was still to be part of the crew. The new vessel was to be named 'Jann Denise', after Bob and Ann's young daughter.

CHAPTER **XIII**

THE TRIP TO LONDON

The 'Fishing News', the trade paper of the fishing industry, announced an exhibition at the Olympia Hall in London. All aspects of fishing were to be displayed. A 'men only' trip was arranged by the fish-selling agent, departing early on Friday morning, returning Sunday night. This excursion was well supported, with a total of sixteen travellers. There were six younger members, including Tom, Baz, Bob and myself, none of whom had been to London before. A definitive group of 'boys from the sticks'.

There was a party atmosphere as the group travelled by rail to Kings Cross Station and a large amount of strong drink was consumed on the way, despite the occasional grumble at the cost of the beer, by the older men. The underground was a revelation, as we attempted to find the way to our hotel in Sussex Gardens. The splinter group of youngsters were to use the Circle line several times during the weekend; on one occasion travelling the wrong way, stopping at eighteen stations, when it would have been nine had we gone in the opposite direction.

Much to our dismay, on arriving at the hotel, we discovered we'd been allocated a room that slept four persons, in two double beds. Not thinking to challenge this arrangement, we accepted it with stoicism. I was to double with Baz. Once the shock of this unforeseen problem had diminished, the humorous aspect of the situation appeared. Expressions of, "keep yer 'ands t' yerself."

236

"Don't pinch all t' blankets."

"No fartin'."

"Don't bring a woman back wi' yer tonight, though y' can bring two," were bantered to and fro across the room.

The exhibition was quite spectacular to our inexperienced eyes, with many stands displaying all that was new for the modern fisherman. The latest design of trawl nets and V shaped boards were critically examined by the older hands. Hi tech radios, including the latest VHF sets with multiple channels, allowing skippers to exchange information on private frequencies; a new innovation. Another revelation was an echo sounder with a bottom lock and expansion feature. Sounders gave notoriously poor performance in bad weather, due to the unpredictable rolling of the vessel. This new equipment would eliminate the problem. It would also highlight the first three fathoms of water above the seabed, expanding it to ten times the normal display size. This would enable the user to define fish, hard down on the seabed.

By eight o'clock in the evening the younger element of the party could wait no longer to see Soho. We'd heard so much about strip clubs, but none of us had ever been to one. We were like lambs to the slaughter. After quickly perusing the dozens of clubs, looking at the gorgeous photos exhibited outside, not realising the same girls performed in each club on a rota basis, we selected one that offered sixteen exotic acts.

Excitedly, we entered the sleazy foyer of the 'Blue Flamingo', the carpet sticking to our feet; its pattern no longer discernible. A bored girl with straggly blond hair was listlessly chewing gum behind the counter. At her side a large 'bruiser' with flattened nose was dressed in a dinner suit, complete with bow tie. How the tie was fastened was not clear, as the gorilla appeared to have no neck. The bow sat on his lower chin.

"Are you gentlemen members?" he asked, as we eagerly jostled in the entrance, oblivious to the grotty surroundings. Crestfallen, we looked at each other, then at apeman, and shook our heads. "Never mind lads, its only two pounds each to join, the first act's about to start." Our spirits rose as we quickly stumped up the required amount. It was expensive, but it would be worth it. "And of course there's a one pound ten shillings admission charge," he added, assessing our enthusiasm and financial status perfectly. One or two lads hesitated, but were swayed by the majority. What was the point of being members if we weren't going to go in the place? Looking at the bouncer there would be no refunds.

We paid up and scurried down the narrow stairs, laughing and joking like naughty schoolboys. Slipping through a grubby red velvet drape, we entered a dimly-lit room, furnished with a raised stage at the front, screened by a threadbare curtain. The single spotlight shining on the material, highlighted the wear, while making the rest of the room seem darker.

Crammed into the available space, leaving only a narrow aisle at each side were ten rows of ten seats, which appeared to have had a former existence in a cinema. Undismayed that the room was empty, we vied for the central places on the front row. The seats were so close, we could and did put our feet on the stage. A pretty, skimpily-clad redhead, hair in a ponytail, tray in hand, approached the group and asked if we'd like anything. There was much banter and innuendo at this offer, but though she probably meant 'anything', we requested six pints of beer.

In the barmaid's absence Baz was elected 'kitty man'. It was a democratic decision, five votes for and one against. A brief protest from 'Kitty' that he always got the job was stifled, when it was pointed out to him that he worked in an office and was cleverer than the rest of us. We duly forked out two pounds each to Baz for the night's drinks.

Oriental music sounded from the speakers at the side of the stage, quickly growing louder, to indicate the start of the performance. The curtains opened to reveal a quite beautiful, vibrant, smiling blonde, clad in exotic veils, her arms and body gyrating wildly to the music. We cheered loudly, causing her smile to widen further. She was hardly recognisable as the girl from the paybox. As if prearranged, our drinks arrived just as the first of the flimsy garments was being removed. Six bottles of warm, weak beer with glasses inverted atop, were passed along the row with a minimum of fuss, by Yorkshiremen whose love of good ale is legendary.

"Four pounds ten shillings," Ponytail said to Baz, who was nearest the aisle. He coughed his first mouthful of the tepid ale back into the glass at the extortionate charge, then threw a five pound note onto the tray, not wanting to make a fuss when a revealing act was imminent, only a short distance from his face. Pony Tail departed, no change was returned, but 'Kitty' didn't notice; 'Blondie' was dangling her bra under his nose. Her unfettered boobs bounced wonderfully, twelve inches from his exposed tongue. We all cheered loudly. Our eyes were on stalks as the dancer lowered her pants to her thighs. Her hips were gyrating and thrusting suggestively, her pubes only inches from our faces. She allowed the wisp of crimson underwear to fall to the floor before expertly kicking them into Tom's lap. It was fantastic, we'd never seen anything so sexy.

The next performer was a tall brunette dressed as a nurse, with a very short tunic and suspenders. Each of us in turn were allowed to twang them. Bob got a gentle slap round the head and a delightful, "naughty boy," from the lady for twanging her knicker elastic instead.

Eight or nine other customers had now taken seats in the rows close to the front. The strippers followed each other quickly, each routine taking no more than five minutes. They were mostly attractive, pleasant and fun loving, and appeared to enjoy performing before such an enthusiastic, innocent audience, who applauded and cheered continuously. A beautiful, dusky, Asian girl with striking eyes which flashed at each of us in turn, melting our hearts, was a huge success.

It was thirsty work. The warm beer was soon gone. "Ger 'em in Baz," someone to my right called. Baz rolled his eyes, only he was aware of the cost of the beer. Summoning the hovering redhead, he called, "six beers please." The order was quickly fulfilled. Another fiver was placed on the tray, "I'll just get your change," she whispered to our fund-holder, but never did.

It was my turn next to be the centre of attention. Unfortunately it was not an enchanting temptress, but a very large, buxom, African lady with a loud raucous laugh and tombstone teeth who selected me as her stooge. After removing her bra, she began swinging her huge drooping bosoms in my face. Next she held one of the swollen globes out with both hands, pointing it in my direction for a kiss. The lads were laughing at my blushing predicament and egging me on. I had no choice, had I not co-operated, I could have been smothered between both the boobs. I gave the large, pink, raisin-like nipple a gentle peck. In an instant she spun in a semicircle, screaming like a banshee, her tits flew through the air out of control. Now her huge fat bottom, covered in tight black matting, was inches from my face. "Now here," she bawled. I turned my face away and looked in the direction of my mates. They were rolling in their seats, tears streaming, delighting in my plight.

Having reduced me to a red-faced, embarrassed wreck, the curtain closed on the 'African Queen'. "Didn't y' fancy it Nommy, she wasn't that bad," Bob suggested, grinning at my discomfiture.

Other comments came thick and fast, "she'd crack ya like a nut."

"It's somewhere t' park ya bike."

"Motorbike, more like."

"Y' could ride a motor bike in there."

The quips were rude but amusing, even to me at the butt of the joke. Everyone laughed, even the people sat behind joined in the banter.

"Ya' mus' be jokin', I wouldn't be seen dead wi' that." I answered Bob, when I'd regained some composure. I reflected that it was probably the only way I would have been seen with her.

Someone changed the subject. "More beer Baz," came a cry from the right. A state of relative normality had been resumed.

"You'll 'ave t' gi' me another ten bob each, there's only two quid left in t' kitty," Baz replied quietly.

"Don't be daft, we've jus' put two quid in," shot back a reply.

"Yeh' but it's fifteen bob a bottle in 'ere," he said, cringing, awaiting the expected outburst.

"'Ow much?" came five replies in unison.

"Fifteen bob a bottle," Baz whispered guiltily.

"Fuckin' scandalous."

"Robbin' bastards, fo' this piss."

"I'm not stoppin' 'ere."

"And ah thought you were clever." All this and more was simultaneously yelled in Baz's direction.

Pleased to be out of the limelight, I chipped in, "that's five times what it costs at 'ome."

Baz attempted to mitigate, in his own defence. "But everythin' costs more in London, an' we 'ave seen all these smashin' birds." The fact that several lovely, and one not so lovely girls had performed, almost for us alone, was now forgotten. "An' there's more acts t' come yet," Baz went on, but there was a ground swell of unrest.

"Bollocks to 'em," came a retort, followed by the sound of a chair flipping up as it was vacated. "I'm off." Others followed; it was unanimous. The music for the next turn was starting as we walked, single file, down the aisle towards the exit. We tumbled out into the street to find flashing neon lights everywhere. It was daylight when we'd entered. Another pound a man was begrudgingly put in the kitty, then several pubs were tried in the hopeless task of finding good beer in London, before we retired back to Sussex Gardens and bed.

The night was spent restlessly, each of the sleepers at the extreme edges of their beds, back to back. The blankets were raised taut between the occupants as each tried to obtain enough bedclothes to cover his body. Frequent curses split the night as the covers were removed from anyone relaxing their grip of the sheets. The occasional breaking of wind was followed by a chorus of "dirty bastard," from those on the receiving end. Everyone was awake and dressed by seven the following morning, having spent a fitful night in the now fetid room.

The following day was spent sightseeing. Trafalgar Square was impressive, a fitting tribute to our nation's finest maritime hero, we all agreed. Buckingham Palace was thought to be a bit big for one family, but would be great for playing hide and seek. A game could last all day. Madam Toussauds was extortionate. "Its a bigger bloody rip-off than that bloody strip club," someone said, and there were murmurs of agreement.

Later, the consensus of opinion was it would be a good idea to go to the Elephant and Castle on the Saturday night. It must be a good pub, it was named on the map. It was an ordeal navigating the underground to this remote hostelry, having not graduated from the Circle Line since our arrival, but we eventually found our way to the required destination.

"Where's the pub mate?" Tom asked a passer by, as we left the station, unable to see this great establishment.

"Which pub yer looking for lads?" replied the man, in a lovely cockney accent, attempting to be helpful.

"Elephant and Castle o' course."

" You're 'avin' me on son, you're takin' bleedin' liberties, there's no such place."

We looked at each other in dismay. It was Saturday night and we were stuck in an unknown area, with nowhere to go.

"There is a good pub not far away mates," chirped the local lad, seeing the disappointed yokels before him and still keen to help. "There's entertainment on tonight, should be good for a larf."

We brightened up immediately. Following his directions we soon arrived at a large establishment with 'Watney's Red Barrel', signs adorning the facade. Though busy, the interior of the building was quite gloomy with dark walls and high ceilings, stained with nicotine from years of smoke. Old fashioned in appearance, this place had once been elaborately furnished with gleaming brass fittings, ornate mirrors and glazed tiles, though these were now dull and chipped. In its day this would have been a magnificent building, but now it was worn and tired, contrasting dramatically with the customers who seemed very lively.

A raised platform on one side of the spacious room was occupied by three lads, tuning up guitars, getting ready to play. Ear piercing screeches rent the air as they tweaked amplifiers and tuned instruments. The drummer, limbering up behind the three, gave several drum rolls on his snares, with occasional symbol clashes.

This tuneless racket was soon forgotten however, when they struck up, 'Johnny B Good'. The band played some excellent music from the popular groups, Beatles, Stones, Searchers and others. One hit song after another belted out for an hour or so. The audience were singing and clapping along. Any standing room in the pub was filled with couples dancing.

When the group stopped for a break to loud applause, one of the barmen, a short, bald, rotund man with baggy trousers and a striped waistcoat, stepped onto the stage carrying a serving tray, marked with the brewery's logo. At first he was ignored by all present. We thought he was collecting glasses, but realised he wasn't when he took the microphone from its stand.

Still holding the tray this peculiar fellow began telling jokes. He was extremely bawdy and funny. One poor girl, crossing in front of the makeshift stage, on her way to the toilet was asked by the comic, "are you pissing off? Everybody pisses off when I get up." She scurried into the ladies, blushing profusely. Anyone moving from their seats during this performance was castigated. Though bursting, people were riveted to their chairs, not prepared to run the gauntlet to seek relief.

Now perspiring heavily, he took a deep breath then burst into song. It was a rendition of 'Mule Train', as it had never been performed before. As this strange man sang, he accompanied himself by beating his elbows, knees, thighs, bottom and hairless pate with the tray, not gently, but violently. Each time he struck his head, a shower of sweat was launched into the air. At the end of this unique performance the man sagged to his knees, either from sheer effort or concussion no one was sure. The tray, distorted beyond recognition would never be used again. It was an incredible act which brought a rapturous response from almost all those watching. There was a more genteel type of clapping from those sat cross-legged, agonising for the loo. As this amazing performer staggered from the stage, applause still resounding in his ears, there was a rush for the toilets.

The pop group returned from their break to give a terrific second session which rounded off an entertaining evening. We left the building at closing time, full of high spirits and 'Watney's

Red Barrel', to negotiate a course from the 'Elephant & Castle' to Sussex Gardens.

Sunday morning found us at Hyde Park Corner, aptly described as the 'biggest open air lunatic asylum in the world'. I've never seen so many people voicing opinions on such diverse subjects, some of them quite forcibly. Tom immediately took exception to a German, standing on a box, telling anyone prepared to listen, what was wrong with 'strike ridden' Britain. Stopping to face the orator, he yelled, "bugger off back t' where y' come from if y' don't like it 'ere mate, no one's forcin' ya t' stop."

Passers by slowed, and a crowd began to gather as the German, now having someone to debate with replied, "but I haf com' to 'elp you British, to show you how to become more disciplined, more European like us."

"'Itler tried t' do that in 1939, we didn't like it then either," I chipped in. This brought a chorus of laughter from the onlookers. The debate began to get heated as others in the gathering circle began heckling.

"Will you be using buzz bombs again this time?" someone called from the other side of the circle. As the speaker turned to address this cutting remark we slipped away to listen to other performers. Some of the hecklers were clearly local. They probably looked forward to Sunday mornings as part of their weekly entertainment. A speaker with a mouthful of terrible black teeth was rambling on at length about the Armageddon soon to come from the proliferation of nuclear weapons. A little man, close to the front, clasping sandwiches and a thermos flask bawled, "could you give me the name and address of your dentist, so I can avoid him." This was well received by all within earshot, encouraging him to continue.

"Should I cancel my Christmas Club?"

Some of those giving vent to their opinions were religious zealots, expounding extreme views from which no humour could be derived; others were giving political comment, which invited contrary remarks. It was quite refreshing to listen and to join in, to voice or hear an opposing view without fear of provoking a fight. I thought, "this wouldn't happen in any other country, it would create riots or lead to insurrection. The perpetrators would be locked in jail." It made me feel quite proud to be British.

Our weekend in London was drawing to a close. We visited Petticoat Lane, an exceedingly long, busy street market, enjoying the patter of the traders, but keeping hands firmly on wallets, for fear of pick pockets. We had time for a quick beer in a pub nearby, 'Dirty Dicks', which seemed a popular stop off for tourists. It was a dingy building, making a success from its grime. The place probably hadn't been altered or decorated for hundreds of years. It hadn't been cleaned for a considerable time either. A dead cat, long mummified, was on a shelf above the bar. Though fascinating, its appeal was lost on us, and not having the time to seek other hostelries, we returned to collect our luggage. Our expedition to the big city was over.

The following morning we were back at sea. It was a wonderfully fine sunny day. The visibility was such that we could see the entire coastline from Whitby to Flamborough Head. Several laden colliers were in view to the north, heading in our general direction. Our trawl was down and Terry and I were gutting the remaining box of fish from the recent haul, when Bob called to us from the wheelhouse, "this bugger isn't gonna miss us by much."

We turned in the direction of his pointed finger. A black hulled collier, masts in line, was about a mile away, heading straight for us. Its name was visible but not readable. Bob scanned it through the binoculars shouting, "it's called *Corstar*," then grabbed for the hand set of the VHF radio.

"*Corstar, Corstar, Corstar*, this is the fishing vessel *Success*, do you receive." The airwaves were dead. He repeated the message but there was still no reply.

The name was clearly visible now above the foaming bow wave of the oncoming ship. Bob called once more, then flung the wheel hard to port. The *Success* began to turn but only slowly. Dragging the trawl made her sluggish and unresponsive. Terry and I were watching open-mouthed as the ship charged towards us. "Get the raft ready," Bob screamed, waking us from our trance. We dropped our knives, running for'ard to the inflatable life-raft, stored in a cradle near the foremast. The ship was almost upon us as we fumbled for the quick release clip.

"'Ang on!" Bob bawled, as the *Success* inched her way clear of the onrushing ship. He'd managed to clear our boat from the stem of the huge ship but the collier still struck us a glancing blow with her bow, rocking us severely.

Holding onto the mast, Terry and I were yelling at the empty bridge at the tops of our voices as the ship sped past, but to no response. As the stern section of the vessel came in line, a boiler-suited engineer appeared, carrying an oil-can. He looked startled at our close proximity and was perplexed when Terry screamed, "yer fuckin' stupid bastard!"

Chapter XIV

Married Life

October soon came, and with it our wedding. We were to wed in the fishermen's Church of St Thomas, close to the harbour. Baz was my best man and Olga the matron of honour. Alison, now nearly four was a bridesmaid. A coach brought Dot's family from Hull for the occasion. I'd been instructed by my 'wife to be' earlier in the week, that under no circumstances was I to wear white socks for the church ceremony. Though these were popular dress and I wore them frequently, for some unknown reason Dot didn't like them. I hadn't planned to wear them for the wedding, but from my point of view, they were now a 'must'.

Standing at the altar with my best man, I heard the organ strike up, 'Here comes the bride'. I was still slightly breathless, having arrived only minutes earlier from the Leeds Arms, where a competitive game of dominoes with the lads had delayed our departure. There was much shuffling as the congregation stood. Biding my time until I estimated my bride to be close, I hitched the backs of my trousers up, exposing the forbidden socks. As my betrothed drew level at the alter she turned to me, smiling beautifully and through clenched teeth said, "you've got white socks on."

Through a similar communiquè I replied, "I wasn't going to, but you told me not to." The battle for supremacy had begun.

We honeymooned in London for a week, where I was able to show off my vast knowledge of the Circle Line, Trafalgar Square and Petticoat Lane to my lovely wife, who didn't list geography and navigation among her best attributes.

Our first home, close to the harbour, was an upstairs flat, above a souvenir rock shop, closed for the winter. The flat was only available for six months, as it was holiday accommodation during the season. We visited the Town Hall housing department shortly after moving in the flat, requesting that our name be placed on the list for a council house as soon as possible. We had two hundred pounds saved between us and had plans to buy our own house, but that was for the future.

Access to our winter accommodation was from the rear, via a flight of stone steps and a dark passage. It was a cold building, with no available sunlight. The main room was large, with a high, whitewashed ceiling. The only heating was from a coal-burning fire. The kitchen was a brick-floored, glass-roofed annex, formerly an outside yard. A part of this was sectioned off for coal storage. Our possessions, mostly wedding presents and clothes, were stored in tea-chests in the spare bedroom. There was little point in unpacking if we were not staying. We thought we had vacant possession of the flat but quickly realised we were sharing with an extended family of mice, who it seemed were keen on the remains of our wedding cake.

In conversation on the pier soon after taking up residence, I mentioned there were mice in our flat. Soapy suggested I use an old mousetrap that he'd been using in his bait shed. The wooden base was damaged but the spring trap still worked. It certainly did. In the first two weeks it caught thirteen mice. I checked it each morning at four or five o'clock when I turned out for sea. Any contents were dispatched down the toilet. It was checked and re-baited around midday if I was ashore. On two occasions there were two dead mice in the trap together. Dot was a little upset when I used our wedding cake to bait the trap so I bought some warfarin, a pest killer in powder form. Small amounts of this were placed in strategic positions around the flat. The mice devoured it with no seeming ill effect. They enjoyed it so much I switched to baiting the trap with it.

It was a poor winter for fishing, the weather seemed constantly bad. Easterly gales were endless. Few boats sailed and when they did, catches were small. Each bad weather day, a procession of fishermen could be seen, trekking up the main street to the employment exchange. 'Dole money' was calculated on a daily basis, though for some, there were many consecutive weeks of unemployment. When we did get to sea, I saved the lumps of sea coal that were regularly trawled up. It was far superior to the coal we bought, giving off much more heat, and it was free. Unfortunately on one occasion, I mistakenly included a piece of pitch, which burned fiercely before melting, and filled the room with dense black smoke, much to my wife's displeasure.

Dot obtained work as a trainee machinist at a local clothes factory, where her pay was a mere five pounds a week. The regular staff were paid by 'piece work'. A target number of garments was required before Dot could improve her pay to the level of other workers, but her fiver a week was our main source of income for much of that winter.

At Christmas we bought each other fur boots, which were to prove very useful. Early in the New Year it snowed heavily, in a cold spell that lasted several days. Huge icicles hung dangerously from the guttering of all the buildings in the area. Dot wasn't amused at all when I handed her a snowball as she lay in bed one morning, following another fruitless turn out to the harbour.

A few days later we woke to find the house freezing. On going downstairs we discovered a mound of snow, smashed icicles and broken glass piled high on the kitchen floor. The mass had slipped, unheard from the roof at some time during the night. After clearing up the mess, we trudged a mile and a half to the home of our landlady to report the incident. To her credit she quickly organised a repair, but it was a very depressing time waiting for the tradesman.

Spring was looming, and with it the threat of eviction. We had promised to quit our accommodation by Easter but as yet we had no alternative. There was a room at home with my parents, but it would only be a last resort, we valued our independence. I began to visit the housing office at the Town Hall at every opportunity, requesting a house. One week during another unsettled period of weather I was interviewed by a young lady who said, "weren't you here yesterday?"

"Yes," I replied, "an' I'll be 'ere again tomorra." It may have been coincidence, or the staff at the Town Hall may have become tired of my visits, for the week before we were due to leave our first home, we received the keys to a flat on East Mount. I knew the premises well, my Gran had lived in this area when I was small. I'd collected mussel shells from the flats in my school days. There were three blocks, each of three storeys. We were given an end flat, on the middle deck of the middle block.

When built in the nineteen twenties, the flats were ahead of their time. Ours was roomy and light, with a good size living room, three bedrooms, kitchen, bathroom and an exterior coal-bunker. These buildings had been home to scores of families over the years, and held happy memories for me. Many of my school friends had been raised here. Though spacious, with a bow window, the main room had the most ghastly wallpaper, featuring huge yellow and orange flowers. Our first thoughts were to decorate, to make the place more to our tastes. After discussing the matter, we agreed that though the flat was homely, it wasn't ours. We were only renting it and it would suffice for now. The tea-chests of possessions would remain unpacked.

We quickly noticed whenever either of us approached the window to look out, an elderly lady living in an adjacent flat was always seated in her window, usually looking in our direction. After ignoring this perceived invasion of our privacy for a while, I began to wave at her, but with no response. The nosy neighbour became a source of great irritation to me, then became a challenge. One Sunday afternoon, following a lunchtime visit to the pub and a big dinner, I stood in the window, surveying the weather. Dotty was ironing laundry airing on the clothes-horse, by the fire. Looking to the side I spied the old biddy, eyes fixed on our window. "She's there again, dun't she ever go out? 'Asn't she owt better t' do than gawp at us."

My wife was more sympathetic. "She's an old lady, what harm is she doing?"

Eyeing the washing, a mischievous thought crossed my mind. "I'll give 'er somethin' t' look at." Grabbing Dotty by the hand I pulled her to the window, giving her a big kiss in full view of the spectator. When she'd returned to her ironing muttering something about me up to mischief again, I took one of her cardigans from the clothes-horse, throwing it upwards into the window. Next I threw one of my jumpers, then a blouse. This was quickly followed by a shirt, a bra, pants, trousers and underpants. Without allowing myself to be seen by Mrs Nosey, I closed the curtains, leaving lots to her imagination. We then went out for a pleasant walk along the Foreshore for the remainder of the afternoon. The old dear passed away a few weeks later. I hoped my prank didn't have any bearing on her demise.

The launch of the Jann Denise was a very special occasion for Bob and Ann, though tinged with a little sadness. Seventy guests, including Dotty and me, were transported from Scarborough to Fraserburgh by coach for the event. This involved a day to travel the four hundred mile journey north, a second day for the launching, including the subsequent celebrations, then a third for the passage home. Accommodation for everyone was arranged by the boatyard, in two of the town's family-owned hotels. The proprietors were familiar with boat launches and knew how to make the occasion special. It was almost dark when our coach arrived outside the Balaclava Hotel. The other contingent disembarked at the Royal. Although lengthy, the coach trip had included a couple of stops and had been fun, with much banter and interaction between the travellers. All were treating the occasion as a mini holiday.

An excellent meal was served shortly after our arrival, but not before the ladies had unpacked and the men had assessed the bar's McEwan's 'heavy'. It wasn't found wanting. After dinner Dotty and I decided to stretch our legs following the long day of inactivity, so we took a short stroll down the narrow High Street, leading to the huge fishing haven. Little seemed to have changed since I'd been here with the crew of the *Hazael*. The boatyard lay in darkness at the far end of the harbour. This would wait till the morrow. It remained for us to return to the Balaclava's bar where an evening of hilarity and good humour prevailed. A little before midnight I enquired of the barman, "when do y' close?" It was long past the English legal licensing deadline.

With a wonderful deadpan expression he replied, "och we usually ha' a week in October."

"That's OK then, let's 'ave some more," was the general opinion.

Breakfast was much quieter, though still friendly and pleasant. Afterwards the women and children in the party went off to explore the shops, while the men, drawn subconsciously, found the harbour. It was apparent to the locals that a launching was imminent, when dozens of strangers, some clearly hungover, were seen wandering the docks and piers in the early part of the day. The boatyard was first stop for everyone. The towering, corrugated, iron doors were pinned back to display the well-rounded, cruiser stern of the new construction. Gleaming brightly, the four-bladed propeller, in place on the shaft but as yet unconnected to an engine, looked impressive. The underwater section of the vessel was a standard deep red. A six inch band of white separated this from the upper hull colour, an unusual but striking turquoise. Those with a head for heights mounted the flexing, twenty foot, wooden ladder to explore the craft from the deck perspective. Others would wait until it was possible to step aboard following the launch.

Next for inspection by the tourists was the extensive fishmarket, where hundreds of boxes of fish were on display, landed by the many 'seine net' vessels operating from the port. Several of these superb craft were given the 'once over' from the quayside, by the fishermen in the party. The slipway wasn't far away and attracted visitors but as the morning progressed, most of the male contingent could be found seeking a 'livener', in one of the half-dozen friendly waterfront bars.

At noon the entire group, dressed in their finest clothes, made their way to the large, green-painted building, bearing the name, 'James Noble', in bold, white letters above the entrance. Inside the shed, at the bows of the new baby was a makeshift stage, decked in bunting. The smell of new wood and fresh paint filled the air with a pleasant, heady aroma. Proudly, Bob, Ann and their two young children, Steven and Jann mounted the staircase for the imminent naming ceremony. Close behind came Jimmy Noble, his wife

Madge, then the bespectacled, silver-haired, business partner and his spouse.

The crowd quickly gathered around the platform to hear little Jann Denise softly name the new arrival in her own name, asking God to bless her and all who sailed in her, before releasing the champagne bottle. Decorated in red, white and blue ribbons, it arced forward to shatter with a pleasing crump on the forefoot of the boat. Those closest were lightly splashed with a fine spray of the sparkling product.

At a nod from the foreman, shipwrights waiting beneath the craft, in unison, began hammering at the preventer chocks, knocking them away to allow the vessel to move. The same workers quickly scampered away, having assisted in the birth. The new arrival, festooned in multicoloured flags, emerged slowly from the shed to loud applause from guests, curious locals and yard workers. On the deck, attempting to hang on and wave were several youngsters from the party. They'd been given express permission to be on board by the builder, at Bob's request. Keeping a safe eye on the children were several of the workforce, who would be required to manage the vessel and to check its integrity for ingress, once afloat.

Flying proudly at stem and stern were the flags, 'Lion Rampant' and 'St Andrews Cross'. She may be for English owners, but she was Scottish built and unashamedly demonstrated it. Gathering momentum down the well-greased ways, directing and supporting her on her first journey, she hit the water with a splash. Rolling and cavorting ungainly, *Jann Denise* took several seconds to gain her balance. A piper heralded the new arrival's first immersion into the harbour water, with a rousing rendition of 'Skye Boat Song'. The emphasis was clearly on the words, 'Speed bonny boat'. Tears were shed by several of those watching, on the safe delivery of this beautiful craft.

Tradition was honoured to the men who'd created her. A spread of food, a case of beer and a bottle of the finest malt occupied a small part of the now vast, echoing chasm in which the beautiful vessel had grown through the previous months. Tomorrow these craftsmen would lay the keel and begin the first stages of the gestation period, which would produce the next baby from this prolific womb.

The new arrival, now settled, bobbed lightly but as yet lifeless in the water, surrounded by broken timber, the sacrificial wooden supports which had held her upright on her passage to the sea. Two men in a small motor boat were in the process of gathering this flotsam, preventing it from spreading around the harbour. The brightly painted hulk was gently coaxed to the pierside with ropes, thrown from the deck to willing hands ashore. Others, on the stone jetty running parallel to the slipway, held redundant car tyres dangling on lengths of rope. These were protection for the vulnerable wooden skin of the new boat, from the abrasive harbour walls. These fenders squealed as they were compressed between the two rigid masses. The tyres would be hitched to the boat's sides as soon as possible, giving a semi-permanent defence.

Scores of bodies, of both sexes, swarmed aboard the boat the instant she came alongside, level with the pier. Ladies were struggling with or removing their high-heeled shoes, some hitched up skirts to facilitate boarding. Most would be disappointed, there was little for them to see. As yet the 'Jann Denise' was an empty shell. It would be several months before she was finally completed. Though fully-decked, there was a gaping hole in the centre of the vessel, which everyone was staring into. This was to be the engine-room and fish hold. First it was to be the entrance for the fuel tanks, engine, hydraulic pump, batteries and all the thousands of component parts which go into making these complex hunting machines. The shipwrights had finished their task. Now a small army of engineers, plumbers, electricians, carpenters and electronics specialists must work together in harmony to complete the fit out. These tradesmen would bring life to the powerless creature.

The entire afternoon following the launch was taken up with a reception and formal dinner. This seven course feast with baked Alaska for dessert, (whoever heard of putting ice-cream in an oven, it'll melt), was followed by speeches, much like a wedding. Toasts in sparkling wine were made, first by the builder's representative to the new owners, thanking them for placing the order for the ship with Noble's yard. A response was given by a very nervous

Bob, to the builders for their professionalism, the workers for their craftsmanship, the designers for a lovely vessel, and the hotel for the splendid meal. Everyone was then asked to toast the *Jann Denise*. This was supported wholeheartedly, by all. Formalities over, most remained in their places, continuing the celebrations until late afternoon. There was only time for a brief rest and change of clothes before the evening programme of dancing, with music provided by a ceilidh band. The locals proved very adept, light on their feet and confident. They enjoyed watching the tangled mess resulting from English attempts at 'Strip the Willow' and an 'Eightsome Reel'.

At the mid-point of the evening, the dimmed lights were raised to enable the staff to serve tea and sandwiches. Could anyone be hungry following the huge meal in the afternoon? Strangely, the entire stock of sandwiches were devoured before the dancing recommenced. Soon after midnight the proceedings were brought to a halt, though some people had retired earlier. It had been a long, enjoyable day and for Bob and his family, a very special one.

It was a quiet, subdued crowd that boarded the coaches at eight o'clock the following morning. A six thirty call for breakfast had gone unheeded by some. Those who arrived for the meal ate little but drank large quantities of coffee. One or two stragglers required second calls to raise them from their beds. What a contrast from the previous morning. The trip south seemed long, all the jokes had been told, there was not much holiday spirit left, everyone was tired or hungover, wanting to be home. What a relief when we were able to step from the bus at Sandgate, early that evening. "Four in the morning," Bob called to me, as Dotty and I crossed the road to go home. We were back to reality, it was business as usual.

The following weekend after several days at sea, I was sitting in the Leeds Arms with Bob, Soapy and Bill Sheader, playing dominoes. Others were watching the game and joining in the conversation. We were recounting the previous week's events, relating the highlights to those who had not been present. Bill quietly said he and his wife had been invited, through his position as the lifeboat coxswain, to a reception on board the Royal Yacht Britannia in Portsmouth the same weekend. As he described the occasion he made it sound an unforgettable experience. There was lots of food and drink, and many notable, familiar faces. As the proceedings continued, Julie, who hadn't been able to find the ladies room, was becoming a little concerned. "Where d' ya think it'll be Bill?" she asked.

He pointed across the saloon in the direction of Prince Philip. "Go an' ask 'im, it's 'is boat."

The months rolled on; the new boat would soon be ready. Before this, some of the skippers had arranged a 'gentlemen only' evening at a hotel on the edge of town. The cost was to be five pounds per person, which included a meal plus free drink and entertainment. The eighty tickets were in big demand, guaranteeing a sell-out. Bob managed to obtain three. I left Dotty with Ann, at their house, drinking coffee and chatting. Bob and I took a taxi to the venue, collecting Terry en route. My parting words were, "I'll come back wi' Bob and we'll go 'ome together." The event was a huge success, perhaps too good. The beer flowed fast and free. Following an excellent meal of roast beef and Yorkshire pudding a comedian entertained, telling rude jokes which were tremendously funny. He fended off the hecklers with great skill, adding to the entertainment.

The cabaret continued with three lovely strippers, who in turn performed their acts for the enthusiastic crowd. It must have been quite daunting, disrobing before the unruly gathering, though the girls were not in the slightest danger. Nevertheless they took no chances, grabbing their discarded garments and scurrying off to the changing room, the instant the final vestige of covering had been removed.

The beer continued to flow, the landlord had clearly miscalculated the capacity of his customers. As the evening progressed, his stock of booze rapidly diminished. Bravely, he stopped the proceedings to announce that an additional two pounds per head was required if we were to continue drinking. There was a loud protest, but it was good hearted. Everyone was having such a good time, they paid up to placate him. My last recollection of the evening was drinking large glasses of Bacardi and coke when the beer ran out. Everything after that was blurred.

I woke up the following morning with my head pounding and back aching, even my scalp hurt. It had been a hell of a night out. I turned my head slowly and painfully towards Dotty, who was staring back with that look which meant, "don't expect any sympathy from me."

"My 'ead aches," I croaked, vocal cords struggling to perform.

"I'm not surprised, the state you were in," shot back the reply.

"But my back aches as well."

"You fell into bed and you've been laid in the same position all night, you drunken slob, I'm not surprised your back aches."

"Thanks f' the sympathy," I mumbled and began to run the previous evening's events through my fuddled mind.

"Don't you remember anything?" I heard Dot say through the haze.

"I can remember goin', I remember eatin' t' meal, and there was a lot t' drink," I could also recall 'the cabaret' but thought it better not mention that part of the evening. "I jus' can't remember comin' 'ome."

"You were both drunk. You staggered out of the taxi, almost fell into Ann's lovely house. Bob was burbling, but you slumped on the settee, falling so hard it tipped over backwards. You were lying in a heap behind it. It was disgusting and so embarrassing. Can you imagine the job I had getting you home?"

I could, it was a hundred yards up the steep cobblestoned hill, then up two flights of steps. I apologised as best I could under the circumstances but heard Dot say, "it's not me you should be apologising to, it's Ann." As we didn't have a telephone, I promised to say sorry to Ann the next time I saw her. Though feeling dreadful, I offered to prepare coffee and toast for breakfast. I was forgiven, we were friends again.

The following Friday evening we went on a tour of local pubs, where we were sure to meet friends. The first port of call was the 'Leeds Arms', where who should we see, but Bob and Ann. I hurried over, grabbing Ann's hands, probably so she couldn't hit me. "I'm ever s' sorry f' me bad behaviour las' week, Ann. Dot told me what I'd done, I can't remember a thing."

"It's all right Fred," she said kindly, "there was no harm done, but I'll bet your head and back ached on Saturday morning, after Dotty kicked you in the back then dragged you up by your hair."

I looked at my wife, who smiled back sweetly saying, "it served you right."

CHAPTER XV

THE NEW BOAT

The new boat was ready. Bob had spoken to Jimmy Noble who assured him she was A1. There were to be four in the crew. My former shipmate Tom, now ex *Whitby Rose* was to be the fourth hand. He would fit in well having all the essential ingredients, he was a good willing worker, could mend nets and take a steering watch, but most important, he had a similar sense of humour. It's essential to have harmony on a boat. Living in close proximity for days on end can be unpleasant if there's ill feeling. When a man and wife have a fall out either of them can leave the house to cool off and find some space. It's not easy to find solitude on a fishing boat. The only privacy is in your bunk, and then only when there's no work to be done.

Laden with rolled up sea gear, kitbags full of working clothes, plus a blanket, we took the first train to York, changing there for Aberdeen. Bob had an extra bundle, charts with which to navigate the two hundred mile voyage south. The railway north from Aberdeen had recently closed, so the fifty mile onward journey to Fraserburgh was by car, courtesy of the builders. The boat looked magnificent from across the harbour. Her cream masts and lifting pole contrasted smartly with the turquoise hull. The wheelhouse was grained and varnished with vertical, rectangular, contrasting panels, picked out with black edging, which looked very effective. It was mid-afternoon when we arrived, and it was clear that the boat was in a mess. We would't be sailing immediately.

The workforce were still finishing various jobs. There were several welding cables strewn across the decks and numerous empty drums which had contained hydraulic, lubricating and gear oils, some of which had spilled onto the wooden planking. Shavings littered the fishroom, engine-room and cabin floors. These would have to be swept up carefully or would soon block the bilge pumps. Bits of wire cable were liberally scattered throughout the vessel, as were short sections of copper pipe, paint tins and empty cardboard boxes. The interior of the wheelhouse, though much bigger than any I'd previously seen, was congested. Several white boiler suited technicians, specialising in radios, depth sounders, navigating equipment and compass adjustment, were moving in the limited space, each attempting to complete his particular project.

We took our gear below, each selecting a bunk from the six available. The remaining two would become storage lockers, one for the first aid box, lifejackets and distress flares, the other for spare fuel and hydraulic pipes, injectors, grease cartridges and the many other components which can't be obtained at sea. Rope, shackles, twine and other fishing equipment would go in the lockers under the seats around the cabin table.

We set to cleaning the ship, careful not to upset the tradesmen still working. Bob was summoned to the wheelhouse to be shown the various electronic equipment by each of the boiler suits in turn. I was taken to the engine-room, where the installation engineer, an agent for 'Gardners' the engine manufacturers, demonstrated how to stop and start the eight-cylinder machine. He highlighted the dipstick and filler cap, so I could keep the crankcase topped up with lubricating oil. Next he directed me to the oil and fuel filters, situated at various points on the motor. Dirty fuel filters were the main cause of lack of engine performance he advised, needlessly.

The header tank on the fore end was filled with fresh water coolant, which circulated around the engine. This too required frequent checking. He showed me the various power take-offs, which drove the bilge pump and electric generators. Finally he pointed to the two stern tube greasers, which fed treacle thick grease to the propeller shaft. He stressed the importance of giving both handles a single turn each day, ensuring the shaft remained lubricated. My head was spinning with information, crammed from this brief, intensive demonstration. Now it was down to me to keep the boat mechanically free from problems with day to day maintenance.

We sailed from Fraserburgh, flags flying, on the following afternoon, the passage south taking almost twenty four hours. The weather was fine with only a slight swell. A small leak developed from the propeller gland, which, being stuffed with new packing, required tightening. This wasn't a job to be done while the shaft was turning; it would wait until we got home. Normally an intake of water of this rate was a situation the bilge pump could cope with easily, however despite our care in sweeping the shavings and bits of wire, we suffered a pump blockage. This was rectified by disconnecting the four inch diameter rubber pipe from the pump to the bilge, withdrawing it from under the engine, clearing the strainer of dross then refitting the pipe. It was a simple, not unpleasant task, as the bilge water was clean. In older boats this was a distasteful job as the accumulation of years of oil and grease, and small particles from thousands of boxes of fish, all eventually found their way into the bottom of the boat.

The visibility was very clear. We could see Scarborough's headland and castle for miles, long before we reached it. It never seemed to get any closer. Our wives, families and friends were waiting on the pier end, waving and cheering as we finally turned to starboard to enter the harbour. The remainder of the day was spent showing dozens of well-wishers around the boat and taking short cruises round the bay.

The following morning we were in attendance early and spent the day rigging gear. There was much to be done. Constructing the bobbin gear, attaching the trawl, then assembling the sweep configuration was quite labour intensive. We occasionally stopped for a pot of tea and to show more interested parties around the boat. Late in the afternoon, as we were sitting on the fishroom hatch taking a tea break, a black painted keelboat, *Graceful Lady* entered the harbour. This was the boat which Herby now worked on. Her name was something of a misnomer, as the boat was now quite ancient and no longer suited her name. There was no vacant berth at the fish market for landing, so the craft was directed by the pierman to tie alongside the *Jann Denise*, until a place became available. Bill, her skipper, gingerly manoeuvred his boat alongside, ensuring Herby had first put fenders out, to prevent contact between the boats.

Tom took a short end of rope from the adjacent craft, catching a temporary turn midships. There was no point in a more permanent mooring, they would only have a short wait. Bob's offer of a pot of tea to the pair was accepted and the two men stepped aboard, keen to examine the new arrival more closely. They were pleased to wander around while the singing kettle re-boiled, comparing their own vessel point by point as they explored. Both were full of praise when they returned to the deck, now carrying steaming hot mugs.

"They've come a long way since t' steam trawlers," said Bill, sitting on the ship's side. He was a very contented man who enjoyed a yarn. One of three brothers, all skippers, he'd spent most of his life working on steam trawlers, excepting for the war years, when he'd joined the Royal Navy. He eventually transferred to the mine disposal squad, where he served with some distinction. Bill's dad, known to all as 'Old Micky', was on one of the seven Scarborough trawlers, sunk in one day by a German submarine during the First World War.

Working approximately fifty miles north east of Scarborough, these vessels were approached in turn during the night. Each crew was ordered into their lifeboat. Most of these flimsy craft hadn't been afloat for years; all leaked badly. The trawlers were then sunk with demolition charges. Torpedoes were thought too valuable to waste on fishing vessels. Some of the skippers were taken to Germany as prisoners, not to return until the war ended. A ship bound for Aberdeen eventually picked up Micky and his shipmates more than five days later. It was several more days before they finally arrived back home in Scarborough, and as there was no way of communicating with their families, they had all been presumed dead. Not long after this close call, on returning to sea, Micky's next ship was also sunk in a similar manner. Hundreds of fishing vessels were scuttled by U-boats during the 1914-1918 war in an attempt to starve Britain of food.

I smiled to myself as I recalled another story Bill had told while sitting in the tea shack at the back of the fish market recently. He reminisced that as a schoolboy, he was employed by one of the dozens of boatmen·operating from the beach, carrying passengers on rowing or sailing trips. The owner of one of these boats, a keen swimmer, in association with an accomplice, had acquired a six foot shark, caught earlier in a trawl. It had been landed on the fish market but later discarded as worthless. The fish was hidden in the bottom of their boat, which was anchored in the shallow water, close to the gently breaking waves on the shore. Hundreds of holidaymakers paddled or swam in close proximity to their craft. The two rogues, backs to the shore, eased the dead creature, unseen, over the small boat's side where it immediately sank to the bottom.

At the tops of their voices they began shouting, "shark!" while pointing down into the clear water beneath them. The muscular swimmer, stripped to the waist and clasping a huge knife, made a great show of diving over the side to wrestle with the inert predator, stabbing it several times before breathlessly dragging it, badly lacerated, tail first to the shore. His partner called to the gathering crowd of onlookers, that his friend had probably saved the life of a child by his heroic, selfless act. He promptly took a hat round to raise a collection for this brave fellow. It was a stunt the two were to pull several times during the summer. Bill said that on one occasion they even used a dead porpoise, knowing that few people would know the difference.

The landing berth became free and the light strop joining the two craft was released, allowing Bill and Herby to discharge the fruits of their labour. We continued rigging our gear, refuelling, stowing empty fish boxes on board and finally taking ice through the bunker lids set in the deck above the ice pound. By evening we were in full readiness and would sail the following morning.

It was a pleasure to be at sea on such a lovely craft. Of course there were teething troubles, this was to be expected, but there was nothing major; the boat handled like a dream. We thoroughly enjoyed the comforts of a modern vessel. We had a comfortable cabin aft, complete with oil burning stove, constant hot water from a gas boiler and even a toilet, situated below in the engine-room. This was a far cry the old 'bucket and chuck it'.

In a few short weeks we were competing with the best of the boats and were considered one of the 'top ships'. The new boat suffered no breakdowns, it could fish in poor weather when others would make for shelter, we were indeed fortunate. Our earnings were excellent. When labourers ashore were taking home less than twenty pounds a week we were making fifty to sixty, some weeks up to a hundred pounds. Bob still wouldn't sail on Sundays like most of the fleet but it was sometimes Saturday noon before we concluded our week.

Now at last when time allowed, Dotty and I could look in earnest for a home of our own. We were expecting our first baby in a few months and hoped to find somewhere before the due date. We desperately wanted to live in the old town, where we felt part of the community, but houses were scarce. Few people moved, and when a house was for sale, it sold by word of mouth. No estate agent was required, there were no 'for sale' signs posted.

We made an appointment at the local building society, where we were given approval in principal, but we still had to find the right property. At least now we could hunt for a likely place with purpose. Our first opportunity was a two bedroomed, post-war house, beautifully situated below the castle, close to the harbour. We were shown round but informed that others had been earlier and had agreed to buy. We were given the second option. The asking price was three thousand five hundred pounds. It was sold to the first viewer for the asking price.

After other disappointments, it looked as if we would have to remain in our flat longer than anticipated, but then we had a stroke of luck. A friend, aware that we were house-hunting, heard of a neighbouring family who were considering selling. They were to move in with an elderly, widowed mother who lived next door. He approached his neighbours, explaining that we were desperate to find a home and were hoping for 'first refusal'. Dotty having been disappointed earlier, refused to build up her hopes, and sent me alone to look at the property.

Number nineteen had an immediate warmth. It was a family home in every sense of the word. The present occupants, the Browns and their three children, had a friendliness and sincerity that was humbling. I was shown round the three bedroomed house, which seemed ideal for us. Mr Brown said if we wanted it, the house was ours. No one else would be invited to view, it was considered sold. The asking price was three thousand, five hundred pounds, the same price as the property twenty yards down the street. Not believing such luck, I ran home and insisted that Dotty came to look at this house that was to be our new home. We couldn't believe our good fortune, making an appointment with the building society as soon as possible. The deposit would deplete our savings totally, but it mattered not, it would be our own home.

We were hit by a body blow only days later, when the house was valued at only three thousand, three hundred pounds by the surveyor. This was the amount on which they were prepared to make the loan. The asking price had seemed reasonable when compared with the two bedroomed property down the road. The next person to view the property would certainly pay it. Devastated, we went together to inform Mr and Mrs Brown. They were very sympathetic. Following a short discussion in the next room, Mr Brown said, "we'll reduce the cost of the house to three thousand, four hundred and forty pounds. You can tell the building society that the sale price is as their valuation. Give us the one hundred and forty pounds difference when you can afford it." This was accepted with deep gratitude. Nothing was written to verify the agreement. It was a matter of trust with the family who would be our neighbours; two people who seemed pleased to help a young couple starting out in life together.

When the transaction was completed and the moving date agreed, Mrs Brown quietly informed us she would have no need for carpets, curtains, an oven, washing machine and many other household items, as these were already installed in her mother's house. These necessities were gratefully received. The items could easily have been sold, but this fact seemed not to have crossed her mind. We refused point blank when they offered to decorate a bedroom they considered in need of attention. When we told friends how fortunate we'd been, how kind this family had been to us, some wag quipped, "they didn't leave you a joint of meat in the oven then?"

Dotty had suffered backache most of the day, a Friday, and suspected the baby was imminent. Luckily I was ashore to be with her. During the evening she had the first contraction and later, with spasms getting closer, she decided it was time to attend the maternity ward. I rang St Mary's on our recently installed telephone to inform the unit we were on our way, then rang for a taxi. St Mary's Hospital was a large Victorian building, surrounded by various smaller units. Along with the maternity wards, it contained a residential psychiatric home, a convalescent ward and a day clinic for infectious diseases. There were no accident or emergency facilities. A boiler-house for the entire complex was on the left, close by the main entrance. I escorted Dotty, carrying her prepacked bag up the stairs to the ward, where we were greeted by a stern nurse who promptly said, "thank you Mr Normandale, we'll see to her now, ring in the morning." She took the bag from me, guiding me back to the stairs. I'd got the bums rush. I didn't even get the chance to give Dotty a kiss.

It was turned midnight on July fourth. I walked home in a daze, got into bed but slept fitfully. At seven o'clock the following morning, I rang the hospital to discover we had a daughter, weighing in at eight pounds four ounces. Though not allowed to visit until eleven, I was there long before that, eager to see them. I thought they both looked beautiful though Dot said our baby, who we named Paula, looked like Winston Churchill without a cigar.

Still dazed I left the building, stopping to pick up a bunch of flowers that appeared to have been dropped in the garden, close to the maternity ward door. As I looked around for somewhere to put them, a voice called out, "oy what are you doin' up 'ere?" It was Artie, the boiler-man, standing in the doorway of his domain. Crossing the path, I proudly announced that I was a Dad, that Dotty had just delivered a lovely baby girl. Expressing his delight, he congratulated me, shaking my hand. I thanked him, then held up the discarded flowers, explaining that I'd picked them up by the door. Much to my surprise he took them from me with thumb and forefinger and dropped them in the dustbin. "It 'appens all t' time. People come t' pox clinic but pretend they're comin' to maternity ward. T' doors are on'y five yards apart. They dump t' flowers before they go in. Some of 'em come in dark glasses wi' collars up an' their 'eads stuck in newspapers."

It was wonderful to have a family at home and to be in a good, well-paid job that I enjoyed. I'd even stopped thinking about being a skipper for a while. Three months later I was able to knock on the Browns' door holding an envelope containing one hundred and forty pounds. It was accepted reluctantly with the words, "are you sure can you manage it?" On being assured we could, Mr Brown offered to write a receipt. It was with great pleasure I was able to say, "that's not necessary, there was never owt written down, an' I'm sure y'd never ask for it again."

Fishing was buoyant and we expanded our range, working up to forty miles from home, sometimes staying for two or three days. On one trip, Tom brought a camera to record our way of life. A particularly good haul of big cod, each weighing ten to twenty pounds was partly filling the deck, when Tom had an inspiration. He descended the fishroom ladders, requesting we remove the bunker lid on the port side. Climbing onto the pile of ice below, he stuck his head up through the circular hole in the deck, asking Terry and me to pack large cod tightly around him to hide the aperture. He called to Bob to take his photo, 'up to his neck in cod', every fisherman's dream.

During the following year we broke the port record, being the first boat to gross in excess of two thousand pounds for a week's fishing; it was a bonanza. Though earning good money, I was becoming restless. I was twenty three years old, could mend nets, take watches, maintain the engine and I'd even taken the boat to sea for a day when Bob had been unavailable, getting reasonable results. I was confident I had the necessary skills to be a skipper. Acquiring a boat was something I had yet to address. It would be one step at a time.

I was aware there were courses available at the Nautical College in Hull, where I could sit for a 'skipper limited' qualification. Others had studied at the 'Boulevard' successfully. The only prerequisites for the three month tutorial were four years proven sea time, two years of which must be served in fishing vessels, good eyesight and colour vision. I qualified on all counts. This certificate would allow me to take a fishing vessel of up to fifty tons, anywhere in European waters between the Shetlands, Land's End and to twelve degrees west, which is into the Atlantic. This was more than I'd ever require. Most craft in our fleet were below twenty five tons. Their skippers didn't need a qualification of any type, but I felt if I was to be a skipper, I should have a 'ticket'. It may be something I'd require in the future.

I tentatively mentioned my idea to Dotty, now heavily pregnant again, not sure what her reaction would be. My wife had always been aware of my ambition and had been supportive, but now we had a growing family to consider. Her reply will remain in my memory forever. "You'll do whatever you feel is right for me and our family. In years to come you'll never say I was the one that held you back." It was a brave statement from my wife. From a position of security, with a small baby to raise and an addition soon due, she was prepared to sacrifice the safe income we enjoyed, to back her man. This was the incentive I needed. I left the *Jann Denise* at Christmas, to commence school early in January.

Chapter VI

Back to School

I was not to be on my own. Two other men, Herby and Frank, a nationalised Dutchman living in Scarborough, soon to acquire the *Courage* from his father-in-law, were to take the same course. The three of us would commute by train daily to study navigation, signals, chartwork, rules of the road at sea, ships' stability, personal survival, fire-fighting, first aid and other subjects which together would enable a skipper to manage a vessel and crew safely at all times.

The college catered for all aspects of seagoing qualifications. Merchant Navy Officer Cadets, commencing their careers were present, along with Mates and Second Mates seeking enhancement. Deep-sea fishermen from Hull and Grimsby, desiring to command ships which hunted cod in the freezing seas from Newfoundland to the Barents Sea were also in attendance. Compared with these lads I felt quite inferior. The duration of their voyages of three to six weeks bore no resemblance to our trips of two to three days. We shared a classroom with the latter group, some of our work running parallel, though these men, pursuing 'Skipper Full', ocean-going qualifications would be at college long after our course had finished.

On our first day at college we met and teamed up with two fishermen from Bridlington, Mick and Ian, both with aims compatible with our own. Ian, sadly was to be lost off Flamborough Head a few years later, when his boat's trawl snagged a wreck and quickly capsized. At first we were given simple arithmetic calculations to get our brains working again, which proved necessary. Though it was only seven years since I'd left school, it took some time for the knowledge to creep back. Gradually the course became more comprehensive. The five or six tutors were extremely capable, delivering their subjects with the confidence and authority of men who'd been to sea. Herby and I had an advantage over the other class members at first, having been taught navigation, chartwork and signals at school, but this lead was soon eroded.

Dotty had spent an uncomfortable, restless night in bed. At six o'clock in the morning, two weeks after I'd commenced school, she announced the imminent arrival of our new baby. Having made arrangements previously, I summoned my Mum, who lived only a few minutes away, to take care of little Paula, while I took Dotty to St. Mary's. Knowing the routine I was at least able to give her a kiss on this occasion before being escorted to the exit. There was just sufficient time to return home, grab my school bag and hurry to the railway station, where I arrived 'all of a lather', making the train with seconds to spare.

The journey to Hull was about an hour and twenty minutes, so I was most surprised when I walked from the platform to find my mother-in-law waiting for me. She said I had a son, that both were well. He must have been born before I got to the railway station. Following the birth, Dotty had rung her mother, who took a bus ride into town from the outskirts of the city to give me the wonderful news and a big hug. The remainder of the day passed very slowly and I was unable to concentrate. I could hardly wait for the end of lessons when I could visit my enlarged family.

Arriving at St Mary's, I found Dotty and my son in blooming health. He weighed eight pounds eight ounces and we decided to name him Daniel James. She smiled as she informed me that during the afternoon, the ward had received a visit from Charlie Bubbins. The Staff nurse had announced to Dotty that a vicar had come to visit her and our new baby. Perplexed, while other mothers found the situation amusing, she was pleasantly surprised when the Curate entered the room. He'd heard news at the harbour of our baby's arrival and felt compelled to pay a call. After spending some time with Dotty, he'd shaken hands with the other six new mothers in the ward, complimenting all on their offspring. He said that had Daniel been born on the previous day, he wouldn't have been able to visit. He'd had a prolonged game of dominoes in the company of Bill Sheader and Soapy and had difficulty returning to the vicarage. Charlie left the hospital having made six new friends who commented how sweet, friendly and down to earth the 'gentle giant' was. Months later he would christen Daniel James in the Parish Church.

I called at Mum and Dad's house to tell Paula that she had a baby brother, though at eighteen months old I don't think she understood. Soon after, I was in the Leeds Arms celebrating, 'wetting the baby's head'. I was in excellent company and was supplied with many beers by well-wishers, delighted at our new arrival. It was eleven o'clock when, slightly the worse for wear, I stepped out into the street. My eyes finding difficulty in adjusting to the dark, I almost bumped into a middle aged man, hunched against the cold wind, walking steadily up the cobblestoned hill.

As I apologised, my eyes adjusting, I recognised Bob Kitto. He was wearing a dark suit, white silk muffler scarf and a cloth cap. Bob was a similar age to my Dad and fished in the coble, *Betty Sheader*. He was a lovely man, softly spoken with bright mischievous eyes and a wonderful sense of humour. "'Ow y' doin' Bob? What d' y' know?" I asked, as I slowed my pace to his to accompany him up the hill. He was on his way home from the Britannia, his favourite watering hole.

"'Ow am I doin' an' what do I know?" he echoed, considering my greeting. "Well I'm alright an' I know these bloody 'ills are gettin' steeper, I'm 'ardly doin' three knots."

I chuckled at his description of his speed up the hill.

"'Aven't you 'eard the yarn about t' three knots?" he asked, as we made our way unsteadily up the hill together.

"Don't think so," I said, "what's that story?"

His pace slowed to a crawl as he began his tale. "Durin' t' war, we were all in t' Patrol Service, on mine sweepin' duties, based in Lowestoft. Because we were in t' navy, we on'y got paid every second Thursday. It was t' night before pay day."

He continued, recalling how he was quite drunk, leaning on the bar in a pub, the first establishment beyond the dockyard gates, late in the evening. He was approached and propositioned by a prostitute, who seemed to be finding trade a little slow that night.

"Anything you want ducky, it'll cost you five shillings," she whispered through crimson lips.

A long way from home and alone, Bob felt through his pockets looking for the required sum, knowing he hadn't enough. He wouldn't get paid until the following day. "I've only got two," he slurred, holding out the single coin in his hand.

"That'll have to do then lovey," she said, taking the florin then assisting him from the building. The 'midnight typist' found difficulty getting Bob back to her place, even though it was only a short distance. Further problems were encountered getting him up the stairs, undressed and into bed, but this was eventually accomplished. Ten minutes of fumbling, moaning and cursing was followed by Bob looking up from the mess of bedding and asking, "ow am I doin?"

"Three knots," was the instant reply from the less than pleased hooker.

"Three knots?" he puzzled.

"Yes, you're not hard, you're not in and you're not having your two shillings back!"

I bid goodnight to Bob, who lived on East Mount, then walked the few unsteady yards beyond the flats, to my own home.

As my period at college progressed, I began making inquiries at the selling agencies and asking local skippers, if they were aware of any boats tied up in the region, needing a skipper and crew. I was hopeful of finding a crew but had no one specific in mind at the time.

Two weeks before completion of the skippers course, I heard of a boat called *Pioneer*, tied up in Grimsby Dock. She was managed and partly owned by Sam Chapman & Co, fish salesmen. I rang the number with heart beating rapidly, not knowing quite what to expect. A polite, well-spoken gentleman answered the phone,

'Old Bob' Kitto, taken close to Sandgate slipway.
Photo Dennis Dobson courtesy of the Kitto family

Part of Grimsby Fish Dock from the air. Another section of the dock
contained more quay space with other fishing boats tied up. There would
probably be many more vessels at sea. Missing from this photograph is the
huge ice house and giant slipways. Photo Grimsby Evening Telegraph

Pioneer at the Vincent Pier, Scarborough, circa 1973.
Photo F W Normandale

Most of Scarborough's fishing fleet in port. There were 4 vessels at sea
when this shot was taken, circa 1975. Photo Dennis Dobson

announcing that he was Frank Chapman. I garbled that I'd heard he had a boat laid up and was looking for a skipper and crew. I explained that I had experience of trawling, and at present I was studying for my ticket, but would be available in two weeks time if the boat was available, and was suitable. I was sure I could get a crew. He sounded quite pleased at the idea of a crew to man his boat and suggested I come to Grimsby to meet him and to look at the boat as soon as possible. That would be the following weekend. My exams were too close to take time off from schooling before then.

The following Saturday found me on the train for Hull as I'd done each weekday for the past three months, only this time I wasn't going to the college, I was on my way to Grimsby, potentially to get a boat. On arriving at the terminus I walked through the city centre to the riverside, where the Lincoln Castle and the Wingfield Castle, two wonderful old coal-burning paddle steamers ferried cars and pedestrians on the half-hour crossing of the River Humber to New Holland. It was a lovely warm, spring morning. I stood on the deck of the old lady, staring at but not seeing the paddle wheels rotate, as I ran my proposition and answers to likely questions through my mind.

It seemed no time at all before we were tying up at the pier on the south bank. As I made my way to the gate on the main deck to disembark, the hiss of steam from a large rectangular aperture below the bridge caught my attention. Peering through bars which divided the glass free window, I looked down into the engine-room below. A pair of gleaming, silver pistons slowly and seemingly effortlessly, slid back and forth with precision. Oil can in hand, fussing lovingly over this timeless piece of engineering, an elderly man, chest hardly covered by a grimy vest, sweat rag tied loosely round his neck, looked up as I cast a shadow over his charge. His grease-streaked face broke into a smile and he winked, clearly a man enjoying his work. Sadly, progress was soon to change this; a new bridge was under construction upstream. This ferry would soon be consigned to history.

The long pier also doubled as a railway station. A diesel train which linked with the arrival of the steamer, was waiting for the small group of pedestrian passengers. Five minutes later the train set off on the hour long journey to Cleethorpes, via half a dozen small villages with strange names, Grimsby Central, then my stop, Grimsby Docks. I'd been to this famous fishing port once before briefly, but had heard many stories from Scarborough men who'd fished from there.

The Port of Grimsby covers many acres, its various docks and piers are measured in miles. I eventually reached the fish market, where underfoot, dirty, melting ice mixed with slime, was being power hosed into the harbour. This was the only evidence remaining of the tons of fish, discharged throughout the night by hundreds of 'lumpers', dockers whose sole work was the landing of fishing vessels. This fish had been sold by auction to the scores of merchants who plied their trade in this great port. Now, in premises all around the vast dock, an army of filleters armed with razor sharp blades, were neatly stripping flesh from the bones of countless cod, haddock, plaice, sole and a dozen lesser-known species. By late afternoon these fillets would be packed in convenient one and two stone boxes, to be transported by rail and road to a thousand destinations.

I asked the man with the hose if he knew where the *Pioneer* was berthed. In a distinct Lincolnshire dialect he directed me towards a complex of slipways, where several vessels of all sizes were standing high and dry, undergoing painting or repairs below the waterline. Making my way towards these towering ships, I passed under an overhead gantry, conveying freshly crushed ice from the old, dark, four-storey, brick building across the road. A light sprinkling of snow from the conveyor found my neck, making me shudder. This endless supply of freezing preservative was being propelled into the gaping holds of a line of ships, which only hours earlier had disgorged tons of fish.

Looking across the harbour I could see a long row of black, rust-streaked trawlers lying with their stems to the pier, awaiting the next tide. Names in large letters across the sterns of these hardy craft identified them, many with the prefix Ross, the name of the company that owned them. *Ross Revenge, Rodney, Kelly,* and *Kandahar* were all visible. I could see the *Northern Jewel* and *Northern Gem* denoting ships of 'Northern Trawler Company'. Some of the ships were named after football teams, *Everton, Spurs, Arsenal* and *Barnsley*.

These resilient vessels, their tonnage measured in hundreds, ranged the stormy high latitudes, far into the Arctic Circle. Here, throughout the year, their twenty-man crews worked eighteen hours on deck, with only six below, seeking the elusive cod. In the frost-numbing winter months the sun never rose. These men worked in perpetual darkness. Shore leave between these arduous three week voyages was limited to forty eight hours in port. It was little time to spend with families, have a few beers with mates and enjoy the fruits of their labour before heading north once more. This breed of men, old before their time, were well named 'two day millionaires'.

I walked past dozens of identically painted, light blue vessels, equipped for seine-net fishing. These fifty to sixty foot long vessels were part of the huge fleet of this class of craft, which also sailed on three week voyages, ranging throughout the North Sea, carrying only three or four men. These small boats fished for cod and plaice, working non-stop in the hours of daylight. In spring and autumn this was hard but during the mid-summer period the crews worked twenty hour days.

Almost all of these boats were owned by their skippers, men with Danish sounding names, Sorensen, Christiansen, Olsen and Bojen featuring largely. These men or their fathers brought their families from Denmark at the onset of war, making new homes and bringing tremendous knowledge and industry to this already thriving town. It occurred to me that this mass of ships and boats, visible in all directions, was only a part of the Grimsby fleet; there would be many more at sea plying their trade.

I finally found the royal blue boat, LH 397, afloat close to the huge slipway, tucked in behind a cluster of the well-kept seine netters. As I drew near, three men standing close by her looked in my direction. "You must be Fred," a cloth-capped, bespectacled man, whose voice I recognised from the telephone said, as he held out his hand, "Frank Chapman."

Aged in his mid fifties, Frank reminded me of Harry Worth, a bumbling television character, but only in appearance. He introduced his companions, two leading fish merchants, the other partners in the vessel. "Here she is, fifty four foot long, cabin aft, she's a nice boat."

I'd been looking at the vessel as we'd been speaking, but now I could give it a better appraisal. The wheelhouse didn't look original, it looked as if it had come off a drifter, (I later discovered it had). I didn't like the look of the winch, the machine looked large and cumbersome. It had no conventional clutches or brakes. The gallows, from which we would lead the warps outboard were poorly constructed. The heavy-duty leading blocks were not fixed into the deck but shackled to the base of the frame. It was obvious they'd had little use. These blocks would bang on the deck as weight was applied or released on the wires running through them. This action would quickly damage the wooden decking, yet the planks were hardly marked. These were things which would need altering if I was to take the boat, but I said nothing. The burning question, to which I needed an answer burst forth from my lips. "What engine 'as she got?"

"It's a hundred and eighty Kelvin." Frank said.

My heart soared. Brilliant! Kelvins were renowned for their power. Trawling was all about net size and towing speed. Even the best looking, well-maintained craft were no use as trawlers if they didn't have sufficient power. This one would do for me. All other obstacles could be overcome if I had the right engine for the job.

We continued our discussions on the spot. Their questions were fairly predictable. How old was I? Was I married? Did I have any family? Had I a mortgage? Did I think I was a bit young at twenty three to be a skipper? What experience had I? Could I get a crew?

The answers to these questions came easily. This was information that I was going to give, had they not asked. The three seemed pleased I had a mortgage; said it was a sign of commitment. I assured them I could get a crew, though this was more hope than fact. To get a good crew a skipper has to get results, to get results a skipper has to have a good crew. I would get a crew.

"Do you have anything to ask or tell us?" Frank as spokesman asked.

This was my opportunity. "I'll be able t' take the boat in two weeks, I'm takin' me ticket jus' now. I can't make any promises of what I'll earn fo' ya. I can't guarantee any results, but y' know I've a mortgage round my neck, I 'ave repayments t' meet an' a family t' keep, so won't be spending much time in t' 'arbour. I'll do me best." The trio seemed to approve of this.

"I'll need to operate from Scarborough." Disapproving looks from the owners, but I went on, "it makes sense, it's t' area I know best, it's where t' best fishing grounds are. It's a six hour steam each way t' Grimsby an' back. We'd be limited t' dock openin' times, we'd need t' commute by train an' ferry an' they only operate in t' day time." My logic appealed to them and reluctantly they agreed. I didn't blame them for being sceptical. If I landed in Grimsby they'd see what I was landing. Chapman's would handle the settlings and take the commission. Elsewhere there could be opportunities for a dishonest skipper to cheat the owners out of their share, or even to sell fish for cash. They knew nothing of me, so it was a big risk for them to take. I was aware of this so continued, "I won't cheat ya, if we get any cash, you'll get yer share. Selling office'll sent you a copy o' t' settlin' sheet every week. You'll know what we're earnin'." Signs of approval again. I'd convinced them.

Pressing home my advantage I continued, "I'll need t' use me own fishin' gear. It'll save you expense. The stuff you've got aboard now isn't enough. I want t' carry three trawls, I want t' be able t' change nets if I bust one without 'aving t' go back in t' 'arbour. You won't 'ave t' worry about me wastin' shackles, floats an' chain or losing gear in wrecks if it's not yours." This too appealed to them. "I'd take a sixth for me gear." Frank's eyes bulged but I hurried on, "you'd get two sixth for t' boat, an' there'd be 'alf for t' crew."

"A sixth is a large share for the gear, I was thinking more of an eighth or maybe a seventh," Frank countered.

"New gear costs a fortune. I have t' buy nets, doors, bobbins, wires an' loads of other stuff. I'll pay ya for whatever gear you've got aboard if it'll 'elp." I couldn't really afford this, but in a few weeks I hoped to. It helped; it was close, but I'd won. I'd got my boat and a good deal. We all shook hands then headed for 'Sam Chapman and Sons' office, where Frank rang an engineer, arranging for him to show me around my boat. Earlier that morning I'd asked the gear chandlers back in Scarborough if they'd allow me whatever gear I needed on credit. I'd give them my gear share cheque each week until the debt was paid. They saw no problem with this, saying my credit was good and they were pleased to get the trade.

Later, on my way home, it occurred to me that had there been other options available to the vessels owners, I probably wouldn't have been so fortunate, but it was a golden opportunity for me and I wouldn't let them down.

The week of the exams arrived. We were all worried, we might not pass. Our heads were crammed with a thousand and one details. The examiners were particularly hot on 'rule of the road' and the 'uniform system of buoyage'. A wrong answer in either of these departments was fatal. Anyone theoretically passing on the wrong side of a buoy, or making a wrong turning in a close quarter situation with another vessel, failed the examination. These unfortunates were compelled to return to sea for a specified period before being allowed to re-sit the relevant part of the exam.

This wouldn't only be embarrassing, it would be greatly inconvenient. We were all aware that the boats at home were doing well. There was fish to be caught. Our income at present consisted of a small cheque at the end of each week from the White Fish Authority. This government-sponsored body promoted and supported the fishing industry through advertising and with various grant schemes, including the building of new vessels. This weekly cheque, though welcome, only slowed the drain on our family savings. Later I'd be able to recover my rail expenses from the local Education Department, but meanwhile a pass was imperative.

The exams, both written and oral, were taken at the Board of Trade offices in the old part of Hull. The small, narrow, cobbled streets, the ancient buildings oozing character and charm, sadly made no impression on us. There was no room in our heads for unnecessary information as we made our way with trepidation to our fate.

The written exam wasn't too difficult, our instructors had taught us well, but we all in turn had a scare when asked to demonstrate the simple task of donning of a lifejacket. Each of us put the orange coloured life preserver over our heads, passing the attached broad tapes around the back, before tying them at the front with a variety of knots and bows, none of which seemed to satisfy the examiner. Not one of us was aware of, or had noticed a small lace at the collar, which had to be tied to prevent the garment slipping back over the head of an unconscious casualty. The examiner sent the entire contingent back to the school two miles away to learn how to put a lifejacket on properly.

The signals exam was taken 'in house' at the college. It was strictly observed though we had no fears of failing this part. Old 'Nobby' Clark, the instructor was the best in the business. He'd taught thousands of students the art of signalling with the three prescribed methods, morse, semaphore and the international code of flags. We sat in pairs at the back, along with the deep-sea men, as a short message was flashed in dots and dashes from the front of the room, at a speed of eight to ten words per minute. One part of the duo read the letters and breaks while his partner wrote them down. Following this, the roles were reversed and a different message sent.

Nobby then stood at the front with a pair of flags on short sticks, each flag halved diagonally in yellow and red. A letter of the alphabet was signalled by holding one or both flags combined at various angles to the body. The reading of this message was again done alternately by pairs of students. This method of signalling was due to be phased out soon, but was relevant to our exam.

In addition to ten numerals and an answering pennant, twenty six different multicoloured flags make up the international code alphabet. Each one when flown singly has a specific meaning. Flown in groups, these signals indicate hundreds of different phrases. A book of flag groupings and their interpretations was carried on all ships, though radio had made them almost obsolete.

Each day brought more sections of the examination. The first aid part took place at the Hull Infirmary, close to the city centre. The doctor conducting the exam, of Polish origin, seemed very aloof and treated us with disdain. He dismissed the five of us as 'passed' after a brief oral examination, despite one of our number when asked, "what is the best treatment for someone who has consumed acid?" recommended, "make 'im sick."

"So you'd allow the casualty's throat to be burned by the acid in both directions would you. Get out the lot of you, I wouldn't allow a fisherman to treat my dog."

The fire-fighting course was very interesting, though not an examination. We were given practical demonstrations at the fire station of various combustibles which caused and fuelled fires, chemical, oil, electrical and general. We were shown which extinguishers were used, or more importantly not used, for each type of fire. It was spectacular watching water being sprayed onto an oil-fire. Breathing apparatus was worn by each in turn to enter a mock, smoke-filled building to extract a weighted dummy. "Lead with your knuckles, not your palms," we were told. "Then you're not likely to grab any electric wires which may have become exposed."

Personal survival, once more a course rather than an exam, took place at the swimming baths and again the trawlermen took part. Shoeless, we wore old clothes and life-jackets, (properly fastened). The two instructors, both ex-fishermen, released and discharged an inflatable life-raft in the pool. Once inflated, everyone including the instructors jumped into the water and attempted to climb into the raft. For the first person, access was extremely difficult. With soaking clothes and only a section of slack webbing in which to place a foot, strength and build was essential. It became easier for those remaining in the water, when assistance was given by the earlier occupants of the raft. The tough trawlermen were dragging survivors from the water with such force, others inside the raft were in danger of injury as bodies flew through the air into the confined space.

When we were safely inside the orange rubber craft, backs to the tubes, legs facing the centre like the spokes of a wheel, an instructor closed the canopy, joining the halves of velcro fastenings together. The temperature within the confined space soared dramatically. "It's essential in cold weather to keep these flaps closed," he stressed, "hypothermia is the biggest killer. Our combined body heat will help to counter this." He was quite right; the heat had become unbearable, though this wouldn't be the case in the North Sea.

Friday, and the results, finally came. All five of us had passed. The Hull and Grimsby men had further weeks of instruction yet before their ordeal by examinations, but we were now free to return home, successful.

I was delighted when my Uncle Francis, known to all as 'Rusty', due to his mop of ginger hair, offered to come with me in the *Pioneer*. Every skipper needs a right hand man, and he would be mine. Rusty had all the skills required, but more than that, he had the right temperament, was willing and had a sense humour. I'd also 'shipped up' two other men who would make up the numbers, enabling us to work the ship.

Together, Rusty and I travelled to Grimsby, following the route I'd taken a couple of weeks earlier. Two of us would be enough to bring the *Pioneer* home to Scarborough, where we could prepare her to our satisfaction. During the train journey, my shipmate-to-be said he'd been in trouble the previous day with his wife, Nina. It was long past his meal time and he was still in the pub among a crowd of pals, enjoying an extra pint. Nina had walked into the bar carrying his dinner on a tray. Wordlessly, though clearly very angry, she placed the meal in front of him along with a knife and fork.

Unperturbed and determined not to be humiliated, Rusty said, "you've forgot t' salt and pepper." Nina hit him with the tray. They were not on speaking terms when he left.

It was midday when we arrived at our destination. The dock gates had closed. They wouldn't open again until evening. We busied ourselves tidying our new acquisition, stowing deck boards and cleaning the cabin. I checked over the electronics in the wheelhouse, while Rusty shopped for coffee, tea, milk, sugar, bread, butter and corned beef. This would fortify us on the passage home. Frank Chapman visited the boat to see how our preparations were coming along. He expressed concern that the lock gates didn't open until late. He hoped we wouldn't be spending any length of time in the pub prior to sailing. I allayed his fears. Normally the pub would have featured in our programme, but having never sailed a boat in this treacherous river before, I needed to be in full control of my senses. We had no radar and the boat had an early model 'Decca Navigator', with which I was unfamiliar.

"Grimsby Town are playing at home tonight," Frank said, "should be a good match." He was determined to ensure we sailed sober. Rusty and I were spectators at the football match that evening, watching the Mariners gain a convincing victory, which I looked on as a good omen.

My heart was racing as I steered the vessel slowly towards the lock gates. Rusty, oilskin clad against the cold night air, stood for'ard. The gap, which was the entrance to the Humber, looked tiny as we drew near. The fact that big trawlers also came and went through this same slot, was far from my mind. "Good fishing," the lock master wished us, as we entered the opening. He wasn't to know we were on passage to Scarborough. The little blue boat slid slowly past the huge wooden gates, now folded back against the concrete walls. High above us loomed the Riby Tower, its top invisible from my position in the wheelhouse. This gigantic construction, of oriental design, visible for miles in all directions, was the first welcoming sign of home for incoming Grimsby fishermen as they entered the river. This tall building was originally a water tower, using hydraulic power to open and shut the dock gates.

It was eleven o'clock on a very dark night when we cleared the dock, entering the river. The ebb tide grabbed the *Pioneer*, speeding her on her way down stream. A sea of lights, some fixed, some flashing, green, white or red met our gaze. There were lights from the opposite shore, navigation lights from passing ships steaming up and down the busy waterway, and vessels at anchor awaiting entrance to the busy port.

Earlier, thanks to the lessons I'd learned at the Boulevard College, I'd written down the configuration and timing of each of the buoys that we'd expect to encounter on our journey down the river. "Look for a buoy flashin' two red, it should be ahead of us somewhere," I yelled to the silhouette before me, close to panic as the magnitude of my responsibility finally hit me. It was only seconds before my trusty mate yelled back, "I see it, it's there, fine on our port bow." Minutes later we passed the 'Burcom Buoy' and I turned the wheel slightly to starboard, entering the marked channel. We were heading east in the direction of Spurn Point, six miles away. I still felt a little wary as we raced downstream on the following tide. Calling out the flashing sequence of the next navigation mark on my list, I was reassured when it was spotted quickly by my lookout in the bow. We were already working well together. I felt more confident. There was no time to relax yet; there was lots of inbound vessels, heavy with various cargoes for the many Humber ports.

Occasionally we'd be overtaken by ships outward bound, travelling at a greater speed than us. It was quite unnerving as these towering ships came up close from behind, sometimes unseen by me in the wheelhouse. Gradually I relaxed and the situation felt more exciting and romantic. We were a part of this busy scene, going about our lawful business, making our way home.

To starboard we passed a dozen or more ships at anchor, awaiting berths in the busy docks upstream. Immediately after the anchorage we passed the 'Bull Lightship' to starboard. The dark outline of Spurn Head lay to port, lit regularly by the flashing lighthouse of that name. This desolate, low lying strip of land, in constant threat of being engulfed by the breakers from the stormy North Sea, was inhabited only by the crew of the Spurn Lifeboat and their families. These men were the only full time crew serving with the Royal National Lifeboat Institution, such was the perceived threat these waters held.

We were in open sea now and the boat began to lift gently with the swell. There were still buoys to the east to navigate, before we could head north in a safe depth, but these could be seen clearly now with the black backcloth of sky. Rusty had taken the opportunity of boiling the kettle and presented me with a steaming mug of coffee and a bully beef sandwich that would've choked an ox. Nothing ever tasted so good.

I looked at the 'Decca Navigator' for the first time since tuning it to the signal prior to sailing. The central clock flashed a continuous red, green, purple sequence. The red clock, reading from zero to twenty three was slowly increasing as we progressed east. When nineteen was reached I turned the wheel to port, holding my course on north by west. The nineteen lane, which the present course would keep us on, would take us directly to Flamborough Head. This navigation system, which virtually all trawling vessels relied on, was simple to understand and had revolutionised fishing.

At two o'clock Rusty came into the wheelhouse. "Go an' get your 'ead down, I'll take her for bit. What course are we on?" I thankfully relinquished the wheel, giving him the course and lane number, which he repeated back to me. I made my way below to stretch out on the seat locker. This was the first of many times in the years to follow, I'd be grateful to let him take over. When he called me back up, it was five o'clock and broad daylight. We were only three miles from Scarborough piers. There was another pot of scalding coffee standing by the wheel.

It felt good to steer the *Pioneer* into Scarborough for the first time. I could sense the attention she was drawing as we manoeuvred across the harbour to a vacant berth at the North Wharf. I could almost hear the critics at Sandgate Corner and had observed the collective group staring in our direction, I would confound them. We tied up safely at the pierside, our two waiting shipmates assisting with the ropes. We were home.

I'd got my boat, I had a crew, I'd finally achieved my ambition, now at last I was a skipper. Little did I know what was in store. This was only the beginning.

CHARACTERS FEATURING IN THIS BOOK
GONE BUT NOT FORGOTTEN

John (Scotch John) Addison
Bob Appleby
George (Pudding) Appleby
Jim (Ruffan) Bayes
Ces Bean
Tom (Tommy Botch) Birch
Charles (Charlie) Bubbins
William (Filey Bill) Cammish
Ann (Nan) Cammish nee'
 Normandale
Sam (Toddy) Cammish
Joe Dwyer
Richard (Dickie) Elliott
Walter (Pellet) Eves
Walter (Wally) Johnson
George Kennedy
Bobby Kitto
Tommy Leader
Tommy Luntley Snr
Tom (Denk) & Maggie
 Mainprize
Esther Messenger
Gwen Nicholson
Billy (Aye Aye) Normandale

John (Johnny Nom)
 Normandale
Robert (Robbie Nom)
 Normandale
Tom Pashby
William (Will) Pashby
Gordon Pickering
Alan Rennard
Jack Rowley
Tom Rowley Snr
Bob (Sabe) Sabin
George (Joxy) Scales
Micky Scales Jnr
Micky Scales Snr
Bill (Jitta) & Julie Sheader
George (Tarrar) Skelton
George Sutton
Alfie Ward
Harold Wharton
Ernie (Soapy) Williamson Jnr
Ernie (Soapy) Williamson Snr
Arthur (Artie) Wilson
Stan Wilson
Bill (Blondie) Wood
Harry (Pinner) Wray

Others, from the author's memory, though not featured in this book, still remembered.

Johnny Armstrong
Harry Austwick
Albert Blogg
Arthur Blogg
Katie Brearley
George Brockwell
George Cammish
Harry (Whisper) Cammish
John (Long John) Cammish
'Chippy' Canty
Bill (Cappy) Cappleman
Norman Cheetham
Major Clark Snr
Ada Colling
Lily Colling
Frank (Franky) Colling
Jack (Torren) Colling
Matt (Yar) Colling
Joe Cook
Keith Corrie
Robert (Bob) Corrie
Becky Coward
Nick Cowling
Bill (Rall) Crawford
Dennis Crawford
Robert (Bobbie) Crawford
Tommy Crawford
Richard (Dickie) Douglas
Donald (Donny) Dalton
Maurice Dalton
Tommy Dalton
Richard (Dickie) Dalton
Dennis Dobson
Wally & Polly Donkin
Michael 'Snotty' Evans
George Eves
Jim Firman

Albert Fishburn
Jack (Nobbler) Fletcher
Jack Fletcher
Joe (Nobbler) Fletcher
Bobby Goodall
Bobby Gray
Alfie Hall
Bill Haylett Snr
Fred Herritt
Terry Hogg
Bert Hunt
Billy Hunter
Terry Hunter
Tom (Mix) & Iris Hunter
Charlie (Dilt) Jenkinson
Bob (Sleddie) Jenkinson 1
Bob (Sleddie) Jenkinson 2
Matty (Wemp) Jenkinson
Les Jenson
Bill (Bagsy) Johnson
John Kirkpatrick
Ernie Lancaster
Jim & Barbara Lawrence
Barry (Gussie) Longhorn
Castle (Cass) & Mary
 Mainprize
Castle (Big Cass) Mainprize
Jack (Boono) Mainprize
Rafe Mainprize
Albert Mann
Walt Mason
Colin Messruther
Robin Messruther
Billy Moon
Harry (Spaceman) Moon
Arthur Moss
Sammy Moss

Herbert Nicholson Snr
Roy Nightingale
Tom (Tommy Nom)
  Normandale
Tom (Gent) Normandale and
  Florrie
Harold Parker
Harry Pashby
Harry (Bulla) Pickles
Jacky Redman
Bob & Alice Rewcroft
Herbert Rewcroft
Eric Riby
Jimmy Ritchie
Ken Roberts
Diddy Scales
Richard (Dickie Bunny) Scales
Frank (Waffy) Sheader
Fred (Frankeye) Sheader
Harry (Pip) Sheader
Irene (Rene) Sheader
Jack (Jacka) Sheader
John (Johnna) Sheader
Nancy Sheader
Richard (Ginger) Sheader
Richard (Nab) Sheader

Walt & Mary Sheader
Charlie Simmons
Bill Smalley
Bob (Soss) Smalley
Captain Sidney Smith
Dougie Storry
David (Davy) Trotter
Albert Upson
Frank (Frankie) Upson
Harold (Podge) Walker
Sid & Mag Walker
Edward (Teddy) Ward
Amelia (Meili) Walker
Robert (Bob) Walker
Jack (Whacky) Watkinson
Derek Watson
Tommy West
George Westwood Snr
Bob Wheeler
Bill & Winnie Wilkinson
Harry (Teashop Harry)
  Williams
Ruth Williamson
Violet & Jim (Kelly) Wright
Stanley (Ringo) Wright
Maggie Young

There are many, many others, sadly not named here who lived and died following a way of life which has gone forever. If your family member or friend is not mentioned, the author apologises. No one has been intentionally omitted. We, the present generation owe them much. To those from the 'Bottom End' who remember these times, write down your memories. They are all that's left, you're the last of the line. Be grateful you lived through these wonderful times.

In writing this book the author intended to give his readers an insight into the way of life in the mid 1960s and early 1970s as seen through his eyes. It is clearly acknowledged that certain events are not necessarily in chronological order. Some characters depicted are ficticious.